teach yourself...
QBasic

2nd edition

by Chuck Butkus

A Subsidiary of
Henry Holt and Co., Inc.

Copyright © 1994 by MIS:Press
a subsidiary of Henry Holt and Company, Inc.
115 West 18th Street
New York, New York, 10011

All rights reserved. Reproduction or use of editorial or pictorial content in any manner is prohibited without express permission. No patent liability is assumed with respect to the use of the information contained herein. While every precaution has been taken in the preparation of this book, the publisher assumes no responsibility for errors or omissions. Neither is any liability assumed for damages resulting from the use of the information contained herein.

Second Edition—1994

ISBN 1-55828-341-2

Printed in the United States of America.

10 9 8 7 6 5 4 3 2 1

MIS:Press books are available at special discounts for bulk purchases for sales promotions, premiums, fund-raising, or educational use. Special editions or book excerpts can also be created to specification.

For details contact: Special Sales Director
MIS:Press
a subsidiary of Henry Holt and Company, Inc.
115 West 18th Street
New York, New York 10011

Trademarks

Throughout this book, trademarked names are used. Rather than put a trademark symbol after every occurrence of a trademarked name, we used the names in an editorial fashion only, and to the benefit of the trademark owner, with no intention of infringement of the trademark. Where such designations appear in this book, they have been printed with initial caps.

Dedication
To Mom

Contents

Chapter 1: The Basics 1
   The Wrong Way to Learn 2
   The Right Way to Learn Programming 3
   Why Use QBasic? 6
   How to Use This Book 7
   An Analogy for Program Flow 10
   The Definition of a Program 11
   Summary 11
   The Book in Review 11

Chapter 2: Your First Program 13
   Conventions in This Book 14
   Four QBasic Statements 16
   Print 16
   Statement Labels 18
   A Program to Print an Address Label 20
   A Program to Average Three Numbers 20
   Your First Look at Programs 21
   What a Register Program Does 22
   WildWater Works Register Program 22
   Summary 23
   The Book in Review 24

Chapter 3: QBasic 25
   Using the Right Tools 26
   Working Backwards 26
   Starting QBasic 27
   Typing in a Program 30
   Saving a Program 33

Opening an Existing Program *35*
Testing a Program *36*
The QBasic Environment *38*
Setting QBasic Options *38*
Browsing the Menus *40*
How to Move Directly to a Menu *47*
Summary *47*
The Book in Review *47*

Chapter 4: Diagrams and Programming 49

Solving the Wrong Problem *50*
Programs "Flow" Just Like Rivers *50*
Program Flow and Logic *54*
The Nature of Programming *56*
The Nature of Computers *58*
The Program Blueprint *60*
QBasic Help *64*
Summary *68*
The Book in Review *68*

Chapter 5: Data Names and Data Types 71

Layout and Naming *72*
What is Data? *74*
Why Have Data Names? *75*
Data Types *77*
Data Names in QBasic *80*
Data Naming Rules *81*
The Data Dictionary *84*
QBasic File Menu and Commands *87*
Summary *91*
The Book in Review *92*

Chapter 6: The QBasic Editor 93

Chris' Newsletter 94
  How the QBasic Editor Helps You 94
  The Editing Keys 95
  Edit and View Menus 97
  The Find Command 97
  The Change Command 98
  Cut and Paste Commands 99
  Copying from One Routine or Program to the Other 101
  Syntax Checking 102
  An Example of Editor Use 102
  Summary 109
  The Book in Review 109

Chapter 7: Program Organization 111
  The Business Plan 112
  Why Use Routines? 112
  Organizing a Program 113
  The 10-part Model Program 117
  QBasic Routines 123
  From Blueprint to Routines 124
  Summary 126
  The Book in Review 127

Chapter 8: Control of Routines 129
  Office Environment Analogy 130
  Routines 132
  Subroutines 133
  Procedures 135
  Global and Local Data 139
  Data Into and Out of Subroutines 139
  Data In and Out of Procedures 140
  The GOTO Statement 143
  Routines in a Program 145

Summary *146*
The Book In Review *146*

Chapter 9: IF Statements 149

Choices in Real Life *150*
Why Use IF Statements? *151*
How IFS Affect Program Flow *153*
The Three Types of IFs *155*
The ELSE *156*
Block IF Statements *160*
Complex IF Statements *161*
Two Rules for IF *163*
Why Work Hard? *163*
Indenting IFs *167*
Summary *168*
The Book in Review *169*

Chapter 10: Loops 171

Non-Computer Loops *172*
The Loop is the Heart (Pump) of Every Program *173*
Three Loops *176*
The Main Routine Loop *181*
Dangerous GOTOs *182*
Summary *183*
The Book in Review *184*

Chapter 11: The Concept of Files 185

Manual File Search *186*
Data File Definition *186*
Record Definition *187*
Field Definition *187*
File Structures *189*
Sequential *190*

Indexed Files	*192*
Linked Files	*193*
File Subject Categories (and How to Design Them)	*194*
File Layouts	*196*
Summary	*198*
The Book in Review	*199*

Chapter 12: Random Files 201

A Frustrating File Search	*202*
Random File Definition	*202*
Opening a Random File	*202*
Locating a Record	*204*
Reading and Writing	*206*
Record Layout	*209*
Packing and Unpacking	*213*
Creating a Random File	*214*
Determining the End of the File	*215*
Summary	*217*
The Book in Review	*218*

Chapter 13: Linked File Concepts 221

How a Linked File Works	*222*
Linked File Examples	*222*
The Innards of a Linked File	*226*
Linking Backward	*231*
Linking Forward	*231*
Linking Forward and Backward	*231*
Link to the Master	*231*
Linking to a Document	*232*
The Last Record Used is Critical	*232*
The Master Link in the Chain	*233*
Linking the Links	*233*
Summary	*244*

The Book in Review *245*

Chapter 14: Keyboard Input **247**
Fast or Correct? *248*
Editing — It is Critical *248*
Editing Levels *249*
Error Messages *256*
Screen Neatness *263*
Summary *265*
The Book in Review *266*

Chapter 15: Reusing Edit Procedures **267**
No Two Alike *268*
Reusable Edit Procedures *268*
LINE INPUT Statement *284*
LEN Function *285*
String Processing Functions *286*
MID$, LEFT$, and RIGHT$ Functions *287*
Summary *290*
The Book in Review *291*

Chapter 16: Print it Out **293**
The Unreadable Sales Report *294*
Start at the End *295*
The (Lack of) Value in the Printed Output *295*
Types of Page Layouts *297*
Rules for Laying Out a Page *298*
Print Formats *299*
FORMAT Statement *299*
LPRINT, LPRINT Using Statements *300*
TAB Function *301*
CHR$ Function *302*
Commas and Semicolons *303*

Width Statement *303*
Summary *304*
The Book in Review *305*

Chapter 17: Screen It Out 307

The Disoriented Customer Data Screen *308*
Begin at the End *309*
The (Lack of) Value of Screen Output *309*
Screen Layout *311*
Color, Underlining, and Blinking *312*
Ten Mistakes to Avoid *312*
Keep it Simple *313*
Print Formats *313*
FORMAT Statement *313*
PRINT and PRINT USING Statements *314*
The TAB Function *316*
Commas and Semicolons *316*
CHR$ Function *317*
CLS Statement *317*
Locating a Point on the Screen *317*
The COLOR Statement *318*
The Only Criterion *320*
Summary *320*
The Book in Review *321*

Chapter 18: Calculations 323

The Cost of Service *324*
Where Computer Calculations Start *324*
Operators *325*
Combining Strings *326*
Division by Zero *326*
What is Calculated First in a Formula *327*
The Use of Parentheses *328*

Using the Right Data Types to Get the Correct Answer 330
Rounding and Presenting the Correct Answer 331
CINT, INT, FIX, and CLNG Functions 333
Math Functions 336
String Functions and Calculations 336
Date Calculations 337
Summary 340
The Book in Review 341

Chapter 19: Tables 343
Chris' Train Schedule is a Table 344
Locating the Elements in a Table 345
One-dimensional Tables 345
Two-dimensional Tables 346
Three-dimensional Tables 346
Uses of Tables in QBasic 346
Defining a Table 347
Subscripts: Keeping Them Straight 349
Dimensioning a Table 350
Getting Values into Arrays 351
Data and Read Statements 351
Printing Out a Table 352
A Table within a Random File Record 353
A Comprehensive Example 353
QBASIC Limitations 355
Summary 356
The Book in Review 357

Chapter 20: Debugging 359
Avoiding Mistakes 360
Single Stepping 360
Stop the Action 361
Action 362

Quick Look, Quick Change, Then Action *362*
A Comprehensive Example *362*
Debugger Hints *365*
Summary *366*
The Book in Review *366*

Chapter 21: Menu Programs 369
Chain Statement *370*
What a Menu Program Does *371*
The WWW Menu Program *372*
The Book in Review *373*

Appendix A: QBasic Selected Statement Summary 375

Appendix B: Sample Data Dictionary with Rules for Naming Data 379
Naming Rules *379*

Appendix C: Blueprints 383
Step 1. Purpose *383*
Step 2. End Result (OUTPUT) *383*
Step 3. Necessary Data (INPUT) *384*
Step 4. Hidden Data (HIDPUT) *384*
Step 5. LOGIC *384*
Sample Blueprint #1 .... *385*
Sample Blueprint #2 .... *386*

Appendix D: Model Program Structure 389
From Blueprint to Routines *396*

Appendix E: Sample Routines 399

Appendix F: Linked File Routines 405
Read the LastUsed *405*

The Query Routine *406*
Before Calling the Routine *409*
The Routine Itself *409*
Update the LastUsed *409*
Write a New Linked Record *410*
Update the Master Record *411*
The Assembled Routines *411*

Index **415**

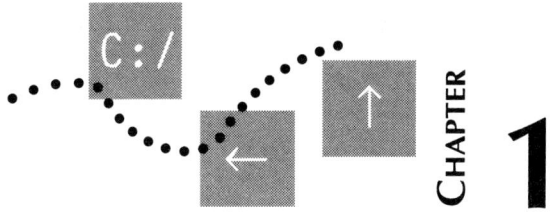

The Basics

This chapter teaches you about the wrong and right methods of learning programming, and why it is important to first understand the problem, then plan and effect the solution. The topics in this chapter include:

- The wrong way to learn
- The right way to learn programming
- Why use QBasic?
- How to use this book
- An analogy for program flow
- The definition of a program

The Wrong Way to Learn

Suppose you see some videos on white water rafting and decide to try it with three of your friends. You go down to your local sporting goods store and buy a four-person raft and four paddles. You are ready for the weekend.

The next Saturday you and your friends meet at the river. After spending one and one-half hours blowing up the raft, you discover that the *four-person* raft is really only big enough for two.

Slightly dejected, you leave the river.

The next week, you trade in your raft for a six-person raft, and buy a pump. In only half an hour, the raft is inflated, the four of you hop in, and off you go on your adventure! You quickly hit a sharp rock and puncture the raft. (It's a cheap raft, not a real white water one.)

Even more dejected, you leave the river.

The following week you buy a book called *Rafting Rivers Rapidly*, and read the first two chapters. These chapters say that you need a specially built raft for white water, and a good four-person raft costs about $1,700. You order one, wait two weeks for it to arrive, and make it back to the river on the third weekend. Your friends pump up the boat in no time, everyone jumps in, and you're off! You keep getting stuck on rocks for the first hour, and actually progress only one quarter mile downstream. Finally, you hear the roar of white water, push off the last rock, and seek your high adventure.

Since no one knows how to control the raft, let alone pick the right path through the white water, the raft hits a rock, flips, and knocks everyone out. As you and your friends swim safely to shore, you watch $1,700 go floating downstream.

Totally dejected, you leave the river.

You now read the entire book, and realize that it takes training and skill to run white water, more than you can glean from just reading. So you set up a raft trip with WildWater Works, Inc., your local rafting company.

You didn't take the **time** to learn. So you wasted both your time and money.

The Right Way to Learn Programming

The previous example is a little exaggerated to bring out a point. You would never do something as foolish as risking your life (and those of your friends) without fully understanding what your are doing. Most of us, at one time or another, have done something incorrectly because we did not properly plan and learn. Some folks risk their careers or their businesses with programs and programmers that fail because of haphazard work and a desire to get going before they know what they are doing. Computer work is similar to a construction project in that it requires both building (programming) and design skills. And you have to know what you're building before you start!

In short, take the time to:

1. Learn to program with QBasic.
2. Understand the problem.
3. Know what you want for a result.
4. Plan the project.
5. Stick with the fundamentals.
6. Work thoughtfully.

Time to Learn

Had you bought a good white water book in the first place, you would have realized that you need training to safely run white water. You could have gone to special schools and practiced on rivers with professional instructors.

Learning programming is similar. Listening to tapes while you sleep will not teach you to be a programmer. Skimming computer magazines will not do it. Neither will a book titled *Become a Master Programmer in Only One Weekend*. There's nothing magic about programming. It takes common sense, time, and practice.

NOTE
Take the time to learn and practice programming before you try to do a program of your own.

Time to Understand

Remember the four-person raft that was too small? Buying the six-person raft was not the solution. It was still the wrong raft, which solved the wrong problem.

Solving the wrong problem is a common occurrence with many programmers. They happily put together a series of programs that accomplish nothing toward the solution to the problem. It's not just difficult, it's impossible to program a solution to a problem that you do not understand.

Never think about programming something until you understand the problem.

Time to Know

You were seeking white water thrills as an end result. Before jumping (literally) into it, you should have booked a trip with a professional group to see what it was all about. Maybe you would not even like it. After a couple of trips, you would begin to see what you like (or don't like) about white water.

Many programmers do not take the time to determine what kind of report or information needs to be produced in order for a program or system (series of programs) to be useful. A report can be useless because just one piece of information is missing.

Take the time to define the end results of your program or system. Put it on paper before you start.

Plan the Project

If you had initially bought a book on white water, you would have read that every rafting trip must be planned. First you have to walk the river so you can look at each section, and see the safe way through. In some cases, like a 30-foot waterfall, you better beach and walk around it. You plan your route, equipment, and supplies.

What if programmers put together a payroll system and start it up in the middle of December? Can you imagine what a mess it would be to put in all the year-to-date numbers, train everyone how to use it, cope with the holiday absences, and get all the end-of-year reports out? They would not be able to do it. If they do all of their programming correctly, yet do not plan for the right time to start (like the first of the year), the plan will not work. Plans should be put on paper so that they are not forgotten or misunderstood.

Minutes spent in thoughtful planning, then written down, can save you hours, maybe days, and sometimes the entire job.

Stick with the Fundamentals

You could have tried flat water rafting before jumping into the rapids. That way, you would learn the basics of paddling and raft control. You would learn to walk the river and to plan your trips. Or you could ride with experienced people to learn the basics. You don't need it, right?

That's the way it is for a lot of programmers. They want to write the fancy stuff before they can write even a simple program. In QBasic, you should not expect to learn the ins and outs of every statement, how to present fancy screens or printouts, or how to work with complex file structures. Stick with selected statements that do the job, and use them over and over until and unless you find a good reason to use another statement type.

It's better to know a few statements thoroughly than to try to impress yourself and other people by using the complex, esoteric ones.

Work Thoughtfully

Programming requires careful thought both before and during the programming stage. Once the project is defined, you should be careful to watch for things that have been missed during the design stage. Programming projects fail because:

- Data is missed
- There is too much data
- There is insufficient room for data
- Many reasons that should have been picked up by a thoughtful programmer

 NOTE Following bunch of rules is no substitute for continually thinking about what you're doing, and why you're doing it. Not every situation is covered by a rule.

You can apply these lessons throughout the book to teach you to become an outstanding programmer. You do not accomplish this in one weekend, but in a month you will be crafting sensible programs that accomplish tasks well, without unneeded complexity or frivolous design. You start out with very simple programs, and you gradually:

- Design programs
- Blueprint your design (put it onto paper)
- Learn to use the right tools (QBasic statements)
- See results
- Build your confidence as a programmer, and be on your way to becoming a truly outstanding programmer

The concepts in this book, if followed and expanded upon, can accomplish this. However, you need to do a thoughtful job on your own, instead of following instructions by rote, or having someone else do it for you. By working on your own, you master the fundamentals. Then big projects seem to magically shrink down to a workable size.

Why Use QBasic?

What programming language should you use? ALGOL? C? COBOL? FORTRAN? Pascal? Why program in BASIC? Following are some of the reasons:

- It is universal. There are over one hundred million personal computers (PCs), most having BASIC bundled with the hardware.

- BASIC is well supported. It is the most developed and regularly upgraded software language.
- BASIC is the most powerful of the high-level languages. You no longer sacrifice power in exchange for ease of use.

And Why Use Microsoft's QBasic?

- **The environment.** Once you are into the QBasic software, you have available all the tools you need for every programming task. You can do your program writing, testing, changing, and retesting all with the same familiar screen.
- **The power and ease of use.** QBasic is perfect for beginning programmers. It has all the power you need for most personal programming applications. It also handles business applications. It is easy to use because it is integrated directly with DOS 5.0 and 6.0.
- **The building-block process.** QBasic encourages you to write routines, rather than program one line at a time. Each of these routines is a building block of your program structure. Just as QBasic encourages building blocks (not line-after-line of code), so does this book. The approach you'll learn starts with a block diagram, then develops and tests each section of a program separately. Using this Structured Programming method, you avoid the biggest problem: confused logic.

With *teach yourself... QBasic*, you define the overall structure of a program and then fill in the pieces, one at a time. You then test each block *before* going on to the next. This block method works better than writing program statements as fast as you can.

The problem with instant writing is, when you suddenly remember you want to change another part of the program, you *jump* to do that, then forget where you were. Then, your change probably messed up perfectly good logic.

The building-block approach gives you the discipline to finish what you're doing.

How to Use This Book

In this book, you can focus on grasping the fundamental idea of everything you do. Understand what you are programming (rather than worrying about which new statement type to use today); then do it.

Good programming requires:

- A concept of both the problem and the solution
- Good design work
- Thought while programming
- Regular practice

When you finish this book, you will have a head start on becoming a good programmer. But it doesn't end there. You need to continue practicing and enhancing this approach to become a great programmer.

As you read *teach yourself... QBasic*, think about these things:

1. Read each chapter thoughtfully. Make the time to study, not just to look at the sample programs. By investing your time initially, you save months of programming time later on.

2. The sample programs illustrate the building-block approach to programming. This approach is both easy to learn and quickly produces working programs. Take the programs in their building-block order; do not jump around the book.

3. Do the exercises. Do not just think about them; write them out. It helps enhance both understanding and memory.

4. You may wonder why you are not working on-screen all the time, starting with Chapter 1. In the same way that raft guides begin their crew in gentle water, then progress to dangerous rapids, this book guides you into the actual use of QBasic. Like most computer languages, QBasic may seem strange at the start. Remember, this is not an instruction manual. You are going to gradually build your knowledge of QBasic, program design, and program structure by actually using them.

5. You may not understand everything you read the first time. This is no reason to panic. Reread what you do not understand several times, then go on. You might not feel ready to use each statement right away. Use it anyway. Use it until you have a good feel for how it works, even if you do not understand it completely. Focus on the big picture and ignore the details. There may be times when you do not see the point of an example. In each case, do the exercises, and go back to the original muddle. If you still do not understand the example, make a note, then go on. When you

are through with the next chapter, go back to that example and read it again. If it is still not clear, repeat the process after reading each succeeding chapter.

6. Never memorize detail. It gives you false security. It is better to understand general concepts. No matter how much detail you have memorized, a new problem crops up. The best way out is to think. Learning to program is like learning a foreign language. Of course you don't understand everything at first, but example after example clarify the meaning for you. Sometimes the examples intentionally lead you to make a mistake and then fix it, so that you gain confidence in your own problem-solving skills.

7. Do not be insecure that other people are using fancy functions, commands, and program statements that are not included in this book. Rather than explain four ways to do the same thing, this book selects the one or two that are the easiest and most efficient. It is better to expertly use a limited number of tools rather than to fumble with the many tools that might work. It saves you the time of looking up that rare fancy statement to see how it works.

8. Do not read between the lines. Do not project your own ideas onto what is read. Clear your mind each time you pick up the book, and read what is there and no more.

9. Read this book carefully now, and program for several months. Then reread it. The things that seem puzzling at first will seem simple after you have had some experience in programming.

After you have thoughtfully read this book, you will marvel at how quickly you can design and write programs that really work. All you have to do is zero in on the task and its simple solution. I hope the exercises in this book keep the learning light and give you a chuckle. You will be proud of your own accomplishments as you solve the problems raised in these funny examples.

Here's a surprise: Start at the end of the program and work backwards. Instead of leaping in to code line number 1 without a design, you begin at the end by designing the output of the program. Just ask the right questions. Once the output is designed, the rest of the program can be *blueprinted* (both logic and data specified on paper). After the program is blueprinted, you begin writing the actual program. Try this method a few times; it works.

An Analogy for Program Flow

You probably wonder why this book starts with that exaggerated white water example. The reason is that computer program flow relates well to water flow in a river. To keep continuity throughout the book, it begins with a white water example, and all further examples throughout the book relate to WildWater Works, Inc. This imaginary white water rafting company was founded by three people—Chris, Pat, and Terry. The sometimes exaggerated examples use this imaginary company to help you to learn to use QBasic to solve problems.

Chris, Pat, and Terry are all MBA graduates who went to work for large companies and met while white water rafting on the Hudson River one weekend. Realizing how much they enjoyed the rafting, they decided to pool their savings and form WildWater Works, Inc. With their combination of white water and business knowledge they felt that they could make a lot of money while having fun. They bought four rafts, paddles, gear, insurance, and went into the rafting business.

They rented an old barn to use as office space and to store all the equipment and rafting gear, and provide changing rooms for the guests. Chris is the marketer and handles all advertising and promotion. Pat is the river manager in charge of all the rafting trips and the equipment. Terry handles the administrative work such as bill-paying and scheduling.

After one year of hard work and a lot of fun, they realized that they were not making enough money. They were having so much fun, that they forgot to use their business backgrounds. They need to get more repeat business and to manage their trips better. They have to make more money on each rafting customer and manage their purchases better.

They decided to buy a computer. It came with DOS 6.0 and QBasic.

That did not guarantee their success. A lot of computers are used improperly and create, rather than reduce chaos.

But Chris, Pat, and Terry are sharp people who realize that they cannot really manage well without a computer. Of course, the computer is worthless without the necessary business programs (software). Fortunately Terry is an accomplished systems analyst/programmer, and knows QBasic. You will be working along with Terry for many of the examples.

The Definition of a Program

Since this book is about writing programs, it seems logical to end the first chapter with our definition of a program:

A *program* is a series of statements (precise instructions), which the computer looks at and executes in order until it reaches the end result: a report.

A *report*, as used throughout this book, means any data that is written onto any medium, such as paper, computer screen, or computer floppy or hard disks.

Summary

1. Study the sample programs.
2. Write out the exercises. That's what programming is all about.
3. This is more than an instruction manual: it is your learning tool for programming. You are the most important ingredient.
4. Reread unclear topics and use the examples and exercises to make them clear.
5. Understand the concepts, do not memorize.
6. Do not try to impress anyone with fancy programming tools. Use a few tools well.
7. Do not read between the lines. The hardest part of programming is to make things simple. As you read this book, you develop that training in simplicity.
8. Reread this book six months from now. You learn a lot more the second time.

The Book in Review

This is the first in an accumulation of the major points of every chapter. At the end of each chapter, you will find a repeat of the themes of the preceding chapters, merged with the concept you just learned. These are the *building blocks* of your programming knowledge in QBasic. Here is your first basic building block.

1. **Design and program thoughtfully.**

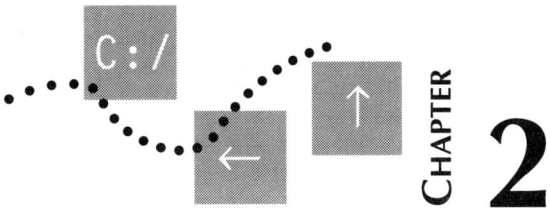

CHAPTER 2

Your First Program

This chapter explains the conventions this book uses for programs, keyboard commands, and text. It introduces you to some simple QBasic programs. The topics include:

- Conventions in this book
- Four QBasic statements
- Statement labels
- A program to print an address label
- A program to average three numbers
- Your first look at programs
- What a cash program does
- WildWater Works cash register program

Conventions in This Book

Before you look at the QBasic programs, there are a few special highlighting techniques for which you need explanations:

- You will see a QBasic program line that is very long, and takes up two or more lines in this book.
- There are specific keyboard input instructions:
  - pressing a specific key or keys
  - typing a specific word or words
  - typing a word or words that varies with the data in the program.
- Sometimes you see that a word (in a sentence) is part of a QBasic program statement, not part of the English text that you're reading.
- You need to be able to distinguish between words that are QBasic *commands* and words that are not.

To do all of this clearly, here are the eight conventions used throughout this book.

1. A QBasic program line can be up to 254 characters long. You cannot fit more than 60 characters on a line. So the line ends with an underscore (_) when it continues onto the next line:

   ```
   PRINT custlastnam$; TAB(20); custfirstnam$;TAB(40);_
   custdob; TAB(50); custphone#; TAB(65); custlastpurch
   ```

2. When you are asked to press a particular key, you see the word *Press* followed by the key name in bold like this:

   Press **Caps Lock**.
   Press **Space**.
   Press **Tab Tab Tab** (press **Tab** 3 times).
   Press **Enter**.
   Press **Shift** (and hold it as you Press **Enter**).

3. Whenever you are asked to type in a specific word(s), you see the word *Type* followed by the words for you to type in bold print:

   Type   **Good Rafting**, press **Enter**.

Type **11.95**, press **Enter**.

4. Normally at the end of each Type instruction you press the **Enter** (**Return**) key. If for some reason you should not press it, Enter will not be displayed at the end of the line. So the examples above would look like this:

Type **Good Rafting**
Type **11.95**

5. To keep the examples clear, you may see Type only on the first line of several lines requiring typing:

Type **Break a paddle**, press **Enter**.
Good Surfing, press **Enter**.
Good Swimming, press **Enter**.

6. You see words within the following brackets :{ }. They usually bracket a generic term (such as *file name*). Do not type the word or words that you see within the brackets; instead, type the specific values that fit the situation. Here are two examples:

   1. Type {today's date}

   You type today's date in 2-digit month/day/year format. For example, if today's date is June 1, 1994, you type:

   060194

   2. PRINT {some text}

   You type the text to be printed, for instance:

   PRINT "Whitewater is Wonderful!"

7. The words that the computer recognizes as *commands* to do something (called *reserved words* in QBasic, since they are reserved for QBasic's use— you cannot use them as data names) will be capitalized within English sentences:

```
PRINT
INPUT
IF...THEN...ELSE...
GOTO
```

8. If QBasic does not recognize a word as a command, it figures that the word is something whose value can change within the program. These *variable*

names (all the words in a QBasic program that are not reserved words) are within English sentences in lowercase and italicized like this:

price
retailprice
lastname$

Four QBasic Statements

QBasic programs are made up of statements that instruct the computer to do operations such as:

- Get data from the keyboard
- Display data on the computer screen
- Print data onto paper
- Perform calculations with data
- Read data from a disk
- Write data onto a disk
- Go to a statement (other than the next one in line)

Each statement type you need is explained thoroughly later in the book. To start your programming knowledge, here are PRINT, INPUT, GOTO and Calculation statements. You will use these four statements in some programs.

NOTE

Grasp the general idea of this section. Do not worry about the detail of the statements; they are covered thoroughly in later chapters.

Print

The PRINT statement displays data on the computer screen. (Chapter 5 covers data types and data names completely.) For the first example, assume that *price* has a value of 19.95. Then this statement:

```
PRINT "The cost will be "; price
```

displays as:

```
The cost will be 19.95
```

on the computer screen. In this example, the data name *price* contains 19.95, and "The cost will be" is a text label.

This statement:

```
PRINT "T-Shirt Sales for WildWater Works"
```

displays as:

```
T-Shirt Sales for WildWater Works
```

on the computer screen. This example has only the text label "T-Shirt Sales for WildWater Works." It has no data. Note the quotes around the text labels. They tell the computer to print exactly what is contained within the quotes.

This statement:

```
PRINT price
```

will display as:

```
19.95
```

on the computer screen. This example has only the data value of 19.95 in price. There are no text labels.

Input

The INPUT statement gets data into a computer program using the keyboard. When an INPUT statement is executed in a QBasic program, the computer stops and waits for you to type in data.

This statement:

```
INPUT "Please enter a new selling price";saleprice
```

displays this on the computer monitor:

```
Please enter a new selling price ?
```

and waits for the operator to key in a value, which it saves in the data name *saleprice*.

This statement:

```
INPUT price
```

displays this on the monitor:

```
?
```

and waits for the operator to key in a value, which it saves in the data name *price*.

GOTO

The GOTO statement tells the computer to go to a statement other than the next one down in the program. (Program flow is covered completely in Chapter 4. The GOTO statement is explained thoroughly in Chapter 8.)

This statement:

```
GOTO calctrip
```

causes the computer to go to the statement line that has the name *calctrip:* as the first nine characters in the line.

Calculate

Calculations in QBasic are represented in the same way that formulas are shown on paper, with + (add), – (subtract), * (multiply), and / (divide):

```
c = 100
```

gives *c* a value of 100.

```
b = c * 3
```

gives *b* a value of 300 (*c* is 100; and it is multiplied by 3).

```
a = b + (c / 5)
```

gives a the value of 320 (when *b* is 300 and *c* is 100).

Now that you have seen a few statement types, you will be introduced to statement *labels*. A label is either a name or a number that uniquely identifies a program line in QBasic. A label is always at the start of the line.

Statement Labels

You may have seen BASIC programs where each line started with a number:

```
1000 INPUT "Enter a value for the cost ";realcost
```

```
1100 sellprice = realcost * 1.75
1200 PRINT"Cost is ";realcost,"Selling price is "; sellprice
1300 GOTO 1100
```

Any statement line that is referred to by any other statement in a program must have a label as the first characters of the line. You have two choices in labeling a statement in QBasic:

1. Name the statement line. For example,
   ```
   nextcost: INPUT"Enter a value for the cost ";realcost
   ```
2. Number the statement. For example,
   ```
   1000 INPUT "Enter a value for the cost ";realcost
   ```

In QBasic, you can mix statement line names and numbers, as long as all statement labels are unique. It is better to name, rather than number, the lines for easy reading. (Every program always has at least two readers: the computer and the programmer.)

The computer is rather smart. It can find statement lines anywhere, and it can remember them all. It makes no difference to the computer if you name or number statement lines, as long as each statement label is unique.

But people are smarter. Programmers (you included) can figure out that a statement numbered 140 comes somewhere after number 100. You can also guess that statement 4000 is roughly half-way through a program whose line numbers run from 10 to 8200. And you will remember the statement numbers of frequently used routines. But programmers do not retain that information for long. If you come back to the program after a lapse of eleven months or maybe after a two-week vacation, will you remember at what number the date-testing routine begins? Probably not. It is too hard to remember what numbers represent several dozen routines in a big program. And when you're working with several programs, the number 1900 probably represents something different in each program.

As the programmer, you need to be able to look at your work and follow the *flow* of the program logic. However, the logical flow is different from the numeric sequence of the statement lines. As control keeps jumping back and forth, the numbers of the statement lines mean less and less. So it is better if you use line names rather than numbers. Throughout this book you see line names as labels, for the above reasons. But the final choice between names and numbers is yours.

A Program to Print an Address Label

The following program could take the place of a typewriter in printing an address label for an envelope. (Except it prints on the screen, rather than the printer.) The program:

1. Asks for five different data items—name, address, city, state, and zip.
2. It then asks the program user it should print it out.
3. If the user types in a **Y** and presses **Return**, all the data is printed on the screen.
4. It then goes back to the beginning and asks for more data.
   Study it—you run it in the next chapter.

```
getnext: INPUT"Key in the name ";nam$
INPUT"Key in the address";street$
INPUT"Key in the city ";city$
INPUT"Key in the state";stat$
INPUT"Key in the zip ";zip$
INPUT"Print it out, (Y or N) ";i$
if i$ <>"Y" THEN GOTO getnext
PRINT nam$
PRINT street$
PRINT city$;" ";stat$;" ";zip$
GOTO getnext
```

A Program to Average Three Numbers

Here is a little a program that:

1. Asks for three numbers to be typed in.
2. Averages them.
3. Displays the answer on the monitor.
4. Goes back to start and asks for three more numbers.

It could be used for averaging bowling scores. Try to understand how it works. (You run it in the next chapter.)

```
getnums: INPUT"Key in the 1st number ";numbr1
INPUT"Key in the 2nd number ";numbr2
INPUT"Key in the 3rd number ";numbr3
avg=(numbr1 + numbr2 + numbr3)/3
print numbr1;numbr2;numbr3;"   ****   ";avg
GOTO getnums
```

Your First Look at Programs

The first time that you look at any large, unfamiliar program you may as well be looking at the cockpit of the space shuttle. There is so much to figure out. How do you make sense of it all?

1. Break it up into small, workable pieces.
2. Look at the REM statements.
3. Slow down and relax. You can do it.
4. Draw blocks around the sections or *logic groups* (statements that appear to belong together because they are the same type of statement, make up a routine, or they all are indented the same). Try to identify what each block does in one simple sentence. This is the block-line method.
5. Look at the REM statements, which are the original programmer's REMarks or comments, to help the reading programmer understand how the program works.
6. Remember that every program:
   - Reads data
   - Processes it
   - Puts out some form of report (on the screen, to the printer, or onto disk)

What a Register Program Does

The next program that you see is called a *Cash Register* program. It has six major steps. The program:

1. Asks for a price of an item.
2. Asks for the number of items being bought at that price.
3. Repeats steps (1) and (2) until no items are left.
4. Prints a subtotal.
5. Calculates sales tax.
6. Prints the total amount of the sales transaction.

WildWater Works Register Program

Here is a simple register program. It is a little too plain for real use by WildWater Works. But it's a good program to use as an example, because it has several parts. We dress up the program later. Try to figure out how it works. (You enter and use it in the next chapter.)

```
REM -- program "WWWreg.bas" -- created 060194
    CLS : REM -- clear the screen
    PRINT "* * * * * WILDWATER WORKS * * * * *"
    PRINT "* * * * * REGISTER  PROGRAM      * * * * * *"
    subtot = 0: REM — zero out the subtotal

REM -- (Step 1- asks for the price)
getprice:
    REM — get the price of an item
    INPUT "Please enter the price of the item"; price
    REM — If price = 0 (no more items) got to subtotal
    IF price = 0 then goto subtotal
REM — (Step 2 - asks for number of items)
    INPUT "Please enter the number of items with that price"; numbr
    REM — multiply to calculate the extended price
    extpr = price * numbr
    REM — print the extended price
```

```
    PRINT "extention is "; extpr
    REM — add to the subtotal
    subtot = subtot + extpr
REM — (Step 3 — goes back to repeat the process)
    REM go back and get more
    GOTO getprice
REM — (Step 4 - prints the subtotal)
subtotal:
    PRINT "Subtotal is "; subtot
REM — (Step 5 - calculate the sales tax)
    slstax = .05 * subtot
    PRINT "Sales tax is "; slstax
REM — (Step 6 - print the total)
    grandtot = subtot + slstax
    PRINT "Total amount is "; grandtot
END
```

Look at the Step numbers in the program, and find the statements that do the functions of each step.

Recall this statement from Chapter 1: You might not instantly understand everything you read in this book. You needn't worry about what goes on in each statement line; that's not the purpose of the examples. You need to develop a *feel* for how these sample programs work.

If you are comfortable with the Register program's workings right away, great! Go back for an even closer look, and try to figure out more of the detail.

If, after half an hour you are confused with the Register program, clear your mind and go on. You will understand it by the end of the next chapter because you will be running it.

Summary

1. Use names, not numbers, for line labels.
2. The first time you look at a program:

   - Group statements into sections and draw blocks around those sections. Identify in a single sentence what each block does.
   - Look at the REMark statements.

The Book in Review

1. Design and program thoughtfully.
2. **To examine any QBasic program, break it up into blocks.** Then, study each block separately, and finally, look at the logic that controls all the blocks.

CHAPTER 3

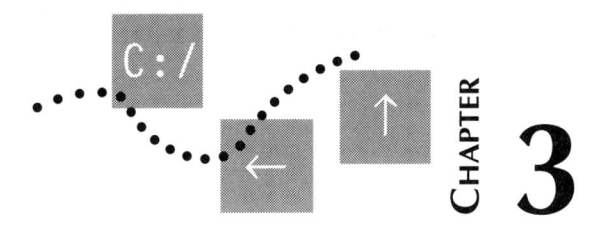

QBasic

This chapter provides exercises that you can perform to build some short programs in QBasic. You will use more examples from WildWater Works, Inc. to build your skills. You will learn about:

- Working backwards
- Starting QBasic
- Typing in a program
- Saving a program
- Opening an existing program
- Testing a program
- Working in the QBasic environment
- Setting QBasic options
- Browsing menus

Using the Right Tools

Remember the last time you worked on your lawn mower, bicycle, or truck without having all the right tools at your fingertips? You found that you wasted more time than you spent actually working.

WildWater Works is in that very situation. It is working on the old school bus that WildWater Works, Inc. uses to haul their customers to and from the river. It was a really cold raft trip (typical Adirondack March weather), and the icicles that were hanging from the customers' hair and beards never melted on the half hour bus ride back to the barn! So Pat is installing an extra heater in the rear of the bus— a warm customer is a happy one.

Pat takes all the tools out, bumping the heater in the process so it's out of alignment, only to find the ratchet missing. That's right—Terry used it to repair the generator last week. Pat goes into the office, finds the ratchet right next to the generator, and goes back to work.

Pat realigns the heater, puts the bolt through, starts to try to tighten it up; it will not go. The vice grips are needed to hold the nut Looking through the pile of tools strewn on the ground, Pat realizes that the VICE GRIPS ARE GONE!

Oh, yeah. Chris was using them to put together the miniature river display — the one with flowing water that shows the different classes of rapids. Pat goes to the van, gets the vice grips, then back to the bus. "Now, where was I??"

Computer programming is much like a complex repair task. There are thousands of detailed steps, and you to have know which one you are on. QBasic provides you with both the tools and the working environment to get your programs finished without wasting time. Once you start programming in the QBasic working environment, you never need to leave it until you are finished. You'll see. You start using it in this chapter.

Working Backwards

You can work along with Terry to write the register program from the previous chapter. Although simplified, this program accomplishes what a cash register does.

For each program, Terry starts at the end, then works backwards, asking a series of questions:

Q: What is the purpose of this register program?
A: To add up purchases, calculate sales tax, and print the total amount of the sale at WildWater Works's clothing headquarters.

Q: What output report(s) are produced?
A: The calculated extended price, sales tax, and total purchase amount.

Q: What input is needed for this report?
A: Price and number of items purchased.

You can work on your own computer, as Terry writes the menu program for WildWater Works. You go into the QBasic environment, write the program using the Editor (a fancy name for a word processor for programmers), and then run it. Once more, don't worry about understanding everything. If you run into a problem, this book shows you right away how to back up and try again.

Starting QBasic

Just a quick couple of sentences on computer disks: A directory on a computer disk is like a chapter in a book. Directories are normally formed to separate different kinds of programs, just as chapters in a book cover different topics. If you installed DOS 6.0 according to the instructions, QBasic is in the DOS directory. You need to get into the DOS directory (or whatever directory that contains QBasic), and then type **qbasic**. For example,

Type **cd\dos** (to get into the DOS directory).
      qbasic (to run QBasic).

(If you have a problem starting QBasic, check file directories to locate the right directory; then consult your DOS and QBasic reference manuals.) You can also get into QBasic by calling in **dosshell**, and selecting **MS-DOS QBasic**.

The program displays the MS-DOS QBasic Startup Screen, as shown in Figure 3.1 on the next page.

Press **Esc**.

28 • TEACH YOURSELF... QBASIC

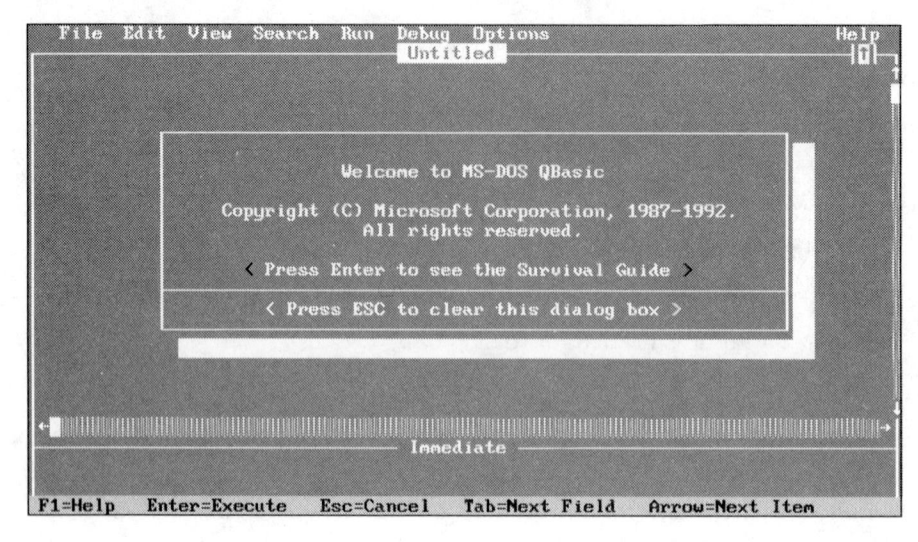

Figure 3.1 The MS-DOS QBasic startup screen.

The program displays the following screen, displayed in Figure 3.2, which is your work space. The large window is where you write and edit your programs. There is nothing in the editing window yet, and it is labeled "Untitled." At the bottom of the screen is a smaller opening, labeled "Immediate." You use that in a later chapter.

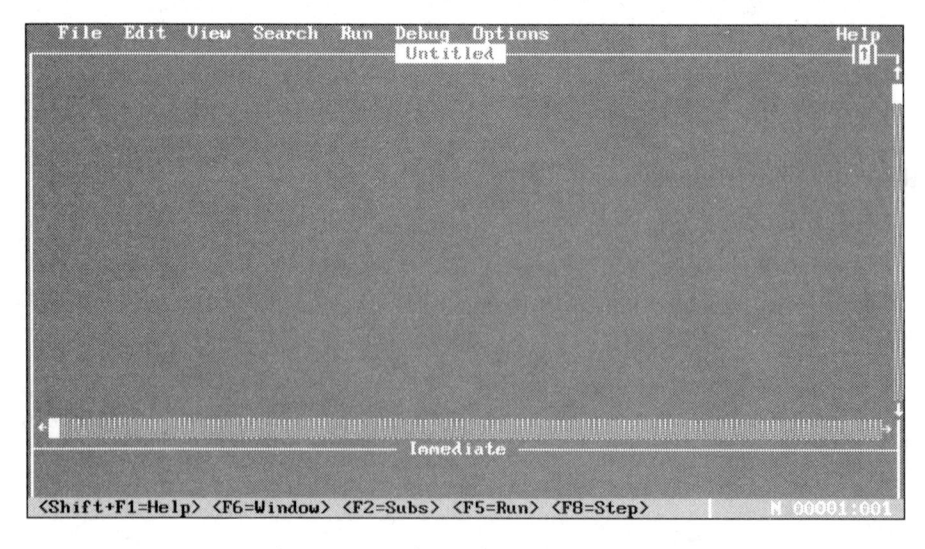

Figure 3.2 The QBasic work space.

There are a lot of QBasic commands. To make it easier to select from the possible choices, they are combined into different menu lists. The names of the menu groups are shown across the top of the screen.

These group labels across the top of the screen are your ALTernative choices in QBasic. They are always accessed by pressing **Alt**.

This first exercise in using QBasic:

1. Shows you how to exit QBasic.
2. Gets you back into QBasic.
3. Has you type in a new program.
4. Saves a program.
5. Runs a program.

The first menu selection is the File group.

Press **Alt**.

The File option, which is the first menu group at the top left of the screen, is now reverse-highlighted, as shown in Figure 3.3. QBasic is ready to perform whatever operation you select from the File menu.

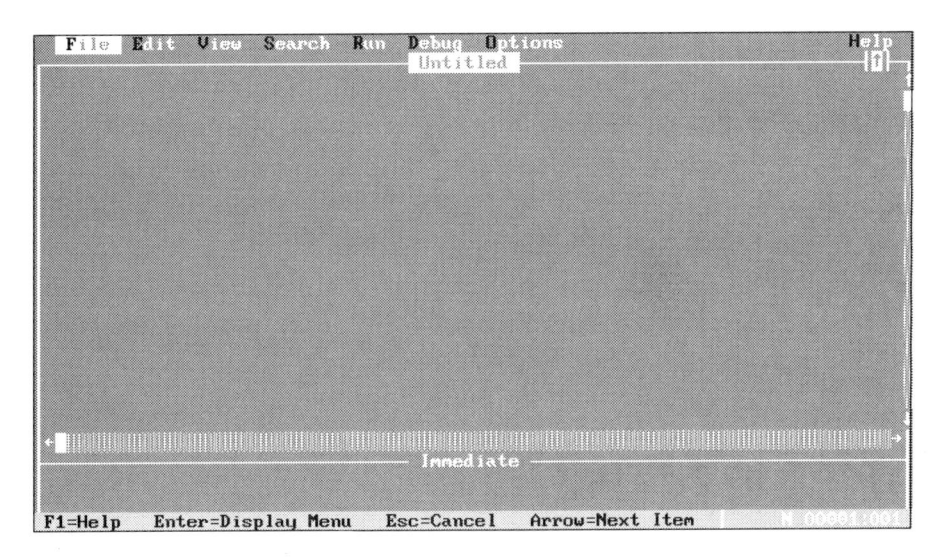

Figure 3.3 *The reverse-highlighted File option.*

To select the File menu, press **Enter**.

The program displays the File menu, as shown in Figure 3.4.

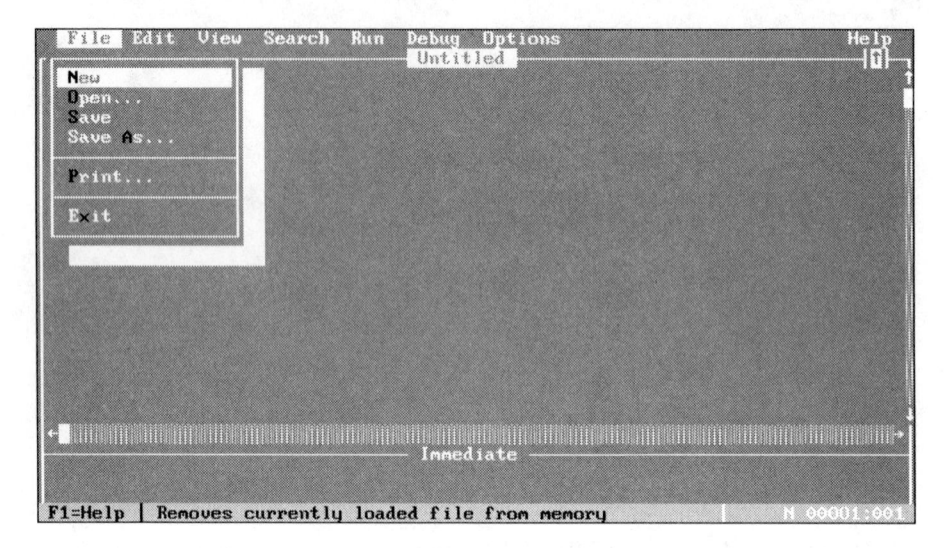

Figure 3.4 The File menu.

The first entry on the File menu, **New**, is highlighted.

First, we are going to get out of QBasic. then we will get back in. Notice that the last entry on the File menu is Exit. The quickest way to get out of QBasic is to type the letter that is highlighted and underlined in the word "Exit."

Press **X**.

You have exited QBasic. So remember, in the very worst situation, if you are totally confused, have no idea where you are, what to do—and have to start all over again, you have an ALTernative: file exit. When you are in QBasic, press **Alt**, press **F** (for the File menu) then **X** (for Exit), and you are out.

Typing in a Program

Now, reenter QBasic.

Select **MS-DOS QBasic** from the DOS shell, or type **qbasic** and press **Enter**, if you are at the DOS prompt.

Press **Esc**.

The large window of the working (program writing) space redisplays, as shown in Figure 3.5.

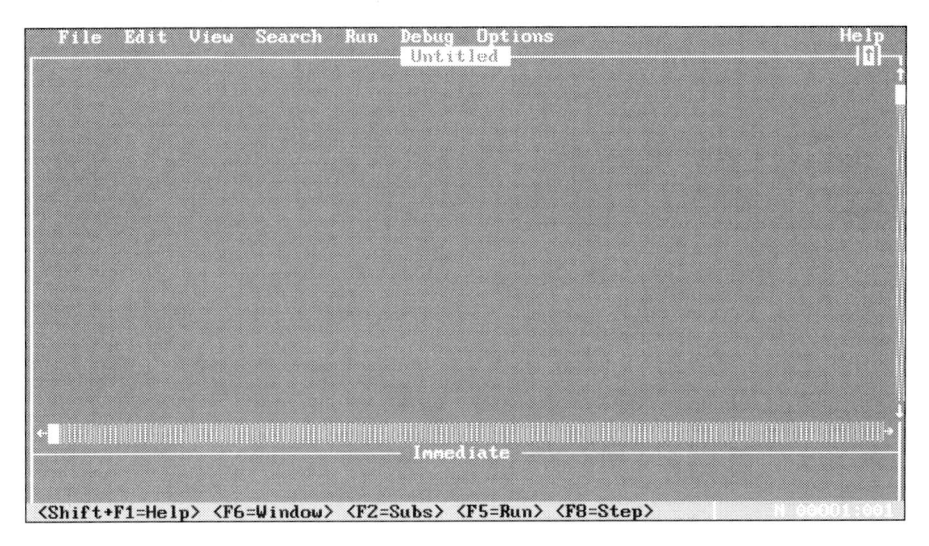

Figure 3.5 The QBasic work space.

To type in a new program file, select the File menu:

Press **Alt**, **Enter**.

The program displays the File menu as shown in Figure 3.4.

The first selection is the one you want, and it is already highlighted, so press **Enter**.

The program displays the work space again.

The cursor is in the top left corner of your working window, ready for you to begin typing in your first program. Terry has a certain convention when writing the first line of a new program; it's a good idea for you use it, too.

Type   **rem — program register.bas {today's date}**

This is a REMark statement with the program name and the date of creation. It should be the first line of every program. Next, watch the "rem" at the beginning of the program line as you

Press **Enter**.

Notice that the line became "REM." QBasic automatically capitalizes its reserved words while leaving everything else (variable names) exactly as typed. This makes programs easier to read and scan. If you have an error message after you press **Enter**, follow the steps below:

1. Press **Enter** once more to get rid of the "OK" box.
2. Check the line that you typed against the REM example above.
3. Use the arrow keys (right side of keyboard) to move to the error.
4. Use **Backspace** or **Delete**, or retype characters to fix the mistake.
5. Press **End** to move to the end of the statement line.
6. Press **Enter**.

Guidelines for Typing in Programs

As you type in program statements, remember these things:

1. To save yourself time and grief, carefully read the program statements that follow and type them exactly. Look at your spacing and punctuation. A colon (:) looks a lot like a semicolon (;), a comma (,) is close to a period on the keyboard (.). If you substitute one for the other, QBasic instantly objects.
2. If you make a mistake, QBasic may tell you, as soon as you press **Enter**, by flashing an error message and an "OK" box. When that happens, press **Enter** again and the error message no longer displays. Then, compare your typed program line with the text that you should have typed. Use the **Arrow** keys, **Backspace**, or **Delete** to correct your statement line.
3. You can always correct a mistake before QBasic catches it by using the **Arrow** keys, **Backspace**, or **Delete**, then retyping.

Now type in the program:

```
REM -- program "WWWreg.bas" -- created 060194
```

```
    CLS : REM -- clear the screen
    PRINT "* * * * * WILDWATER WORKS * * * * *"
    PRINT "* * * * * REGISTER  PROGRAM     * * * * *"
    subtot = 0: REM — zero out the subtotal
REM -- (Step 1- asks for the price)
getprice:
    REM — get the price of an item
    INPUT "Please enter the price of the item"; price
    REM — If price = 0 (no more items) go to subtotal
    IF price = 0 then goto subtotal
REM — (Step 2 - asks for number of items)
    INPUT "Please enter the number of items with that
price"; numbr
    REM — multiply to calculate the extended price
    extpr = price * numbr
    REM — print the extended price
    PRINT "extention is "; extpr
    REM — add to the subtotal
    subtot = subtot + extpr
REM — (Step 3 — goes back to repeat the process)
    REM go back and get more
    GOTO getprice
REM — (Step 4 - prints the subtotal)
subtotal:
    PRINT "Subtotal is "; subtot
REM — (Step 5 - calculate the sales tax)
    slstax = .05 * subtot
    PRINT "Sales tax is "; slstax
REM — (Step 6 - print the total)
    grandtot = subtot + slstax
    PRINT "Total amount is "; grandtot
END
```

Congratulations, you have just typed your first program in QBasic.

Saving a Program

Now you can save the program. Murphy's Law particularly applies to computer programming, so Terry always saves a program on the disk before running it. (A lot of things can cause a program to hang up. If the program was not saved, you can lose all the programming work done; then you have to start over.)

Get the File menu:

Press **Alt, Enter**.

QBasic displays the File menu, as shown in Figure 3.6.

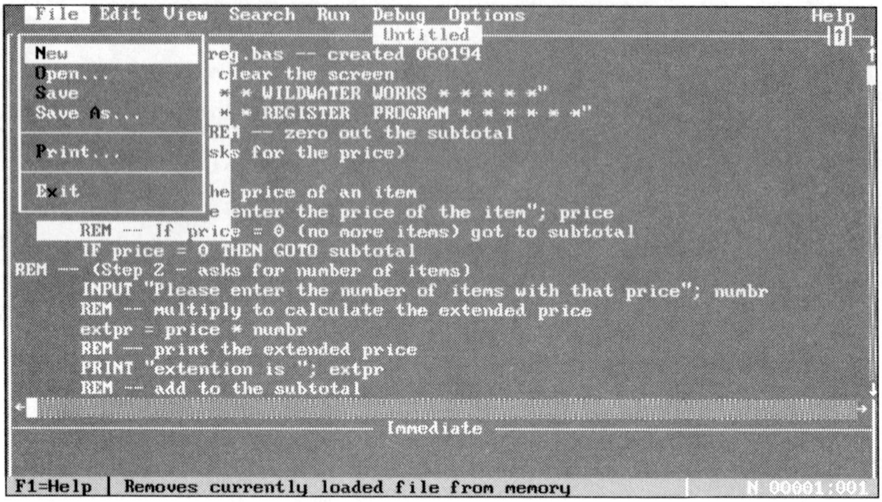

Figure 3.6 *The File menu.*

The File menu offers two ways of saving a program. Select the first, "Save":

Press **S**,

or press **Down Arrow** twice, then press **Enter** and the Save box pops up, as shown in Figure 3.7.

The cursor is now inside the File Name box, waiting for the file (program) name to be saved. Use "WWWreg" as the program name.

Type **WWWreg**, then press **Enter**.

QBasic saves this new menu program under that name. It also puts the name at the top of the editing window, replacing the "Untitled."

Now you can leave QBasic.

Press **Alt**.

Type **F**, **X** to help you practice the exit and entrance.

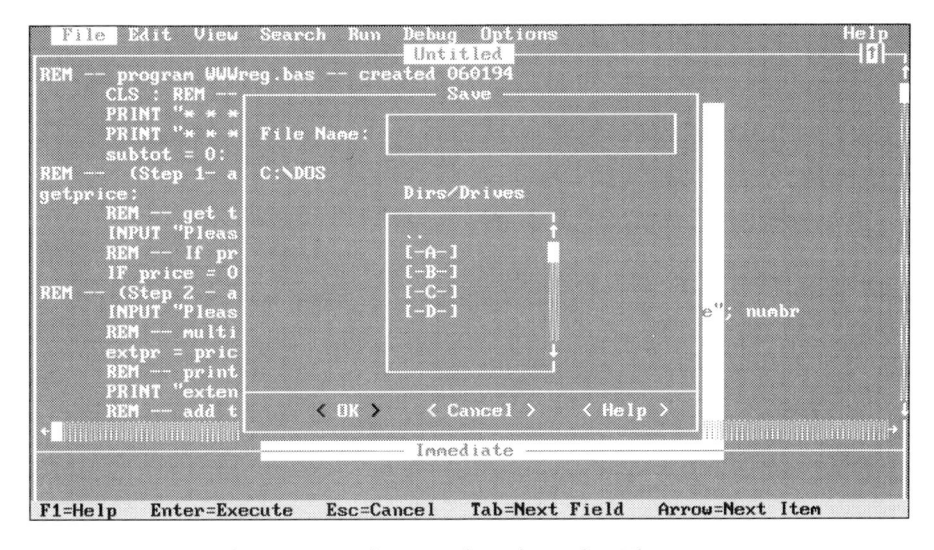

Figure 3.7 The Save box from the File menu.

Opening an Existing Program

Run WWWreg.bas to see how it works. Reenter QBasic:

Type **qbasic**, press **Enter**, or select it from the Dos shell.
Press **Alt**.
Select the **File** menu.
Press **Enter**.

QBasic displays the File menu, as shown in Figure 3.6.

The first time you picked the File menu, you wanted to type in a new program. This time, you want to open a program that already exists. To select that option, you can either

Type **O** (for Open Program) and press **Enter**,
or
Press **Down Arrow** and press **Enter**.

The cursor is in the File Name box, waiting for you to type the name of the program you want to get.

Type **WWWreg**, press **Enter**.

QBasic displays the WWWreg.bas program in your work space.

Testing a Program

You are ready to run your first program.

>Press **Alt**.
>Type **R**.

QBasic displays the Run menu, as shown in Figure 3.8.

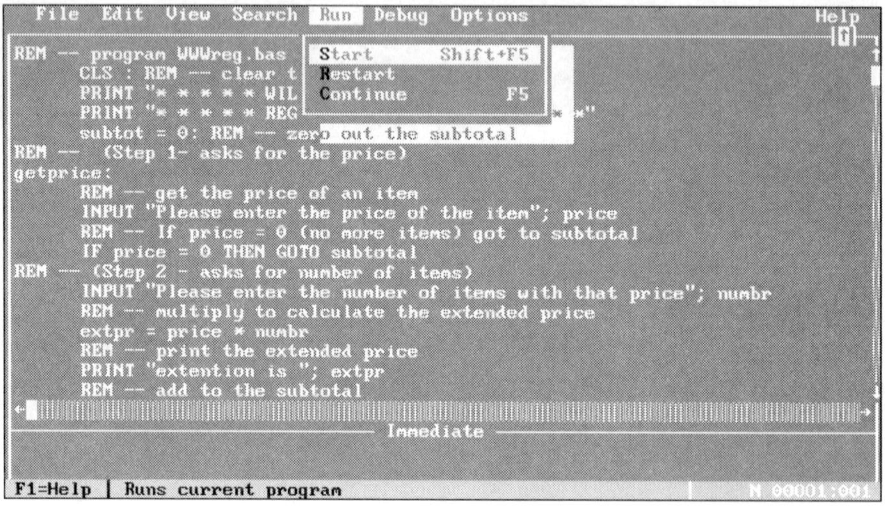

Figure 3.8   The Run menu.

>Press **Enter**.

If your typing was perfect, this is what you will see on your computer screen:

```
* * * * * WILDWATER WORKS* * * * *
* * * * * REGISTER PROGRAM* * * * *
Please enter the price of the item?
```

The program is asking you to type in a price

>Type **10.00**, press **Enter**.

```
Please enter the number of items with that price?
```

The program is asking for the number of like items.

    Type **3**, press **Enter**.

    The program prints:

```
extention is  30
Please enter the price of the item?
```

Type **0**, press **Enter**.

    The program prints:

```
Subtotal is   30
Sales tax is  1.5
Total amount is  31.5
```

You have just run your first QBasic program.

- If the program is perfect, then skip to the section below called, *It Runs!*
- If anything works differently from what is described above, then skip to the section below called, *It Does Not Run...*

It Runs!

Congratulations! Reward yourself, and skip to the next section.

It Does Not Run...

The usual problem is that something was not typed in correctly. Look at your program listing on-screen. Compare your program carefully with the listing above for WWWreg.bas. Correct any errors as explained in the Guidelines.

    Then, save the corrected program file again:

Press **Alt**.

Type **F**, **S**.

    After you save the program, try running it again (press **Alt**, type **R**). If you do not get the results described above within 45 minutes, save the program file on disk. You will come back to it later.

The QBasic Environment

The strong point of QBasic is its many tools. The tools help you with every programming task without leaving the QBasic environment. QBasic is an all-inclusive working environment where you can:

1. Write a program.
2. Test a program.
3. Change a program.
4. Get a program (from disk) to change or test.
5. Save (to disk) a program you've changed or written.
6. Run a program with data to get a report.
7. Merge part or all of a program with another.
8. Bring in pieces from several programs, and quickly cut and paste (move around) selected statements into a working program.
9. Build routines to use later in thousands of programs.
10. Quickly correct errors.
11. Print a program.

Setting QBasic Options

Before you become immersed in QBasic, you need to set some options to suit your way of working. It's a little bit of a side trip, unrelated to anything you have been doing, or will be doing. However, you should get the right options set before you go any further. You perform this procedure only once, and you never have to do it again, so this book will not waste time and space explaining it.

To set the QBasic options, get into QBasic, if you are not already there

Press **Alt**.
Press **O**.

The program displays the Options menu, as shown in Figure 3.9. If the Options menu does not display,

Press **Esc** several times, and start again.

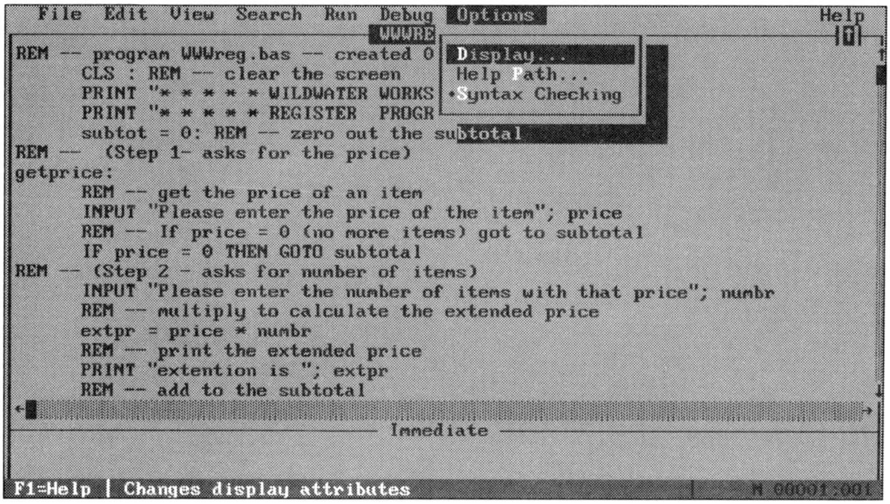

Chapter Three: QBasic • 39

Figure 3.9   *The Options menu.*

Once you see the Options menu, confirm that there is a dot just to the left of the Syntax Checking line.

If the dot is beside Syntax Checking, press **Esc**, and skip down to the paragraph about the Display command below.

If the dot is not to the left of the Syntax Checking line, move the cursor down to the Syntax Checking line.

Press **Down Arrow** twice, then press **Enter**.

The Options menu no longer displays.

Now, press **Alt+O**.

The program displays the Options menu again. A dot should now be to the left of the Syntax Checking line. If it is not, go back one paragraph, and do it again.

If you have a color monitor, you can change the colors by selecting the Display command. You can change the colors any way you want. When the colors are the way that you want,

Press **Esc** and exit QBasic. The options are set.

Press **Alt**.

Type **F**, **X**.

Now you can browse through QBasic.

Browsing the Menus

Now switch from programming for a little while, and explore your QBasic tool kit. This is just a quick *bus tour* around everything in the QBasic menus—a first glance at the environment. Do not expect to understand what you are looking at, just read the menus for an idea of their features.

Get out of QBasic. Then get back in.

The File Menu

Press **Alt**.

Type **F**.

The program displays the File menu, as shown in Figure 3.6. (If it does not, get out of QBasic and start again.)

The File menu is your means of moving programs to and from the Editor, the disk, and the printer. The menu is covered in detail in the next chapter.

The Edit Menu

If you are still in the File menu,

Press **Right Arrow**.

If you are out of the Menus (back in the Editor),

Press **Alt**.

Type **E**.

The program displays the Edit menu as shown in Figure 3.10. Since most of its functions are duplicated elsewhere, use only the New Sub line, which is explained in Chapter 8.

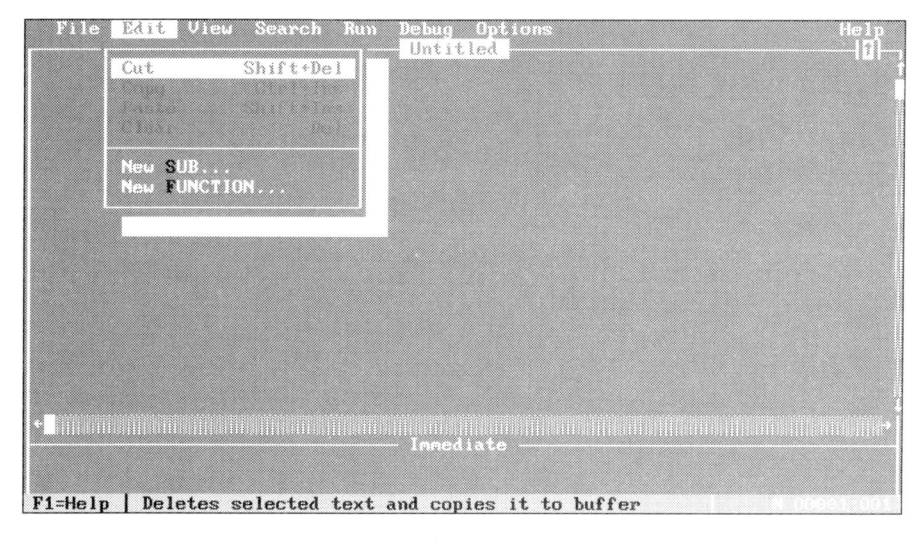

Figure 3.10   The Edit menu.

The View Menu

If you are in the Edit menu, then

   Press **Right Arrow**.

If you are back in the Editor,

   Press **Alt**.

   Type **V**.

   The program displays the View menu, as shown in Figure 3.11 on the next page.

   You can use the View menu to move back and forth among the routines in a program. There is more information on that later on.

42 ● TEACH YOURSELF... QBASIC

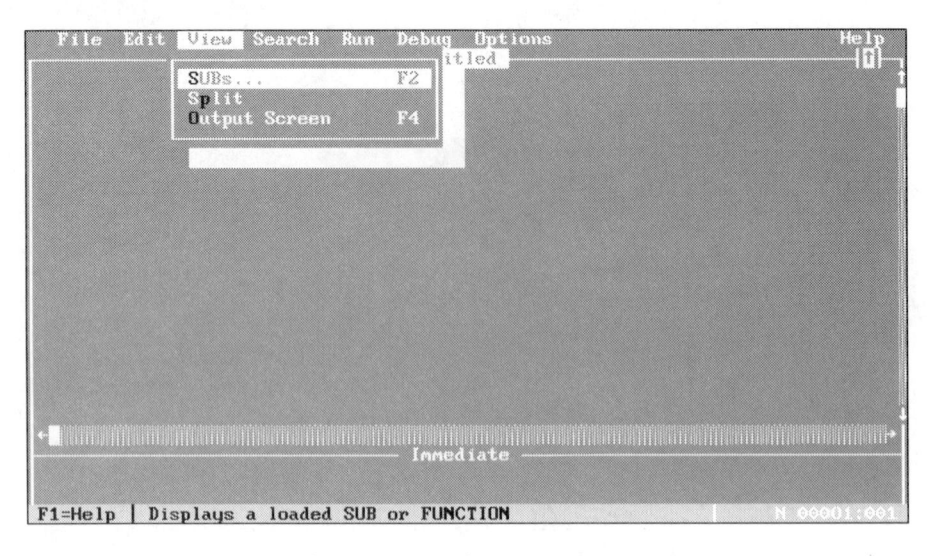

Figure 3.11   *The View menu.*

The Search Menu

If you are in the View menu, then

>Press **Right Arrow**.

If you are out of the menus, get back into the Editor.

>Press **Alt**.
>Type **S**.

The program displays the Search menu, as shown in Figure 3.12.

You use the Search menu to find a specific variable name or line label. This feature:

- Finds all the places where a variable name is used in a program
- Checks where new values are assigned
- Changes a variable name

Chapter 8 contains more information about the Search menu.

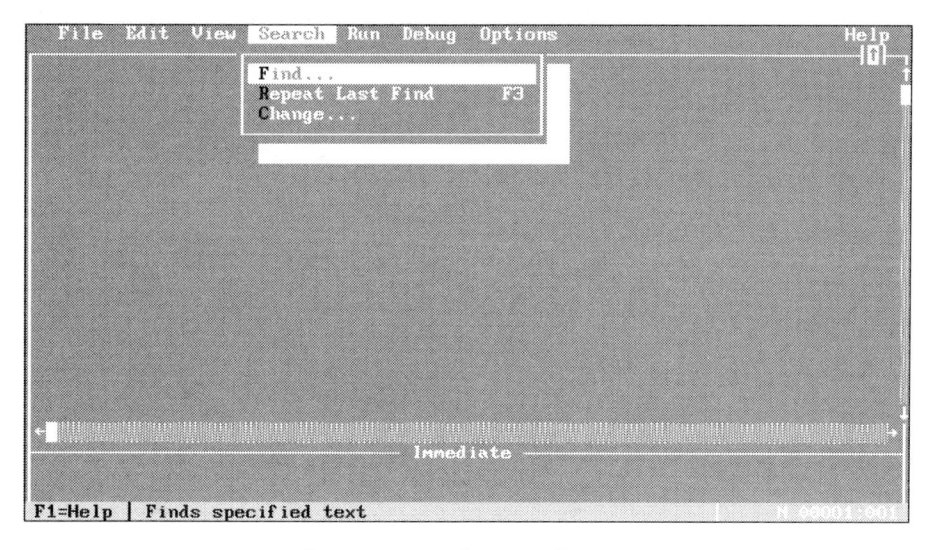

Figure 3.12   The Search menu.

The Run Menu

Now, while you're still in the Search menu,

>Press **Right Arrow**.

If you are out of the menus,

>Press **Alt**.

>Type **R**.

The program displays the Run menu, as shown in Figure 3.13 on the next page.

The Run menu runs a program that is within the Editor, or on disk. Chapter 21 explains this menu.

44 • TEACH YOURSELF... QBASIC

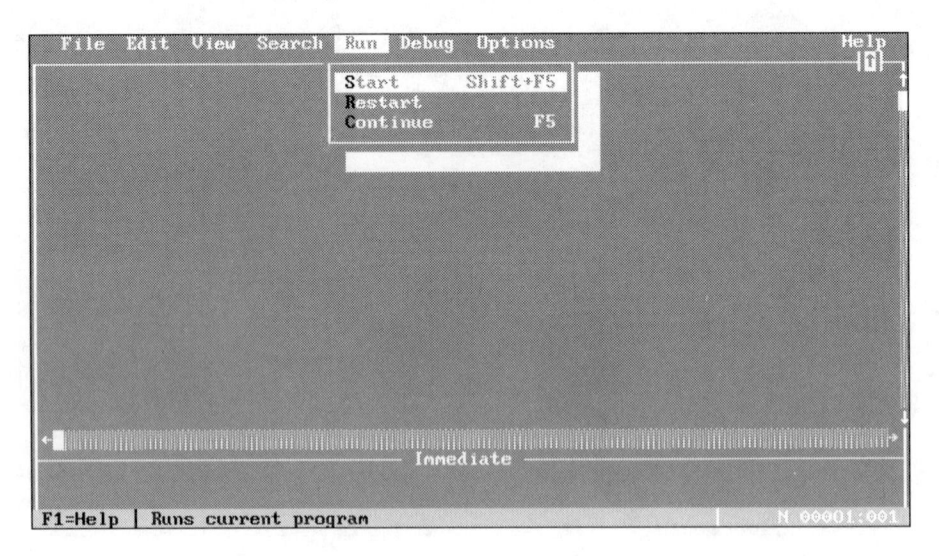

Figure 3.13 The Run menu.

The Debug Menu

If you have not left the Run menu, then

> Press **Right Arrow**.

If you went back to the Editor,

> Press **Alt**.
> Type **D**.

The program displays the Debug menu, as shown in Figure 3.14.

This menu helps you test your programs. Chapter 20 fully describes the Debug Menu.

CHAPTER THREE: QBASIC • 45

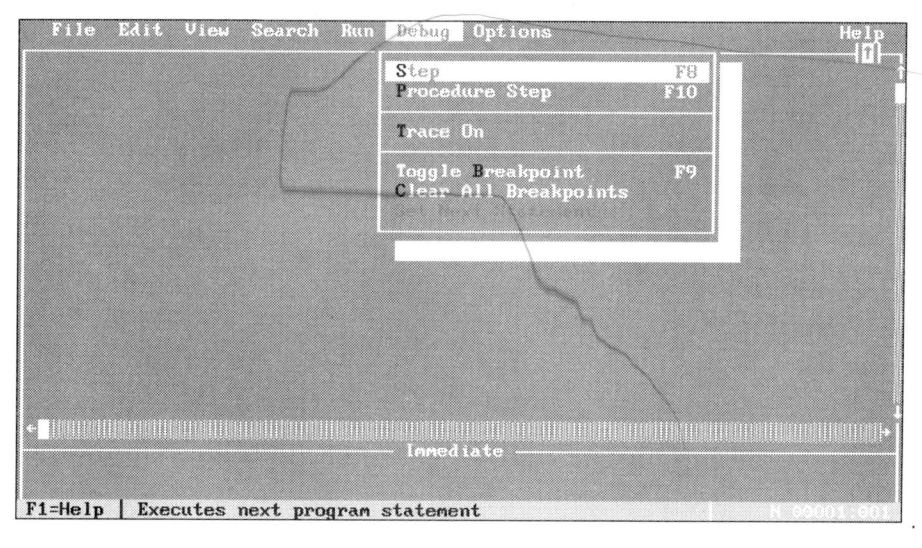

Figure 3.14   *The Debug menu.*

The Options Menu

If you have not left the Debug menu,

    Press **Right Arrow**.

If you went into the Editor,

    Press **Alt**.

    Type **O**.

The program displays the Options menu. You already know about the options discussed earlier in this chapter in the section entitled "Setting QBasic Options."

The Help Menu

If you stayed in the Options menu,

Press **Right Arrow**.

If you are now back in the Editor,

Press **Alt**.

Type **H**.

The program displays the Help menu, as shown in Figure 3.15.

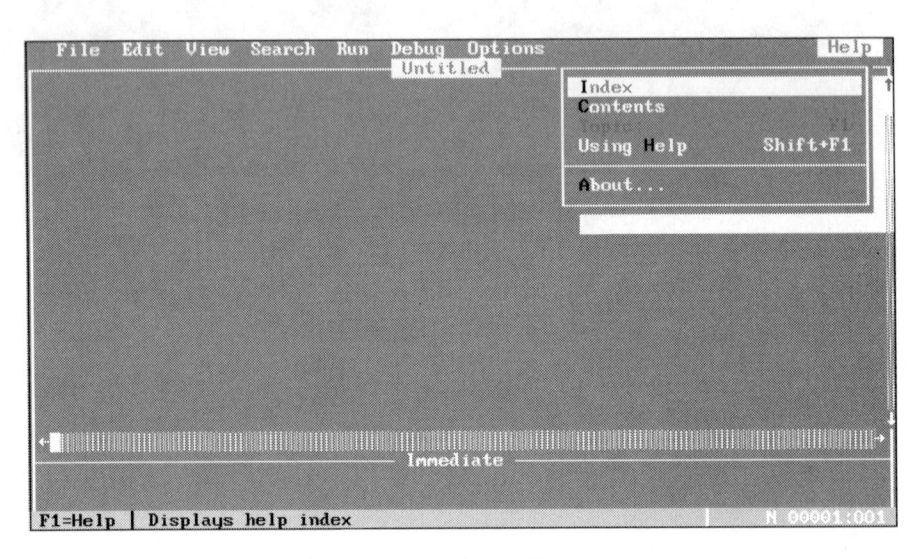

Figure 3.15   The Help menu.

The Help menu provides you with instant information about QBasic commands, menus, special keys on the keyboard, and the general use of QBasic. All Help text is displayed on the screen for your scrutiny, then with the press of a key, you are back in your program.

(In Chapter 4, you are helped in more detail.)

Now, press **Esc** to go back to the Editor.

How to Move Directly to a Menu

In this chapter, you first picked the file menu, then pressed **Right Arrow** to look at each menu. To get directly into a QBasic menu, you

Press **Alt**, then type in the first letter of the menu you want.

Summary

1. Read the book thoughtfully.
2. Type accurately. Fast and sloppy costs you more time in testing.
3. Do not be too concerned when you make mistakes. They are easy to fix in QBasic.
4. Save your programs onto disk using the File Save—*before* you run them.

The Book in Review

1. Design and program thoughtfully.
2. To examine any QBasic program, break it up into sections using the block-line method. Then study each block separately, and finally look at the logic that controls all the blocks.
3. **QBasic gives you a complete working environment that encourages writing programs in a building-block fashion.**

Chapter 4

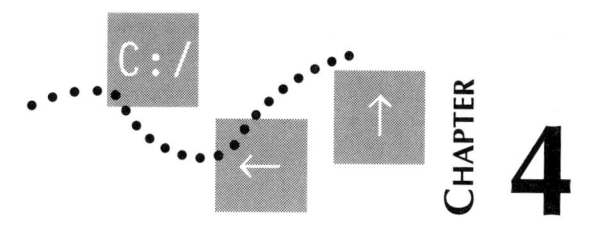

Diagrams and Programming

This chapter introduces you to program flow. You learn how to structure program logic properly so that your programs are solutions to the problems you need to solve. You learn about:

- How programs "flow" just like rivers
- The nature of programming
- The nature of computers
- The four secrets of good programming
- The program blueprint
- QBasic Help

Solving the Wrong Problem

Chris determined the problem. The firm needed to get literature on WildWater Works (WWW) out to a broader marketplace—the Boston area. WWW had a 10% return from their previous mailings. The problem is that quality mailing lists are hard to find and generally expensive. However, Chris found an excellent mailing list company. They provided WWW with 5,000 names, already on labels for 5 cents apiece. So, they had literature printed up, stuffed the envelopes (one week of solid work every evening), applied the labels, and sent them out...

Four weeks later, not one reply! Chris checked on the source of those labels and discovered that the list was really from the membership rolls of Couch Potatoes, Inc.

Chris solved the wrong problem. WWW got a lot of cheap names on a worthless list. What they needed was a smaller, qualified list, which they could have gotten from *Rapids Runner* magazine.

A lot of programmers make the same mistake as Chris. Writing the program without understanding the true problem and defining its solution is the biggest mistake that programmers make.

Just as you should think before you speak, you should understand the logic of your program before you write the first statement. In Chapter 3, you were asked to read, type, and run an already written program (WWWreg). Now, you are going to solve problems by designing programs. Typing in programs, like you did in the last chapter, is the easiest part of the job from here on.

Programs "Flow" Just Like Rivers

Water always flows in one direction—downward, to its ultimate destination, the ocean, as illustrated in Figure 4.1. There are changes of speed and direction; in white water the flow can be reversed for a short stretch.

The force behind the flow of water is gravity. There is a similar force in computer programming called logic. *Logic* controls program flow.

Water almost never flows in a straight line; neither do programs.

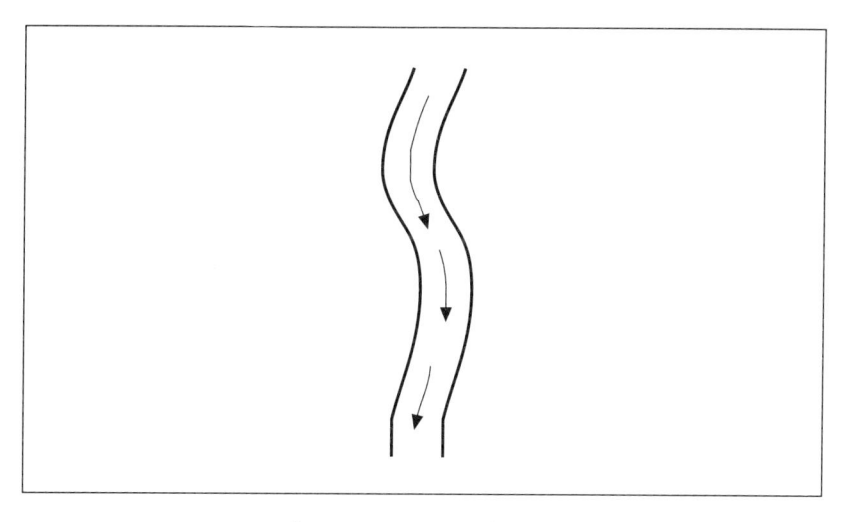

Figure 4.1   Smooth flow.

Branches and Routines

A fork, or stream branch, diverts the flow of a stream, but once the water is past the branch, it joins the main flow once more, as shown in Figure 4.2.

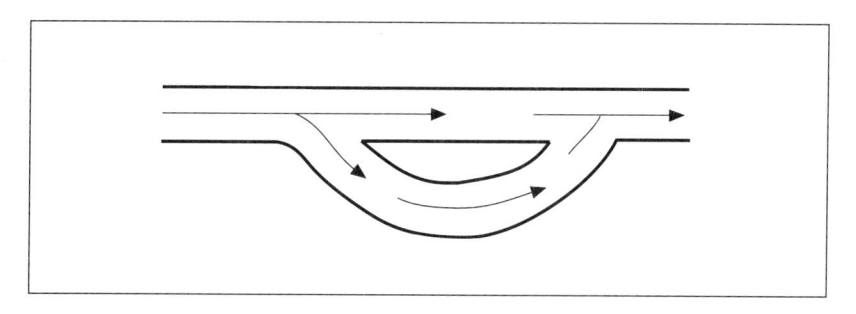

Figure 4.2   A stream branch.

A program routine is like the branch of a stream. The routine sidetracks the program flow for a while, then rejoins the main flow, as shown in Figure 4.3 on the next page.

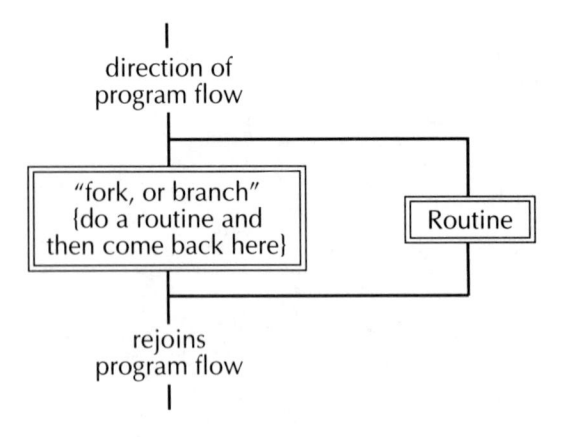

Figure 4.3   A Program routine.

Water Gates and IF...THENs

A water gate harnesses the power of the river to do work.

> IF the gate is shut, THEN the water follows the main flow.
> IF the gate is open, THEN it diverts water to accomplish a task,

like turning the water wheel at the gemstone mill behind WildWater Works's barn (corporate headquarters).

Once the water flow has done its job, it rejoins the main river.

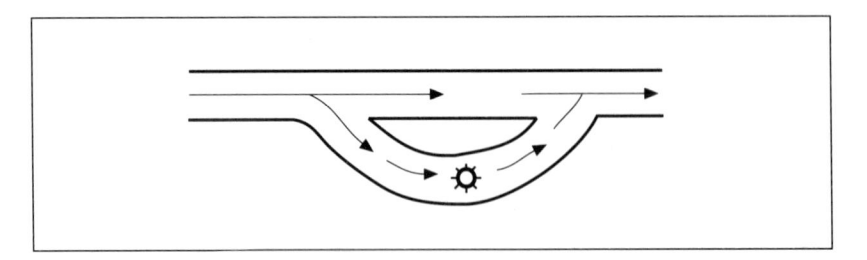

Figure 4.4   A water wheel and gate.

The IF...THEN statement is similar to a water gate. It tests the truth or falsity of a condition:

IF... {a condition is true} THEN {do some work}. (Chapter 9 explains IF statements.)

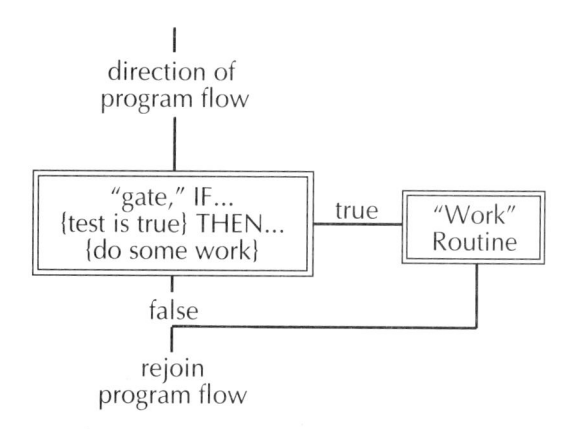

Figure 4.5   An IF...THEN statement.

Pumps and Loops

What about upward water flow? In any pumping system, human-made force temporarily overrides the force of gravity. When that external force is gone, the water resumes its downward flow.

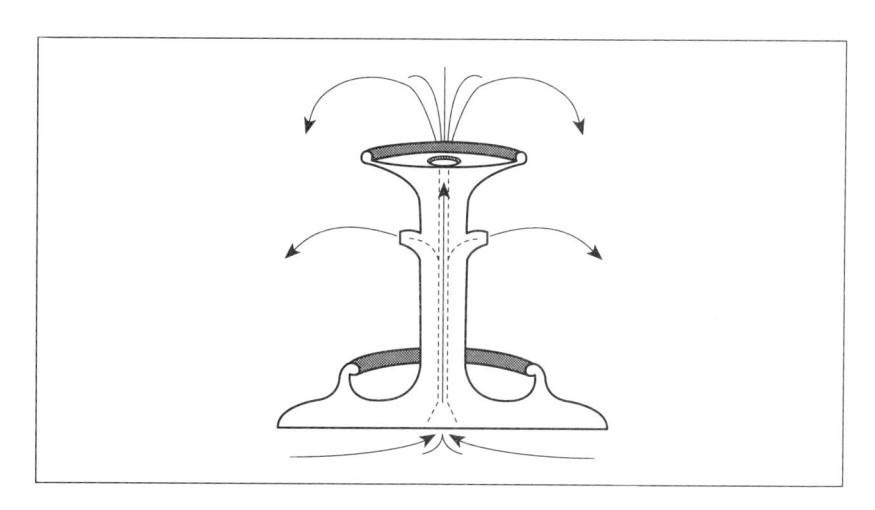

Figure 4.6   A pump flowing water upwards.

Pumping systems, such as fountains, are similar to a loop in a program. In Figure 4.7, the loop statement forces the program to go back and repeat some process.

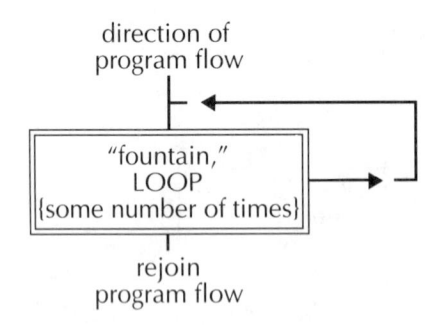

```
         direction of
         program flow
              │ ◄─────────┐
              ▼           │
        ┌──────────────┐  │
        │  "fountain," │──┘
        │     LOOP     │
        │{some number of times}│
        └──────────────┘
              │
            rejoin
         program flow
```

Figure 4.7 *Looping to repeat a process.*

Program Flow and Logic

Except for temporary diversions,

- gravity moves water down to its destination, the ocean
- your program logic flows data through the program to its end result, the report

Keeping the flow analogy in mind, slowly reread the definition of a computer program.

> **NOTE** A *program* is a series of statements (precise instructions), which the computer looks at and executes ONE AT A TIME until it reaches the end result: a report.

(Remember—a report can display on the screen, on the printer, or as a disk file.)

The computer is very fast; it can do millions of instructions per second. However, it can do only one thing at a time.

The computer starts with the first statement, reads the instruction, and executes it. Then, it looks at the next statement and executes that. The computer goes down the program, processing each statement sequentially (statement 2 after statement

1, statement 3 after statement 2, and so on) until a statement tells it to go elsewhere in the program. Then, it goes to that part of the program, processes the first statement it sees, then the next ones until it is told to go somewhere else.

The order in which the computer sees your QBasic statements is *program logic*.

- You are the programmer.
- You control the sequence of the computer's execution of statements.
- Your logic controls the computer.

It is your logic, not the computer's.

Good logic flows smoothly, as shown in Figure 4.8.

Bad logic, (shown in Figure 4.9 on the next page) like white water, can sink you.

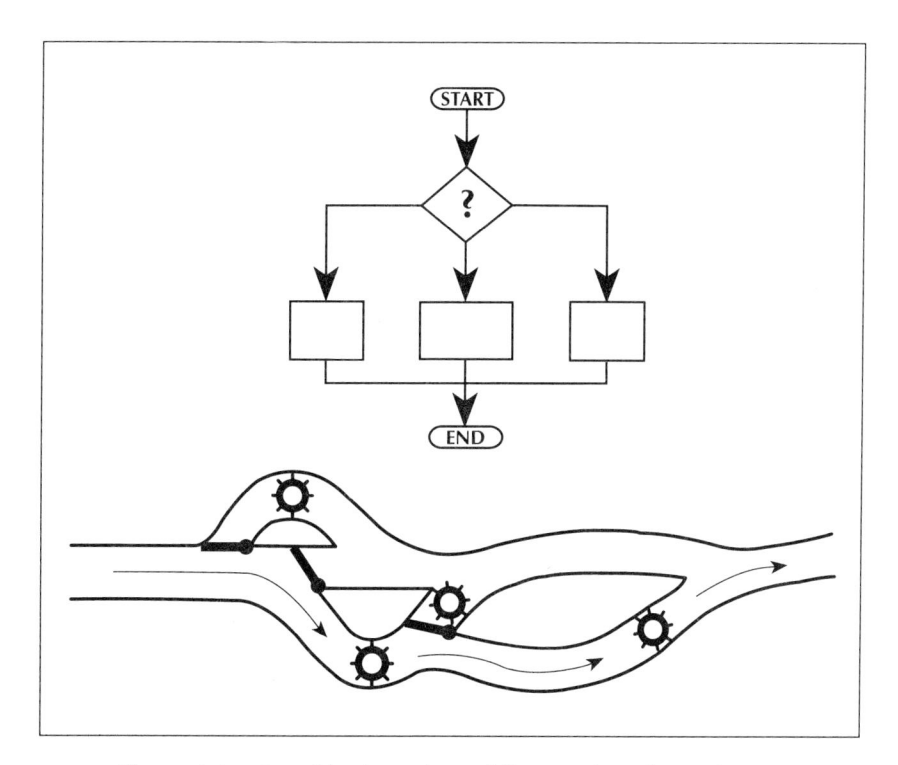

Figure 4.8 *Good logic and good flow with paths and gates.*

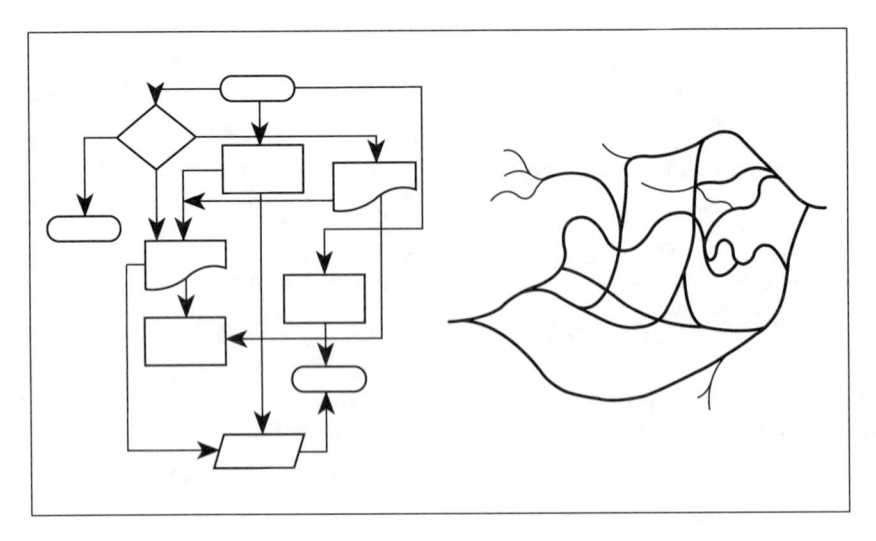

Figure 4.9 Bad logic and the White Water River.

The Nature of Programming

Programming is the translation of ideas into a computer language. A program is comprised of these four elements:

- **Structure**. The building blocks or routines that your program is broken up into.
- **Logic**. The flow of the program, which connects and flows through these blocks, or routines, to produce a *report* on screen, paper or disk.
- **Statements**. The actual QBasic *sentences* that make up each block.
- **Variable names**. The names that you give to each data item that is read into the program, calculated in the program, or written onto a *report*.

These four elements give you four challenges:

1. **The structure of the program must be clear and exact.**
    a. Your computer does not automatically clarify a design that is vague. A poorly defined program will not work.

    b. Some programmer (maybe even you), may read your program next year. If the structure is confusing to you, how can a total stranger figure it out?

2. **The logic flow must be perfect.**

    a. The computer cannot read your mind, but it can read your program. A computer only executes program statements, such as PRINT, INPUT, GOTO, and IF…THEN. The computer does not know that your calculation is adding when it should be subtracting, or that your program is stuck in an endless loop. (That's when your logic causes a computer to repeat a loop forever.) In other words, it does not guess what you meant to say—it does only what you tell it to do in your program.

    b. The computer cannot figure out your intended program logic. It does exactly what you tell it (even if the instruction sequence is completely wrong) without criticizing. Unlike a person, a computer cannot say "I know what you mean." A logic error is the worst programming mistake to make because it's the hardest to identify. Only you can find an error in logic by breaking your program into little pieces and testing each separately. Each program's logic must be clear to you before you begin writing it in QBasic. Do not write the program until you fully understand:

- what task the program is going to do
- how the program is going to do the task

3. **The language must be correct.** Computers cannot figure out things with imagination, guess at incorrect spellings, interpret a badly structured statement, or fill in missing words. Your *sentences* (program statements) must follow all the rules of QBasic. (Rules for writing different kinds of statements are explained in later chapters.)

4. **The variable names, after being used once, must be spelled the same throughout the program.** The computer considers them as new names if you do not use the same spelling. Remember, computers are only as smart as their programmers.

The Nature of Computers

While a computer does not check your program logic, it does check each statement for correct computer grammar, according to QBasic's rules. The computer does this by reading one word at a time and anticipating what acceptable words can follow. When it finds something wrong, it stops.

This gives you two insights regarding computer languages:

1. QBasic statements are like simple English sentences. Our language is flexible, but computer languages are not. QBasic can only work with a few, very simple statement types in a specific word order. Have you ever been approached by someone who spoke broken English? Think about the simple vocabulary and sentences you used to communicate. English is a foreign language to your computer.

2. Every word or symbol in a program statement is considered (by the computer) to be either a *reserved word* or a *variable name*. Reserved words are the action verbs (PRINT, READ, LINE INPUT, GOTO), or special functions (DATE$, COLOR) that QBasic accepts as commands. The variable names that you pick for data items are the nouns that are acted upon by the verbs (reserved words). Everything that is not a reserved word is a variable name to the computer. Never mix up reserved words and variable names.

NOTE: Be careful not to misspell your variable names throughout the program. Give a computer a name it does not understand, and it either stops dead or considers the word to be a new, undefined data item.

QBasic is very picky about how you present ideas to the computer. The secrets below will help you avoid problems.

Four Secrets of Good Programming

Here are the secrets for precision in programming:

1. **Simple structure**. Good program structure is simple and clear. If your design is not, your program probably will not work. It is far better to have

good structure from the start. To help you start, the next section describes the blueprint, a tool you use throughout this book.

2. **Simple flow**. Work hard to make the program logic, or flow so simple that any programmer can easily understand how the modules connect and the statements within them flow. Look at the river in Figure 4.9. If your program logic flow looks like that, you need to rewrite it.

3. **Simple statements**. Use the simplest program statements and keep in mind what makes good, clear technical writing:
   - Do not use a big word when you can use a small one.
   - Turn complex sentences into simple ones.
   - Avoid unnecessary words.
   - Keep paragraphs short.

   Good program writing has similar attributes. Rather than memorize 200 statements, use the simple ones that best get the job done. That's easier than repeatedly looking up and comprehending the more complex statements that you use once a month. You waste less time.

4. **Simple names**. Use simple, meaningful variable names to identify your data being named. You should be able to identify what the data is by its name. Use names like:

Data	Name
The city in your customer record	custcity
the state	custstate
the ZIP code	custzip
The retail price in the part file	partretail
the wholesale price	partwholsal
the cost	partcost

   Avoid unnecessarily long names. You learn all about variable names in the next chapter. For now, let's look at program structure.

The Program Blueprint

In spite of what you have been told by other people, the writing, typing, and running can be the simplest part of programming. It is harder to understand the problem, define it, and structure the solution. This process is called *blueprinting* because the process is similar to blueprinting a bridge before it is built.

Blueprinting a program defines:

1. The *purpose(s)* of the program.
2. The *end results* (OUTPUT) of the program, probably a report on the computer screen, printed on paper, or written to a file on disk.
3. The *source* (INPUT) of the data that is needed to produce the OUTPUT report.
4. The *source of the hidden data* (HIDPUT—explained in a bit) necessary for the formulas that produce the OUTPUT.
5. The *block diagramming* (LOGIC) that produces the OUTPUT.

Follow the details on how to blueprint. This is the big picture, it is conceptual; do not expect to know the detail of some of the processes until later on in the book. Get the concept. You get a lot of practice later.

Step 1: Purpose

State in one simple sentence the single major purpose of your program (no ANDs, ORs, IFs, commas). Then, list the major tasks that this program is to accomplish, defining each task in one simple sentence. If the program has only one simple task, this section is one sentence.

Step 2: End Result (OUTPUT)

On paper, lay out each page to be displayed on the screen or printed by the printer. If you plan to save a data file onto disk, specify on paper what the disk file contents are to be. (Look at the disk file as if it were a report on paper.) List each data item that is output.

Step 3: Necessary Data (INPUT)

Look at the OUTPUT data (Step 2) in the end result, and determine its source (where it comes from—another file, a calculation, or keyboard input). As you are doing this, give meaningful data names to the OUTPUT data this program creates.

Step 4: Hidden Data (HIDPUT)

If a calculation (formula) is involved, then determine the source (as in Step 3) of all the data contained in the formula. The source could be data in another file, another calculation, or keyboard input. Keep going until every piece of data in the formulas has a source within the program. Otherwise, you will have formulas that will not work. Whole systems have been programmed that did not work because one piece of data had no source within a program, making all the reports based on that data worthless.

Step 5: Logic

Put your logic into simple block diagrams. Each block diagram should fit onto a single 8.5-inch by 11-inch sheet of paper; if it does not fit, then your logic is probably too complex. Remember the essence of good programming: *make it simple*. If you cannot fit all the functions or procedures on one sheet, then put the major logic onto one sheet and the other (more detailed) routines on other sheets. In any case, force yourself to be constrained. That is the purpose of using 8.5-inch by 11-inch sheets rather than large paper for the logic. Fitting the logic on small sheets forces simplicity.

The rules of block diagramming are:

1. Put each step within a block.
2. Connect the blocks with arrows to show the direction of program flow.

Two sample program blueprints follow: You block diagram your programs from here on. When you finish this book, you will be an ace at block diagramming.

Take your time. The time you spend blueprinting to define the problem and its corresponding solution pays you back tenfold at the programming stage. Conversely, every minute you think you save by not defining the problem costs you ten or more minutes at the programming stage. Five minutes can save an hour.

Sample Blueprint #1

Chris finally bought a mailing list from *Rapids Runner* and decided to put the list on the WWW computer. Here is the program to enter the names, shown in a program blueprint.

PROGRAM NAME: mailkey1.
PURPOSE: To key the magazine mailing list into your computer.
OUTPUT RESULT: File on disk, containing 3,000 names and addresses.

The name of the file is "mail." The description is:

Data Name	Description	Location in File (positions)	Maximum Length
mailname	prospect's name	1-30	30
mailaddr1	1st line of address	31-60	30
mailaddr2	2nd line of address	61-90	30
mailcity	city	91-110	20
mailstate	state	111-112	2
mailzip	ZIP Code	113-121	9

INPUT: Source for all data is keyboard input. The operator of the program keys in all the data items for each prospect.

Data	Source
mailname	key entry
mailaddr1	key entry
mailaddr2	key entry
mailcity	key entry
mailstate	key entry
mailzip	key entry

HIDPUT (data hidden in formulas): None.
LOGIC (block diagram:

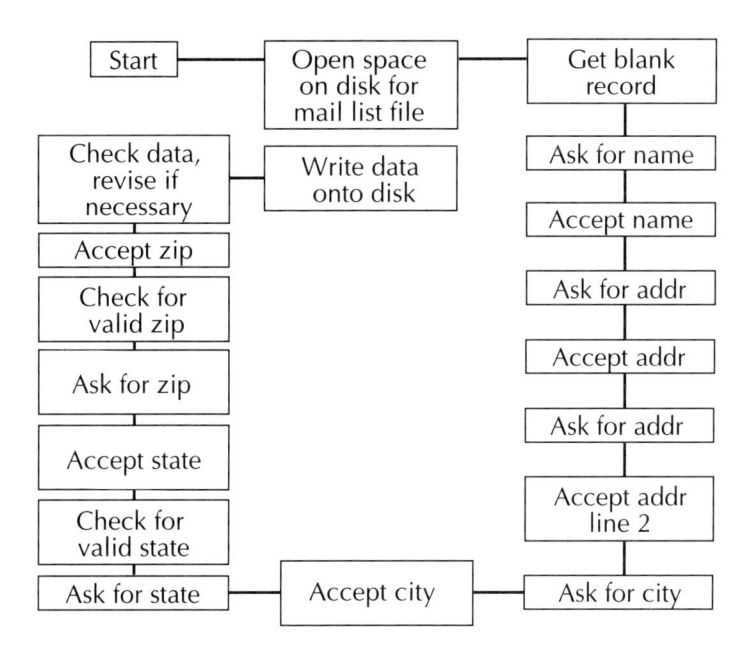

```
Start → Open space on disk for mail list file → Get blank record
                                                      ↓
Check data,     Write data                       Ask for name
revise if   ←   onto disk                             ↓
necessary                                        Accept name
    ↑                                                 ↓
Accept zip                                       Ask for addr
    ↑                                                 ↓
Check for                                        Accept addr
valid zip                                             ↓
    ↑                                            Ask for addr
Ask for zip                                           ↓
    ↑                                            Accept addr
Accept state                                     line 2
    ↑                                                 ↓
Check for                                        Ask for city
valid state                                           ↑
    ↑                                                 
Ask for state → Accept city ←─────────────────────────
```

Sample Blueprint #2

This is the blueprint of the program Chris is using to print out mailing labels to WildWater Works's potential customers.

PROGRAM NAME: maillabl.
PURPOSE: To print mailing labels for all the people in your MAIL file.
OUTPUT RESULT: One mailing label for each person.

```
Chuck Butkus
999 Route 9
Clifton   NJ   11111
```

INPUT (data sources): All the data for the label is found in the file called MAIL, which is on your computer disk.

Data	Description	Source
lablname	prospect name	mail file
labladdr1	1st addr line	mail file
labladdr2	2nd addr line	mail file
lablcity	city	mail file
lablstate	state	mail file
lablzip	zip	mail file

HIDPUT (data in formulas): none.
LOGIC (block diagram):

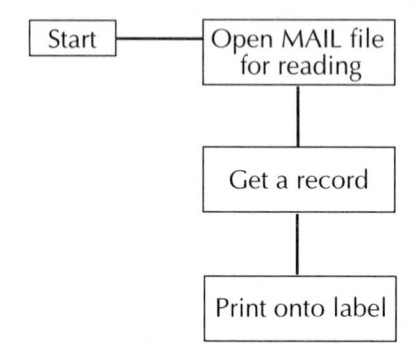

```
Start ─── Open MAIL file
          for reading
              │
          Get a record
              │
          Print onto label
```

The program blueprint is a way to ensure that the data names and program logic are clear and simple. If you produce a clear program blueprint, the programming is easy. A cloudy blueprint can produce a wildwater-like program.

QBasic Help

Rather than pulling down the Help menu, then selecting an item on the menu, follow these steps to get on-screen help:

1. Press **Shift + F1** for general Help. (Press **Esc** to exit Help.)
2. When you need help on a specific topic, like a reserved word, an error, or even part of a QBasic menu, just move the cursor to the word or text for which you would like help, and:

Press **F1**.

The program displays Help specific to that topic.

Press **Esc** to exit Help.

Using Help

Press **Shift** and press **F1**.

The program displays the HELP: Using Help section of QBasic. Read the text in the Help box.

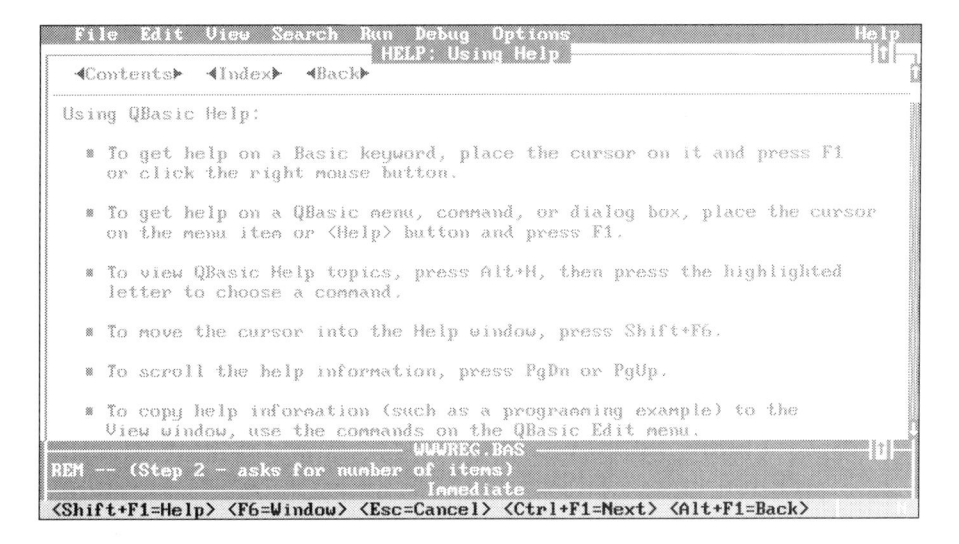

Figure 4.10 General Help.

Help Contents

Since the cursor is on Contents,

Press **F1**.

The program displays a screen of topics, as shown in Figure 4.11 on the next page.

Move the cursor around the Help box, put it onto a topic, then

Press **F1**.

66 • TEACH YOURSELF... QBASIC

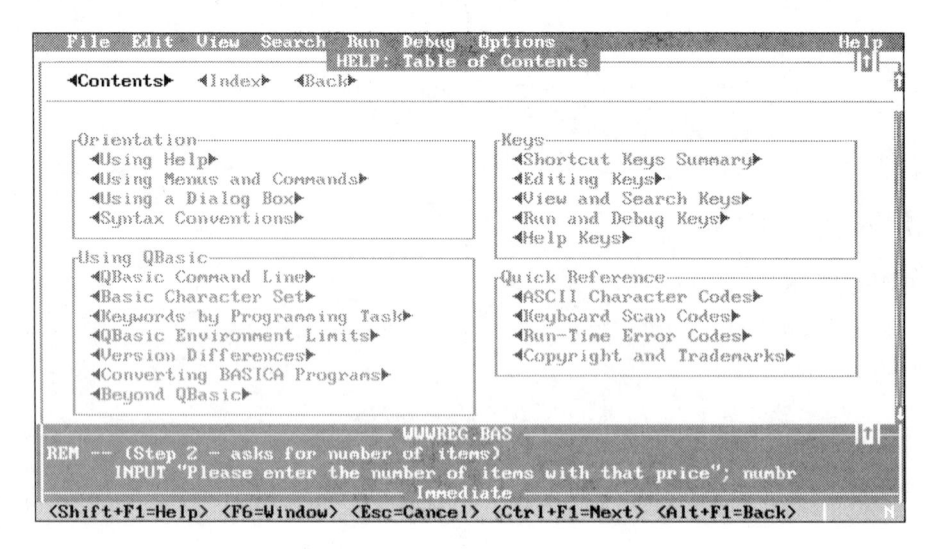

Figure 4.11 Help contents.

The program displays help on that topic. Then, move the cursor back up to the Contents (third line from the top) and

Press **F1**.

The program redisplays a screen of topics. Browse the topics, by selecting with **F1**, then returning to the Contents until you are comfortable with this part of Help.

Help Index

Move the cursor onto the Index (banner line of Help) and

Press **F1**.

The program displays a screen with an index of topics about which you can get help, as shown in Figure 4.12.

Move (using the Arrow keys) to one of the words and

Press **F1**.

You see the details on each topic. Browse through this area of help, just as you did with the Contents. When you are comfortable,

Press **Esc** to get back to the work space.

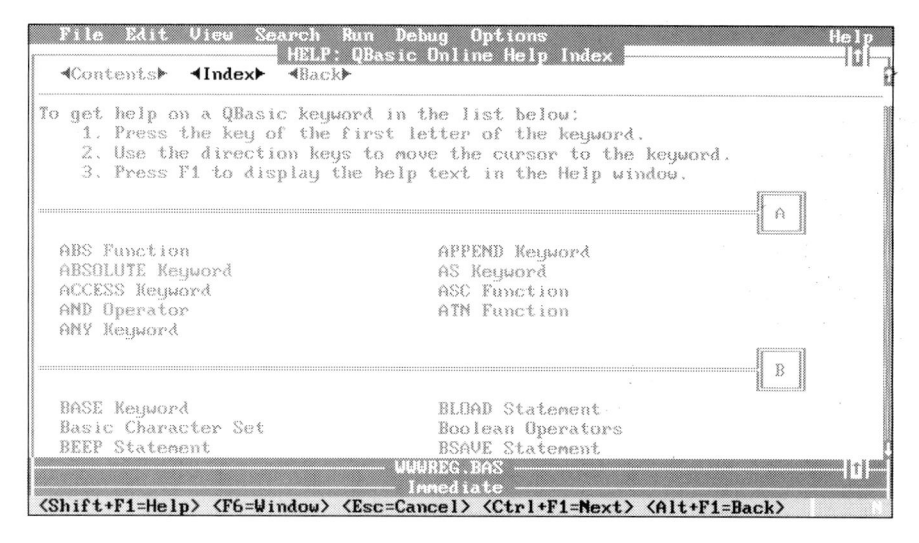

Figure 4.12   Help Index.

Specific Help

While programming, you might be unsure about the correct use of a QBasic construct or a reserved word. If so, move the cursor to the program term in question, and

Press **F1**.

The program displays Help on that topic. When your question is answered,

Press **Esc** to return to your program.

Now, reenter QBasic, and try this with WWWreg:

1. Press **Alt**.
   Type **F**.
2. Move the cursor to Open.
   Press **Enter**.
3. Type **WWWreg,** and press **Enter**.
4. Move the cursor to various parts of your program and
   Press **F1**.

- Browse through the Help on this topic.
- Press **Esc** to exit Help.
5. Repeat Step 4 until you are proficient at finding Specific Help. If you still are not comfortable with Help, keep repeating this section until it is second nature.

Summary

1. Programming demands that you present perfect logic using exactly correct language.
2. QBasic restricts you to using only reserved words and variable names, in a limited number of statements.
3. The secret to good programming is to use meaningful variable names, in the simplest program statements, in programs written with good logic connecting a sound structure.
4. Make sure that your logic is correct. It is the most difficult error to find and fix.
5. Use a program blueprint (your logic must be perfectly clear).
    a. State your major *purpose* in one simple sentence. If the major purpose contains several sub-purposes, state them in one sentence each.
    b. Specify the *output* of your program. List each data item that is *output*.
    c. Determine the source, or *input*, of each data item in your *output*.
    d. Find the source for any *hidput*, the data items that are in the formulas that define your *output*.
    e. Put your *logic* into a block diagram that shows the program steps.

The Book in Review

1. Design and program thoughtfully.
2. To examine any QBasic program, break it up into blocks. Then, study each

block separately, and finally look at the logic that controls all the blocks.

3. QBasic gives you a complete working environment that encourages writing programs in building-block fashion.

4. **Blueprint your program before you write the first line of code.**

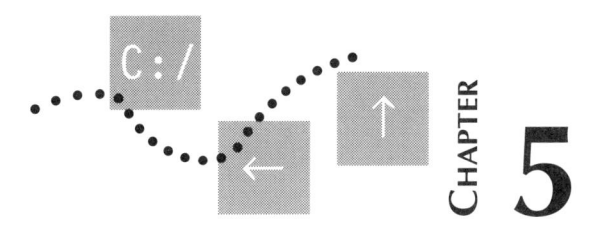

Data Names and Data Types

This chapter teaches you why it is important to follow rules in programming. You learn how to organize and name the data in your program. The topics include:

- The definition of data
- Why have data names
- Data types
- Data names in QBasic
- Data naming rules
- The REM statement
- The data dictionary
- QBasic file menu and commands

Layout and Naming

You and Chris are looking (for the first time) at a map of downtown Tangletown. There is a meeting with a corporate prospect from Twisted Twine, at A-963x Winding Street.

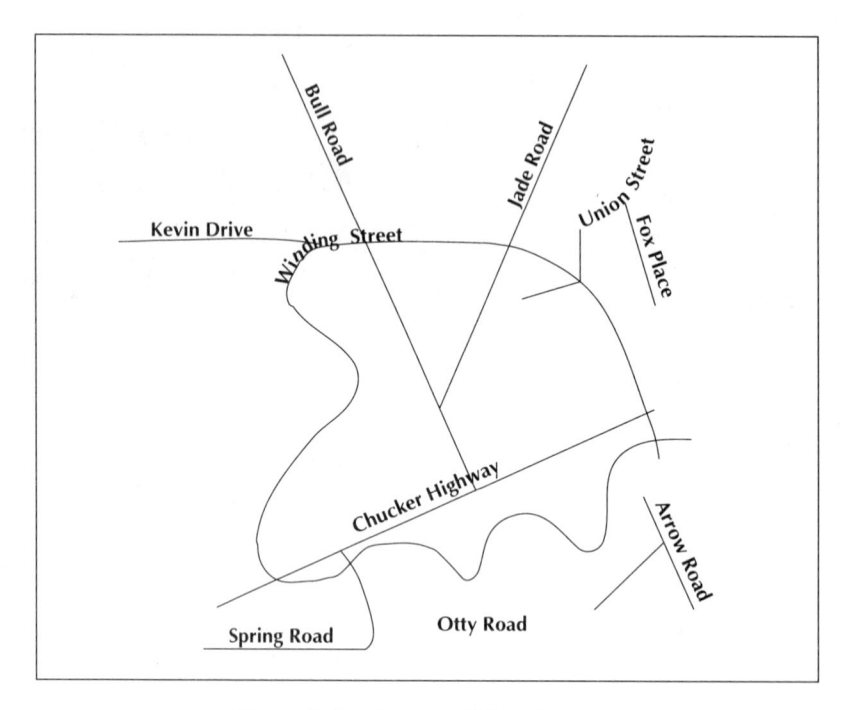

Figure 5.1 A map of Tangletown.

If you are having a problem finding that address, good. That's the idea. Skip this and go on.

The following week, you and Chris are driving into Checkerton, USA. You are looking for Brawny Building Block, Inc. at 100 East 101st street.

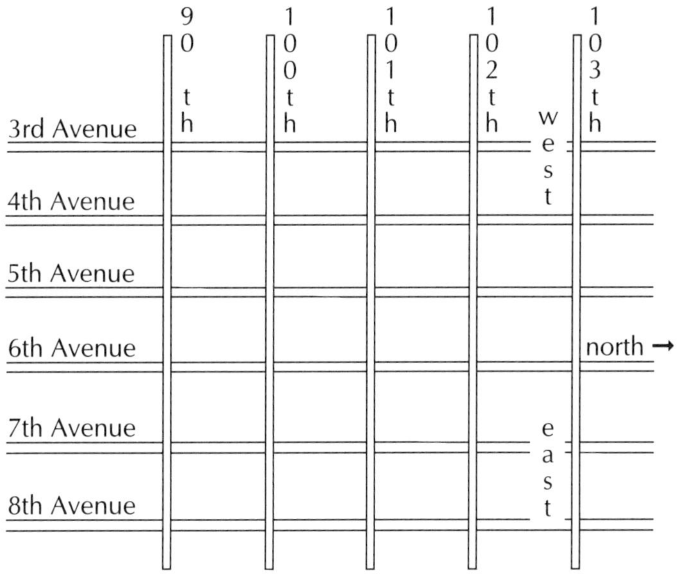

Figure 5.2 *A map of Checkerton, USA.*

Easy, huh?

Getting a sense of direction is a lot easier in Checkerton than in Tangletown because you can reason where a street or number is likely to be. The streets run east-west, and avenues run north-south. The building numbers are also systematic: low numbers begin at Fifth Avenue and increase the further east or west you go from that road. Unlike Tangletown, in Checkerton you can start anywhere and then confidently search based on the organization of the layout and the names.

Finding your way around a city can be easy or frustrating, depending on the layout and the naming of the streets. Searching through a program listing can also be easy or difficult, depending on program structure and data names. Ask yourself:

- How clear is the program structure (Chapters 4 and 7)?
- How clear are the data names (this chapter)?

Picking up a listing of another person's program is like looking at a map of an unfamiliar city. After a few minutes, you should get a sense of the overall layout, or program organization. Then, you work at understanding the variable names. Even your own variable names can make you wonder how you came up with them when you look at your programs a month after you wrote them. Can you remember, 14 months after writing a program, what zxk% represents? Or valu? valuE of what?

You more quickly understand and modify a program with meaningful data names than even a well-documented program with muddled data names. (Examples of good and bad names come later.)

Good data names are not important; they are *critical*.

What is Data?

Like ingredients to a recipe, data is the collection of ingredients that your computer uses to *cook up* the finished product that you see as a report on paper or on screen. Data items are the raw ingredients that computer programs blend and present in different reports on screen, on disk, or at the printer. Data items are the detail from which averages, percentages, and counts are derived for reports. The major function of any program is the processing of data; without data, programs are worthless.

Here's a quick example of data, and its use in a program. Suppose you and Terry did some consulting work for another raft company, The Dunking Daredevils. You have to calculate how much they owe WildWater Works and send them a bill:

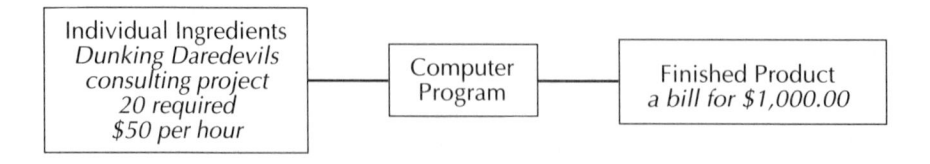

```
┌─────────────────────────┐         ┌──────────┐         ┌──────────────────┐
│ Individual Ingredients  │         │ Computer │         │ Finished Product │
│  Dunking Daredevils     │─────────│ Program  │─────────│ a bill for $1,000.00 │
│  consulting project     │         │          │         │                  │
│      20 required        │         └──────────┘         └──────────────────┘
│      $50 per hour       │
└─────────────────────────┘
```

How is the bill produced from the raw ingredients? First, the data is put into the computer, using a program that accepts keyboard input. Next, the data is stored on disk, for later processing by other programs. Eventually, a computer program uses the stored data to produce a report (like the bill above). The flow of data through a computer, and its eventual compilation into reports, looks like this:

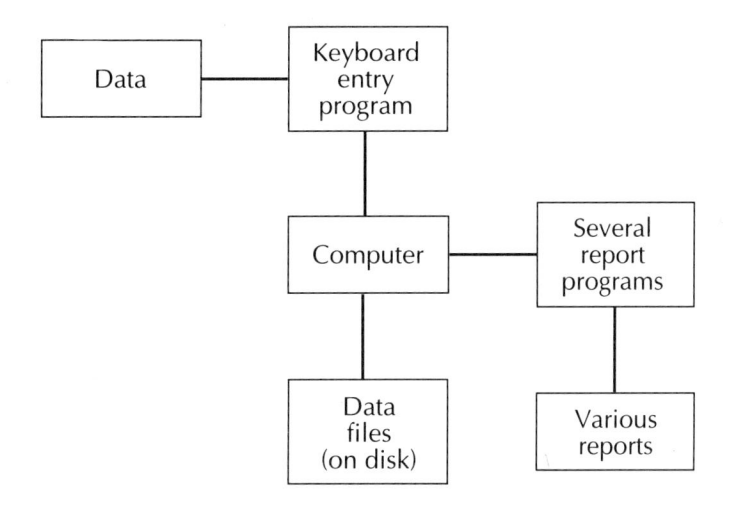

```
Data ── Keyboard entry program
              │
              │
         Computer ── Several report programs
              │              │
              │              │
         Data files      Various
         (on disk)       reports
```

Now here is why names make a difference in this process.

Why Have Data Names?

Your computer's memory is really a checkerboard of locations. Like the map of Checkerton, the memory locations are identified methodically, so that the computer stores and retrieves information precisely. No matter how large the memory (it might have 256 million locations), the computer can keep track of everything in every location.

Before placing a data item in a memory storage location (field), the computer has your program assign a variable name to that location. The data item then occupies that location, which the computer remembers as having that variable name. Now a data item can be recalled from its memory location by telling the computer to find a particular variable name. The variable name identifies which data item occupies a physical location (field).

Take a look at a sample of a "block" in memory while a program is running on the next page.

	location/field "company name"
	location (empty)
	location/field "street address"
	location/field "city"

There is a program running in the computer, and this small block of memory (four fields out of millions) has some activity. Three of the four fields have variable names. The program is not currently using the fourth location as a field for data.

WildWater Works, Inc.	location/field "company name"
	location (empty)
Ripping Rapids Road	location/field "street address"
Rocky Top	location/field "city"

Seconds later, the computer operator has entered data for another company. Now the fields have totally different values:

Dunking Daredevils, Inc.	location/field "company name"
	location (empty)
Flipping Falls Road	location/field "street address"
Muddy Meadows	location/field "city"

Just as the occupants of a building can change with time, so can the values residing within the fields. Inside a computer, these values are always changing. In a computer program, the field names remain the same, while the occupants (specific values or data items) can change every millionth of a second.

060194	location/field "date" at time 1
060394	location "date" an instant later

Since data processing is accomplished within computer memory, the computer must know where all the data dwells in that memory. The computer must be able to find, process, and put back any data item at any time.

In QBasic, you define a field by giving it a name. Even though you, the programmer don't know where it is stored in memory, the computer finds the location every time you use the name in your program. Actually, in giving a field a name, you also have to give that field a data type.

Data Types

The programmer's life would be easy if all data could use the same data type. No such luck. QBasic has several numeric data types, and one for text data.

QBasic distinguishes between two major data types:

- numeric (number characters)
- alphanumeric (letters, numbers, symbols, or a combination of the three)

The alphanumeric, or string, data type will not work for calculations in QBasic. Strings also take up a lot of memory and disk file space for each data item that contains only numbers in that string. So QBasic has numeric formats (data types), which take up less space and are used in calculations.

These four numeric formats, plus the string type, brings to five the total number of data types that you use in QBasic programming. The five data types are:

1. Short integers (%)
2. Long integers (&)
3. Single-precision numbers (!)
4. Double-precision numbers (#)
5. Strings (alphanumeric) ($)

Before you read about each data type in detail, take a glimpse at Table 5.1 on the next page, then move on to the explanations that follow. Take your time studying those numbered descriptions, and refer to the examples in the table.

Table 5.1 Data Types

Data Type	Sample Values	Name Format	Sample Names	Typical statement assigning value to a field
Short Integers	123 –30000	{name}%	workcode% numitems%	workcode%= 11 numitems%=14000
Long Integers	1234567890 99999	{name}&	nypop& numitems&	nypop&=20000000 numitems&=563714
Single-precision numbers	1.23 –123.456 .987654	{name}! or {name}	payrate! listprice	payrate!=11.41 listprice=19.95
Double-precision numbers	.1456829666 7390085.641 –60.834917	{name}#	ytdpay# ytdsls#	ytdpay#=29593.97 ytdsls#=52471.61
Strings (alpha-numeric)	"Anne" "96 5th St." "telephone"	{name}$	firstname$ strname$ telnum$	firstname$ ="Jan" strname$="Wilder" telnum$="5551212"

Detailed Explanations of Data Types

The five data types are explained in detail as follows.

Short integers

Short integers are small, whole numbers (no decimals). The permissible ranges of numbers are:

- 0 to 32767 (positive numbers)
- 0 to –32768 (negative numbers)

Integers are typically used for:

- Counting (for example, how many times a loop has been run).
- Any small number that will never have decimal places (for example, age, number of children, or some code).

Try to use integers as much as possible because:

- They use up less space than other numbers (the same space as two alphabetic characters, or two bytes).

- Calculations with integers are accomplished quickly.

The suffix identifier, which goes at the end of all integer names, is %. (See Table 5.1.)

Long integers

Long integers are large, whole numbers (no decimals) that can have a value from:

- 0 to 2,147,483,647 (positive numbers)
- 0 to –2,147,483,648 (negative numbers)

Long integers are used for:

- Calculations involving large, whole numbers.
- Special calculations (beyond the scope of this book).

The suffix, which goes at the end of all long integer names, is &. (See Table 5.1.)

Single-precision numbers

Single-precision numbers are numbers with up to six digits of accuracy (either positive or negative) that can have decimal places. While they can be whole numbers, they need not be. This type is used for most calculations where six-digit accuracy is enough. In business programming, it is good to use this type for small (six-digit or less) numbers. Single-precision numbers may have a suffix of ! , or no suffix at all. (See Table 5.1.)

Double-precision numbers

Double-precision numbers are large numbers (up to 16 digits of accuracy, either positive or negative) that can have decimal places. They can be whole numbers, but do not have to be. This data type is used for calculations where high accuracy is important in calculations. Double-precision numbers must have a pound sign (#) at the end of their names. (See Table 5.1.)

Strings

A string is any alphabetic (*street name*), alphabetic-and-numeric (*K-42-w1q**), numeric (*1234*), or special characters. Strings cannot be used in calculations;

however, QBasic does provide special "massaging" operations with string variables, which you learn about later.

In addition to the numbers 0 through 9 and the letters of the alphabet (both upper and lowercase), the following symbols are acceptable in strings:

! (exclamation point)
@ (at sign)
# (pound sign)
$ (dollar sign)
% (percent sign)
^ (caret)
& (ampersand)
* (asterisk)
( ) (left and right parentheses)
_ (underscore)
+ (plus sign)
= (equal sign)
\ (backslash)
| (pipe symbol).

Strings can be any length from 0 to 255 characters. They are enclosed in quotation marks in QBasic. String names must have a $ (dollar sign) as their last character. (See Table 5.1.)

Data Names in QBasic

QBasic has its own *hands-off* data dictionary of reserved words. As was mentioned in Chapter 2, these words are reserved mainly to denote action verbs. If you use the reserved words for data names, QBasic becomes confused, and either processes your data incorrectly, or stops.

Some of QBasic's reserved words are:

| BEEP | ELSE | GET | MID$ | REM |
| CLEAR | END | GOSUB | NAME | RESTORE |

CLOSE	EOF	GOTO	NEXT	RETURN
COMMON	ERR	IF	OFF	SCREEN
DIM	EXIT	INPUT	ON	STRING
DO	FOR	LOG	POS	VAL

You find a complete list of QBasic's reserved words in your QBasic manual.

Besides the usual reserved action verbs, there are a few special nouns that you cannot use as data names. Examples are:

- DATE$
- TIME$

These two special words return a value when you insert them into a statement. For example, the following statement line produces the output shown (assume that the program is run at 09:27 on May 29, 1994):

```
PRINT "Last modified on "; DATE$; " at "; TIME$
Last modified on 05/29/1994 at 09:27:43
```

Finally, there's a special word, REM, you will be using frequently, as you see later in this chapter.

Data Naming Rules

If there is one rule to remember in naming data items, it is to maintain clear uniqueness. The problems you have to avoid are:

- Using the same name for two different data items.
- Using a data name, which you may not understand when you see it later.

The first problem is likely to occur if data names are short. You may use a name in one routine of a program, then forget that you used it, and use the same name elsewhere (which mixes up the values of that variable).

The second problem can occur if you use a compact data name that seems clear at the time you first write it, but later, you realize it's too cryptic.

There is also the opposite problem. You might think that long, specific data names would avoid both of the problems above. However, long names are easy to misspell, require a lot of typing, and take up limited space on a QBasic line (which cannot be more than 254 characters).

With these problems in mind, use the following six rules for data names, which guide you safely through these critical waters:

1. Names should be meaningful to you, the programmer.
   Not good: `ln    personslastname    y`
   Good: `lnam    yr%`
   Better: `lastname    salesyr%`

2. Names should be short; not more than 12 characters.
   Not good: `st    streetaddress`
   Good: `stradd`
   Better: `street`

3. Names should be consistent.
   a. All data items from the same file should use the file name as the first part (prefix). Use short file names (up to four characters).
      Not good: `customeraddr1    name    prt1prc1`
      Good: `custstr    custnam    part1stprc`
      Better: `custstreet    custlastname    partlistpric`
   b. The same data item seen in several files should have the same suffix (last part) in each name.
      Not good: `cno    pnum`
      Good: `cusno    prtno`
      Better: `custnum    partnum`
   c. All items that are dates should have the same abbreviated suffix, for example, dt, dat, or date.
      Not good: `pdt    hired    bald`
      Good: `paydt    hiredt    baldt`
      Better: `paydat    hiredat    balancedat`
   d. All numbers that identify things, such as *customer number*, *part number*, and *Social Security Number*, should have the same abbreviated suffix, for example, no or num.
      Not good: `cusnmb prt# socialsn`
      Good: `cusno prtno ssno`
      Better: `custnum partnum ssnum`

4. Names should not be cryptic. Use vowels when necessary for clarity.
   Not good: `cutot    dtst`

Good: `currunpdtot  dtsent`
Better: `totunpaid  datesent`

5. For each program, make a Data Dictionary for yourself containing the data names used. Place it at the very beginning of the program. (There is more on this in the next section.)
6. Finally, the Chuck Butkus rule of data naming. Make data names *unique*. Include enough characters to make them clear, but no more.

The REM Statement

The REMark statement, or REM, is exclusively for the programmer's benefit. The program user, the person who is running the program, never sees the REM. The computer ignores the entire REM statement because its contents are only a message to the programmer.

REM statements are English-text explanations of items such as names, calculations, and routines. They are used to explain these things to unfamiliar programmers:

- How a routine works.
- How a calculation works.
- The meaning or value of a data name.

The syntax is simple:

```
REM {any amount of text up to 250 characters}
```

Insert a space, two hyphens, and another space between the word REM and the message text. This helps make REM statements stand out.

Use REMs at the beginning of every program. This opening group of REMs contains the program name, date created, the program purpose, and the Data Dictionary. Then, use REMs sparingly throughout the program, and keep your REM statements concise. A REM at the beginning of every major routine makes any program more readable.

One final note: you can put a REM statement on the same line with another statement, but it has to be the last statement on that line. To do so, separate the REM from the end of the other statement with a colon (:). This signals QBasic to ignore everything after the REM in that statement line.

Notice the suggested format for the REMarks in the following program segments:

```
REM —        program "maillist.bas" — 06/01/94
REM —        purpose: to print mailing list
REM —        data dictionary (may be more than 400 REM_
REM statements)
REM —        contains data item names and brief explanation_
REM of each
REM —        custlastname$ customer last name
REM —        custstreet1$ customer street address, first_
REM line
REM —        custstreet2$ customer street address, second_
REM line
REM —        etc.
REM —        program chains to "wwwmenu.bas"
GOSUB fileopen: REM — open routine
GOSUB main: REM — main control
GOSUB {etc.}
       .
       .
       .
REM •        begin read loop
main:
       .
       .
       .
```

The Data Dictionary

The best way to understand a Data Dictionary is to see one. Look at a sample from a program that handles customer purchases:

```
REM  -        Data Dictionary
REM  -        blaktrip     $ spent on Black River trips
REM  -        city$
REM  -        custbirthdat$ customer's birthdate
REM  -        custfirstnam$ customer's first name
REM  -        custlastname$ customer's last name
REM  -        custstreet1$ customer's street address,
REM  -        line 1
REM  -        custstreet2$ customer's street address,
REM  -        line 2
REM  -        hudstrip     $ spent on Hudson River trips
REM  -        moostrip     $ spent on Moose River trips
REM  -        purchyr%     year of purchase
REM  -        salestax
REM  -        shirtsals    $ spent on shirts
REM  -        st$    state
REM  -        zip%   zip code
REM  -        Work Variables:
REM  -        c%     loop counter
REM  -        tripsubtot#  trip subtotal
```

The Data Dictionary includes all the data names (variables) used in the program. Put them in two major groupings:

- Data names, which are contained in files.
- Work variables (those used by the program but not saved).

Within each grouping, list the data names in alphabetical order.

The previous sample illustrates what makes a good Data Dictionary:

1. Each Dictionary entry gives the data name, then an expanded definition of its meaning. Limit the definition to 50 characters. Do not write full sentences to expand on a data name.

2. Data names should include the character suffix, which defines the data type (as explained in the section "Data Types," earlier in this chapter). The Dictionary entry *zip%* specifies this ZIP code as a short, five-digit integer (instead of a long, nine-digit integer, or an alphanumeric one).

3. When there can be *no* confusion about what a data name represents, grudgingly omit the expanded definition in the Dictionary. See *city$* and *salestax* in the example.

4. The work variables are simple data names for the "utility" variables used in standard routines, as well as the results of calculations and loops performed within PROCESS, SUBCALC, and MASSAGE routines (which you see in the next chapter).

    Since they serve a broader, workhorse function, being used over and over, their naming is less critical. For example, you might decide that **c%** is always a loop counter, in all your programs, forever. (Loops are explained later on.)

A Data Dictionary may take up hundreds of REM statement lines in your program. It is worth the work because a good Dictionary saves you (as a programmer) weeks of work in the long run.

Some last advice: *consistency* throughout all your programs is the key to data naming.

> **NOTE:** Make a Master Data Dictionary, tape it to your computer, and always use it.

As you write the data dictionary for your first program, begin a Master Data Dictionary on a separate piece of paper. Include the data names that you might use again in any future programming project in the Master Dictionary. Do not precede the names with *WWW*; instead use a prefix that applies to a class of files, (like *cust*, *part*, *invn* or *item*) as the first four characters of the name. That way the name is more general and able to be used elsewhere. In any case, use names that work for you.

Now tape the Master Data Dictionary beside your computer for instant reference and updating when you write programs. This way, your data names are consistent not only within one system (series of programs) but throughout all the programs you write. With repeated use, the data names become second nature. It sounds simple, but in the course of a year, this little secret may save you weeks of work.

Refer to Appendix B for help in making a Master Data Dictionary of often-used data names.

QBasic File Menu and Commands

The File menu gets, saves, and prints programs, or program blocks. Here are explanations of some words (relating to the File menu), before you go on.

1. **Environment.** The QBasic on-screen environment used to write, modify, test, and run programs.
2. **Module.** Any program, or part of a program that is loaded and treated as a single unit by QBasic. (It has its own name, and is changed or corrected separately from other programs.)
3. **Program block.** Any section of program statements of a program.

   Now, you are ready to browse through the file menu: first, get into QBasic:

   Type **cd\DOS**, then press **Enter**.
   Type **qbasic**.
   (or get into QBasic using the DOS 6.0 shell).
   Press **Esc**, and you are in QBasic.

Now,

Press **Alt**.
Press **Enter**, and you are in the File Menu. Look at the selections:

1. **New program** command. One that you start from scratch. This command clears all previously loaded program statements so that you can type in a completely new program on a blank screen.
2. **Open program** command. Gets an existing program from the disk and brings it into the QBasic environment. The command clears the environment of any other program statements before bringing in the requested program.
3. **Save** command. Saves the current module onto the disk. The current module is the one that is on the screen at the time the Save command is invoked.

If the current module was originally loaded from the disk using the **Open** command, it is saved under that same name, replacing the original one on disk.

If the current module does not yet have a name (it is a new program recently typed in and has never been saved), then QBasic asks you for the name. If a module with that same name already exists on the disk, the **Save** command can replace the existing one.

4. **Save As** command. Saves the current module onto the disk, but it asks you to key in the name. As with the **Save** command, if another module with that identical name is on the disk, it can be replaced. This command can be used to save differing versions of the same program under different names. In this way, the original version is not destroyed on the disk.

   This command is also useful for something few programmers talk about. There are times when a program that needs to be written is similar to one already done and working. Using QBasic, the programmer can get that similar program into the environment, make changes, then save it as an entirely new program.

5. **Print** command. Prints all or part of the module currently in the environment.

6. **Exit** command. Leaves the QBasic environment entirely.

You can now get into, then out of, each of these File commands. If the program displays a box that reads "`Loaded file not saved. Save it now?`" while doing this exercise,

Press **Tab**.

Press **Enter** and the text box goes away.

New Program

To start a new program,

Press **Enter**.

The program opens and you are in the QBasic environment, ready for you to type in a new program.

Open a Program

To open a program,

Press **Alt+F**.

Move the cursor down to the **Open** option, and

Press **Enter**.

The program displays the Open program box. The box prompts you for a file name. But you can do more than that with this command. It works like this:

Type *****.bas**, press **Enter**.

The program displays a list of all QBasic programs in the DOS directory.

Type **a:*.bas**, press **Enter**.

The program displays a list of all QBasic programs in the a: disk (the first floppy disk).

Type {a directory name}***.bas**, press **Enter**.

The program displays a list of all the QBasic programs in that directory.

Type {the program you want to bring into QBasic}, then press **Enter**.

The previous program statements are cleared, and the specified program is brought in.

Type *****.BAS**, press **Enter**.

The program again displays the program names in the DOS directory.

Press **Tab** to move the cursor down to the program names.

Move the cursor (using the Arrow keys) to the program you want to bring in. Get WWWreg.bas

Press **Enter**.

Press **Esc** twice to leave this command, if you are still in the Open option.

Press **Alt+F**, and then press **Enter** to clear the screen of WWWreg.bas

Saving a Program

To save a program,

Press **Alt+F**.

Move the cursor down to the **Save** option.

Press **Enter**.

The program displays the Save a New Program box. QBasic is prompting you for a name.

Type **xyz1**, and press **Enter** to save (in this case a blank screen). This is the way to save a program that you type in from scratch.

Using Save As

To save a program that you read from the disk and change, first open WWWreg.bas as shown in Open a Program above, then

Press **Alt+F**.

Move the cursor down to the **Save As** option.

Press **Enter**.

The program displays the Save As box. This box works exactly like the Save New box above. Repeat the same process, but with a different name.

Type **xyz2**, then press **Enter** to save WWWreg.bas as xyz2.bas.

Now you have saved a program that you have read from the disk and changed its name.

Printing a Program

To print all or part of a program,

Press **Alt+F**.

Move the cursor down to the **Print** option.

Press **Enter**.

You can print all or part of your program. The selected text option prints the part of the program that you highlighted using **Shift** and the **Arrow** keys. You have to highlight before invoking Print.

To test Print we will put in a new program:

1. Press **Alt+F**, then press **Enter** to get back into the Editor with a blank screen. Then, you put in a tiny program.
2. Type: **a=1**, press **Enter**.

b=2, press **Enter**.
c=a+b, press **Enter**.
print c, press **Enter**.

Now, move the cursor up to the first position on the second line,

b=2, and
Press **Shift** with your left hand, and hold it as you
Press **Down Arrow** twice.

The second and third lines should be highlighted.

Press **Alt+F**.
Move the cursor down to the **Print** option.
Press **Enter**.

Notice that the dot is in front of the Selected text option.

Press **Enter**.

QBasic prints the second and third lines.

Press the **Down Arrow** to clear the highlighted text. Get back into the File menu, select **Print** again, and this time, print the whole program. Exit QBasic. You're done.

Summary

1. Data is essential. Without it, there's no need for computers or computer programs.
2. QBasic requires data names to identify the location of data in computer memory.
3. QBasic has two major data types, numeric and alphanumeric. Numeric is made up of four sub-types, giving a total of five:
   - Short integers (values between −32768 and 32767)
   - Long integers (values between −2147483648 and 2147483647)
   - Single-precision numbers (up to six digits, including decimals)
   - Double-precision numbers (up to 16 digits, including decimals)
   - Strings (alphanumeric characters)

4. Some words are reserved by QBasic. The complete list is found in your QBasic manual.
5. Data names should be:
   - Meaningful
   - Short
   - Consistent
   - Clear, not cryptic
6. Use REMark statements to compose your Data Dictionary, and to make your program understandable for someone else—maybe even you, at some future date.
7. Make up a data dictionary with meaningful data names while you write each program. Combine the dictionaries from all your programs into a Master Data Dictionary, and keep it by your computer.
8. The commands of the File menu are:
   - **New Program**. You are keying it in for the first time.
   - **Open Program**. Retrieve one already existing on disk.
   - **Save**. The current module onto disk.
   - **Save As**. Save the current module under another name.
   - **Print**. All or part of a program.
   - **Exit**. Leave QBasic.

The Book in Review

1. Design and program thoughtfully.
2. To examine any QBasic program, break it up into blocks. Then, study each block separately, and finally look at the logic that controls all the blocks.
3. QBasic gives you a complete working environment, which encourages writing programs in building-block fashion.
4. Blueprint your program *before* you write the first line of code.
5. **Data names should be meaningful, short (but not cryptic), consistent, and clear.**

CHAPTER 6

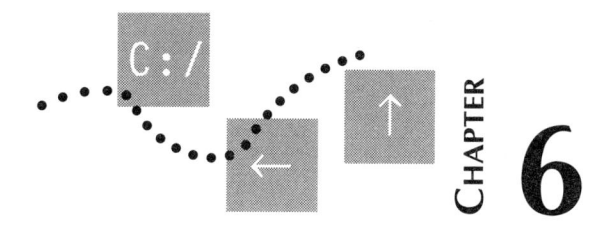

The QBasic Editor

This chapter teaches you how to use the QBasic editor so you can manipulate text in your programs. You build your first precise piece of code in the editor, using its functions. The topics include:

- How the QBasic editor helps you
- The editing keys
- Edit and View menus
- FIND options
- CHANGE options
- CUT & PASTE options
- COPY (from one routine to another)
- Syntax checking
- Example of Editor use

Chris' Newsletter

Chris is writing the WildWater Works (WWW) newsletter while on the road visiting corporations. This time the newsletter turned out to be 10 handwritten pages; that will be about three or four typewritten pages. Chris usually sends the letter back to WWW for Terry to put into the word processor and create the final proof. However, the hotel where Chris is staying has typewriters available, so Chris uses one to save Terry some time. Chris hasn't typed much since college, and these typewriters are old electric ones, but what the heck!

At 4:30 AM, Chris finally finishes the last page perfectly. Just one final proof reading and it is done. Darn! Left out a whole sentence in the first page. All four pages have to be redone. Chris hits the pillow for three hours of sleep. There is a meeting with an important prospect at 8:00 AM for breakfast. The letter will be sent to WWW in the morning so Terry can do it on the word processor.

Chris wasted eight valuable hours in trying to put out a finished newsletter that took Terry less than 1/2 hour with the word processor.

Imagine a word processing typewriter that allows you to insert, delete, move, search for words, search and replace, cut and paste sections of text, and check your spelling and grammar. That is basically what the QBasic Editor (work environment) does for you as a programmer. QBasic is an ideal *word processor* for the programmer. This chapter shows you why.

How the QBasic Editor Helps You

For the past five chapters, you have been working with just Delete and the Arrow keys to make corrections. Now you see how much time the Editor saves.

The editor helps you:

- Correct mistakes.
- Insert additional program lines.
- Delete program lines.
- Find everywhere that a variable is used throughout the program.
- Change a variable name throughout the entire program.
- Move a routine or part of it to another part of the program.

- Copy a piece of code to another part of the program, then change some of it.

Get into QBasic to practice using the Editor, and use the File menu to bring the WWWreg.bas program into your work space.

The Editing Keys

Whenever possible, use the function keys for selection, rather than picking from menus. Moving quickly among menus, commands, and program routines can become confusing, and give you a headache. These are the recommended keys:

Key	Description
Home	Brings the cursor to first position in a program line.
End	Moves the cursor to the last position in a program line.
Tab	Moves the cursor eight spaces to the right.
Up Arrow	Moves the cursor up one line.
Down Arrow	Moves the cursor down one line.
Right Arrow	Moves the cursor one position to the right.
Left Arrow	Moves the cursor one position to the left.
Backspace	Moves the cursor one position to the left, deleting the character in that position.
Delete	Deletes the character at the cursor.
Insert	Puts the Editor into type-over mode. *Never press the key by itself, or you will write over good lines of code.* When you see a flashing block cursor, the Editor is in type-over mode. If you press **Ins** by mistake, and the Editor is in type-over mode, press **Ins** again to put the Editor back into Insert mode.
Page Up	Moves the cursor one screen up.
Page Down	Moves the cursor one screen down.
F2	Enters into module select or delete mode.
Shift+F2	Moves to another module.
Shift <arrow keys>	Select statements, or parts of them, to copy, move, delete or print.
Shift+Delete	Temporarily removes selected statements, or parts of them, from the program.
Shift+Insert	Inserts selected statements, or their parts, that were temporarily removed using **Shift+Delete**.

You can change the number of spaces given to **Tab** by calling the Options menu and selecting the **Display** command, then moving down to the tab stops, and typing the number of positions that you want. You move down to tab stops by pressing the **Down Arrow** four times.

The Arrow keys move the cursor all through the program, without disturbing any of the program text.

The flashing line of the cursor shows that you are in Insert mode, which is the standard mode of QBasic. This means that as you type, all text to the right of the cursor is moved over. This mode makes adding program lines, variable names, commas, and semicolons (you do a lot of this) very easy. Always work in Insert mode to keep things simple. When you make mistakes in spelling, use **Delete** to remove the characters, then type them again, rather than worry about the Insert/type-over mode. It's one less thing to remember.

Modules

A *module* is a separate routine or procedure of a program. There is an example of a module in this chapter, and it is fully explained in Chapter 8.

Using **F2** puts you into Module command mode. This means that once you press **F2**, you can:

- Edit another module.
- Delete any module.

To edit a module,

Press **F2**.
Press **Down Arrow** (or **Up Arrow**) until the module you want is highlighted.
Press **Enter**.

The program displays that group of program code on your screen.

To delete a module,

Press **F2**.
Press **Arrows** until the procedure is highlighted.
Press **Tab** until the Delete is highlighted.
Press **Enter**.

QBasic then deletes the module.

Edit and View Menus

Use the keys explained previously instead of relying on the Edit and View menus. These keys perform most everything that is in these two menus. To keep this chapter and the use of the editor simple, the Edit and View menus are skipped.

The Find Command

The Find command is in the Search menu. You use it to locate specific variable names, expressions, or line labels. If you do not know the entire name or number for which you are searching, enter the fragment that you know. QBasic finds every occurrence of the piece that you specified.

To use the **Find** command,

Press **Alt+S**.

The program displays the Search menu.

Press **Enter**.

The program displays the Find command.

Type in the name or expression for which you are searching.

Press **Enter**.

If that item is in the program, QBasic stops at the first occurrence (beyond the spot where the cursor was before you got into the Search menu).

Press **F3**.

The program stops at the next occurrence. Each time you press **F3**, the program finds that expression or name.

WARNING Be careful when using this command. QBasic assumes that once it has found the expression you are looking for, you might want to change it. If you press any keys other than the Arrow keys, Page Up, Page Down, or the function keys (F1 through F12), QBasic replaces the highlighted expression with whatever you type. Using a mistaken key here is expensive because you may accidentally press a key and change something unknowingly. Hours later, when you run the program, you will find a problem that was not there earlier. At that point, the statement with the error may look like a string of useless characters.

After you locate something using **Find**, the safe bet is to press any **Arrow** key. This removes the highlight and prevents the replacement problem.

Find Options

Usually, you want to search the entire program module for the name, and disregard upper or lowercase. Ignore these features of the Find menu screen at the start.

However, the Whole Word option is a useful tool. When you select this option, it means that the keyed expression (all by itself) is exactly what QBasic is searching for. If that keyed text is part of another word or expression, QBasic passes it by. The Whole Word option is particularly useful when searching for a particular number or a variable name all by itself, apart from its combinations within other variable names.

The Change Command

The Change command works in a similar fashion to Find, with a couple of extensions.

1. You tell it what you want to change the expression to.
2. You choose whether to verify each change, or just automatically change all of them.

To use the Change command,

Press **Alt+S**.

This calls the Search menu.

Press the **Down Arrow** until Change is highlighted.
Press **Enter**.

The program displays the Change command.

Enter the expression that you're looking for, then the expression that you want it to become. Specify whether you want automatic changes, or manual verification of each. In most cases, you should verify every change. This avoids changing something unanticipated by mistake.

Cut and Paste Commands

Now you can get into the QBasic environment for some practice at moving program code around.

First, clear the work space,

Press **Alt+F**, then press **Enter**.

Enter these five lines:

a = 10, press **Enter**.
b = 4, press **Enter**.
c = 5, press **Enter**.
d = c * b + a, press **Enter**.
print "the values of a, b, c and d are "; a; b; c; d, press **Enter**.

Use the **Arrow** keys and **Shift** to select the text that you want to move, copy, delete, or print. First you select it. Then, you act on it (move, copy, delete, or print it).

To select the text,

Press **Shift+Down Arrow**.

The selected statement is highlighted.

When you are done,

Press the **Down Arrow** by itself.

The statement is no longer highlighted.

Repeat this process, selecting text using all of the arrow keys to get comfortable with highlighting.

Moving Text

Follow these instructions to move text:

Highlight the first program statement (a = 10) to be moved, using the above procedure. Then,

Press **Shift+Delete**.

The program no longer displays the statement. This procedure does not really delete the text. It just puts it into a *scratch pad* for possible movement later.

Move the cursor down to the first position where you want the text placed (say at the third statement).

Press **Shift+Insert**.

The program redisplays the statement.

Copying Text

Follow these instructions to copy text.

Highlight the text to be copied. Try the second statement this time.

Press **Shift+Delete**.

The program no longer displays the highlighted statement.

Without moving the cursor,

Press **Shift+Insert**.

The program redisplays the statement in exactly the same spot.

Move the cursor to the first position where you want the text copied (try the bottom of the program).

Press **Shift+Insert**.

The highlighted text is again inserted (copied to a new location).

Press **Shift+Insert** three more times.

Each time you press **Shift+Insert**, the piece of code last (temporarily) removed is copied to a new location.

Deleting Text

Follow these instructions to delete text.

Highlight the text to be copied.

Press **Shift+Delete**.

The program no longer displays the highlighted text.

Although the text is gone from the program, if you made a mistake, and want to put it back,

Press **Shift+Insert**.

The program redisplays the text. This *delete* process is the first half of the Move or Copy processes.

Copying from One Routine or Program to the Other

Moving (or copying) text from one routine to another is easy in QBasic. Here's a quick example:

Get into the file menu, and load WWWreg.bas. Now select any four lines of text using **Shift** and **Arrow** keys.

Press **Shift+Delete** to put the text into the scratch pad.

Press **Alt+F**, then press **Enter**.

The program displays a warning box, as shown in Figure 6.1.

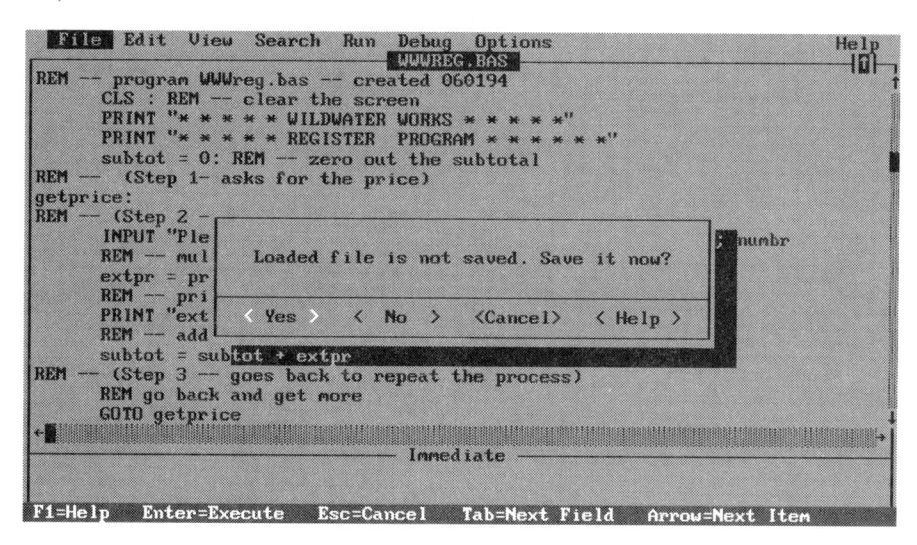

Figure 6.1 Warning box for a file not saved.

Press **Tab** then press **Enter** so that WWWmenu.bas is not changed on the disk.
Press **Shift+Insert**.

Your text is moved from one program to a new program, without disturbing the original program.

Syntax Checking

Normally, syntax checking (automatically testing program statements for proper form) is turned on. This catches errors while you are entering them, not hours later, when you are trying to run the program. To test whether syntax checking is on, look at the Options menu.

Press **Alt+O**.

If there is a dot to the left of the Syntax Checking command, it is on. Get out by pressing **Esc**.

If, for some reason, the dot is not there,

Press the **Down Arrow** until Syntax Checking is highlighted.
Press **Enter**.

Statements are then checked for correctness when you move the cursor to the next program line.

When the Syntax Checker finds an error, it displays a message onto the screen. If you see the error,

Press **Enter** to clear the message, then correct the error.

If you do not know what is wrong,

Press **F1** for on-screen help, then correct the error.

An Example of Editor Use

To familiarize you with the Editor, you are going to type in a program sloppily and then fix it. You would never write a program in this manner, but it is the quickest way for you to use most of the features in one quick session.

> **NOTE** This session is your first really precise work in QBasic. If this becomes a little confusing at times, do not worry about understanding everything you are doing. If you make some mistakes, start over again from

that point. You gain more and more knowledge as you continue using these examples.

First, clear the screen:

Press **Alt**, then **Enter**. If the warning box in Figure 6.1 comes up, Press **Tab**, then **Enter** so as not to save any changes to disk.

Then type in this program:

INPUT "Enter a value for the rate of interest"; i
INPUT "Enter the dollar amount invested in one shirt"; d
INPUT "Enter the number of months in the period"; m
INPUT "Enter the average number of shirts on hand"; a
dols = i * d * m * a
PRINT dols; i; d; m; a
END

Run the program to ensure that it works properly.

Press **Alt+R** and **Enter**.

If it doesn't run, check the program against the one above, correct it, and run it again.

Changing Variable Names

The variables in the previous example have names that are not meaningful. You can change them. Use **Search** and **Change** to make i, d, m and a become *rate*, *costshirt*, *months*, and *onhand*, respectively.

Press **Alt+S**.

Move the cursor down to Change.

Press **Enter**.

The program displays the Change screen.

Type **i**.
Press **Tab**.

Type **rate**.
Press **Tab** twice, **Space**, and **Enter**.

QBasic finds each i, and ask if you want to change it. Each time it asks,

104 • TEACH YOURSELF... QBASIC

Press **Enter**.

The program should now look like this:

```
INPUT "Enter a value for the rate of interest"; rate
INPUT "Enter the dollar amount invested in one shirt"; d
INPUT "Enter the number of months in the period"; m
INPUT "Enter the average number of shirts on hand"; a
dols = rate * d * m * a
PRINT dols; rate; d; m; a
END
```

Next, change the *d* to *costshirt*.

Press **Alt+S**.

Move the cursor down to Change.

Press **Enter**.

The program displays the change screen.

Type **d**.
Press **Tab**.
Type **costshirt**.
Press **Enter**.

QBasic finds each *d*, and asks if you want to change it. Each time it asks,

Press **Enter**.

The program should now look like this:

```
INPUT "Enter a value for the rate of interest"; rate
INPUT "Enter the dollar amount invested in one shirt";_
costshirt
INPUT "Enter the number of months in the period"; m
INPUT "Enter the average number of shirts on hand"; a
dols = rate * costshirt * m * a
PRINT dols; rate; costshirt; m; a
END
```

Next, change the *m* to *months*.

Press **Alt+S**.

Move the cursor down to Change.

Press **Enter**.

The program displays the Change screen.

Type **m**.
Press **Tab**.
Type **months**.
Press **Enter**.

QBasic finds each *m*, and ask if you want to change it.

Press **Enter**.

The program should now look like this:

```
INPUT "Enter a value for the rate of interest"; rate
INPUT "Enter the dollar amount invested in one shirt";costshirt
INPUT "Enter the number of months in the period"; months
INPUT "Enter the average number of shirts on hand"; a
dols = rate * costshirt * months * a
PRINT dols; rate; costshirt; months; a
END
```

Last, change the *a* to *onhand*.

Press **Alt+S**.

Move the cursor down to Change.

Press **Enter**.

The program displays the Change screen.

Type **a**.
Press **Tab**.
Type **onhand**.
Press **Enter**.

QBasic finds each *a*, and ask if you want to change it. In the first case, the *a* it found is part of an input prompt, and you do not want to change it.

Press **Tab** and **Enter** to skip that change. From there on,

Press **Enter**.

The program should now look like this:

```
INPUT "Enter a value for the rate of interest"; rate
INPUT "Enter the dollar amount invested in one_
shirt";costshirt
INPUT "Enter the number of months in the period"; months
INPUT "Enter the average number of shirts on hand"; onhand
dols = rate * costshirt * months * onhand
PRINT dols; rate; costshirt; months; onhand
END
```

Run the program again to make sure that it still works. If it does not, compare your program with the one above and make your corrections. You have more changes to make.

Moving Text

Now we have decided to make the input part of this program into a subroutine (Chapter 8 explains subroutines in detail—this is just your first brief look at one that helps to show how the Editor works.)

First, move the first four statements to the end of the program.

Highlight the first four statements.

Press **Shift** together with the **Down Arrow** four times.

Press **Shift+Delete**.

Use the **Down Arrow** to move to the bottom of the program.

Press **Shift+Insert** to put the INPUT lines back.

The program should look like this:

```
dols = rate * costshirt * months * onhand
PRINT dols; rate; costshirt; months; onhand
END
INPUT "Enter a value for the rate of interest"; rate
```

```
INPUT "Enter the dollar amount invested in one_
shirt";costshirt
INPUT "Enter the number of months in the period"; months
INPUT "Enter the average number of shirts on hand"; onhand
```

Now type a GOSUB statement as the first statement in the program. Move to the very top of the program, and:

Type **GOSUB getinput**.
Press **Enter**.

Next, move to the first input statement, and enter the subroutine name.

Type **getinput:**.
Press **Enter**.

You need a RETURN statement to exit from the subroutine. Go to the end of the last statement.

Press **Enter**.
Type **RETURN**.
Press **Enter**.

The program now looks like this:

```
GOSUB getinput
dols = rate * costshirt * months * onhand
PRINT dols; rate; costshirt; months; onhand
END
getinput:
INPUT "Enter a value for the rate of interest"; rate
INPUT "Enter the dollar amount invested in one_
shirt";costshirt
INPUT "Enter the number of months in the period"; months
INPUT "Enter the average number of shirts on hand"; onhand
RETURN
```

With all theses changes, test the program to make sure it still works.

Press **Alt+R** then **Enter** to run the program. If it does not work, check the changes, make your corrections, and run it again.

Last, give the program a name and date of writing. Go to the very top left of the screen.

Type **rem shircost 6/01/94**.

Press **Enter**.

Then, make the printout a little more readable. Move down to the PRINT line.

Type **PRINT "cost"; TAB(10); "interest"; TAB(20); "shirt cost";_
TAB(30); "months"; TAB(40); "num shirts"**

Press **Enter**.

Now change the other PRINT line to look like this by typing in the tabs:

**PRINT dols; TAB(10); rate; TAB(20); costshirt; TAB(30); months_
; TAB(40); onhand**

The program should now look like this:

```
REM shircost  6/01/94
GOSUB getinput
dols = rate * costshirt * months * onhand
PRINT "cost"; TAB(10); "interest"; TAB(20); "shirt cost";_
TAB(30); "months"; TAB(40); "num shirts" <Enter>
PRINT dols; TAB(10); rate; TAB(20); costshirt; TAB(30);_
months; TAB(40); onhand
END
getinput:
INPUT "Enter a value for the rate of interest"; rate
INPUT "Enter the dollar amount invested in one_
shirt";costshirt
INPUT "Enter the number of months in the period"; months
INPUT "Enter the average number of shirts on hand"; onhand
RETURN
```

Your program is perfect, and you now have hands-on experience with the Editor. Run the program again in a final test. Get an idea (generally) of how the program works.

Summary

1. Use the edit keys whenever possible, rather than the Edit and View menus.
2. Use **Find** to locate each happening of a piece of program text. Make sure that you press (any) **Arrow** when done.
3. Use **Change** to substitute text.
4. Move or copy portions of a program by:
   - highlighting, using the **Shift+Arrow** keys.
   - pressing **Shift+Delete** to put it in the scratch pad location where you want it to be.

Press **Shift+Insert** for each copy of that text that you want.

The Book in Review

1. Design and program thoughtfully.
2. To examine any QBasic program, break it up into blocks. Then study each block separately, and finally, look at the logic that controls all the blocks.
3. QBasic gives you a complete working environment that encourages writing programs in building-block fashion.
4. Blueprint your program *before* you write the first line of code.
5. Data names should be meaningful, short (but not cryptic), consistent, and clear.
6. **The QBasic editor is top shelf. Use the keys, rather than the menus, and you will be productive.**

Chapter 7

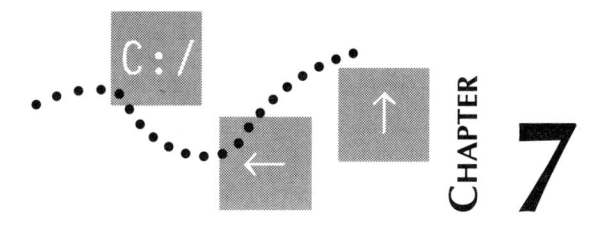

Program Organization

This chapter teaches you about the importance of proper program organization. You learn how to use the blueprint as a basis for writing routines. The topics include:

- Why use routines?
- Organizing a program
- The 10-part model program
- QBasic routines
- From blueprint to routines

The Business Plan

Chris, Pat, and Terry had set up a business plan when they first decided to become entrepreneurs. But they got so involved in their business, that they forgot about it for the first year. Now, they are stepping back and further developing their original plan. It was a good one, but unused for a year. So they wasted quite a bit of time. (This is common problem with start-up businesses.)

Skip this chapter, and you won't waste quite a bit of time programming. You'll waste about half of it. Understand this chapter thoroughly and you'll be a programming hero(ine)! This self-developed approach saves hours of testing. You have seen blueprints. Now you will be able to apply them to a solid program structure.

You should refer back to this chapter after reading each of the ones that follow. It helps you understand why certain statements belong where they are in the program. Each time you come back here, skim the entire chapter. Soon this structured method will be second nature to you.

Why Use Routines?

Chapter 4 showed you how to blueprint a program. Before writing it in QBasic, we use the blueprint to design the routines of the program.

You would think that the billions of computer programs that exist have little in common. Else, why would there be so many? Each program must be completely unique, right? Wrong. A number of things are generic:

- Certain routines occur in most programs.
- The routines work together, and flow together in a predictable way.

As you remember from Chapter 4, before you begin writing a program, you need to ask yourself two questions:

1. What will the program do (purpose and output)?
2. How will it do it (input, hidput, and logic)?

You answered these questions, resulting in the program blueprint. The next step is to determine the program structure. This building-block plan of the routines in a QBasic program does two things:

1. It breaks up the program into a group of tasks ("What will this program do?").
2. It tells you which kinds of statements do those tasks ("How will the program do it?").

This end result of this process is a well-defined, easily written program.

Organizing a Program

Organization gives your program *structure*. Every program needs a sound structure to build upon, a solid framework to which you can attach statements. As with building a house, you cannot construct a program by the seat of your pants. To give you a starting point, use a common structure or pattern for all your programs, a *model* program. (Some sections of the program are not always used.)

Give your program routines meaningful names that are not QBasic reserved words. The names represent the common types of routines that make up your program structure.

Every program:

1. Brings in data.
2. Processes the data.
3. Puts out some kind of report (on screen, to the printer, or onto disk).

This gives you three major functions in every program.

The Major Functions

The major functions in every program are:

- IN
- PROCESS
- OUT

These three major functions are under the control of one master routine called MAIN CONTROL. Your model program organization looks like this:

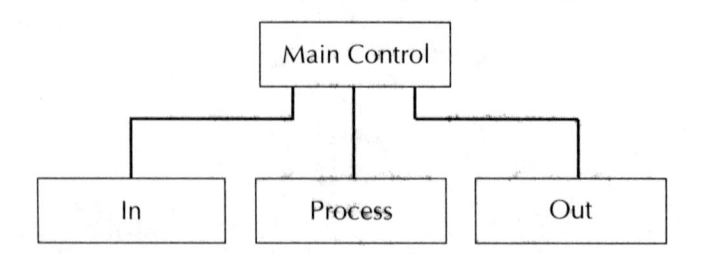

```
                    ┌──────────────┐
                    │ Main Control │
                    └──────┬───────┘
          ┌────────────────┼────────────────┐
     ┌────┴───┐       ┌────┴────┐      ┌────┴───┐
     │   In   │       │ Process │      │  Out   │
     └────────┘       └─────────┘      └────────┘
```

Now you can expand this central structure. If the computer program needs to work with existing data (as opposed to having the user type in everything), then it needs to read in files on disk. You need one standard FILEREAD routine for every disk file that you want to read.

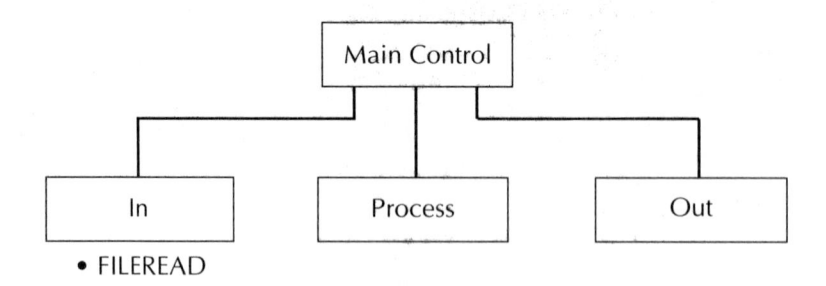

```
                    ┌──────────────┐
                    │ Main Control │
                    └──────┬───────┘
          ┌────────────────┼────────────────┐
     ┌────┴───┐       ┌────┴────┐      ┌────┴───┐
     │   In   │       │ Process │      │  Out   │
     └────────┘       └─────────┘      └────────┘
   • FILEREAD
```

Some programs need only one PROCESS (CALC routine). Others require many small processing routines, all controlled by the major CALC routine. We call these small, subcalculation routines SUBCALCS.

In addition, a program usually has a few small, utility routines:

- Error checking
- Error handling
- Getting keyboard input
- Editing keyboard input
- Date formatting

These utility routines take data and manipulate (*massage*) it to make it more presentable. They are in a program area called MASSAGE routines.

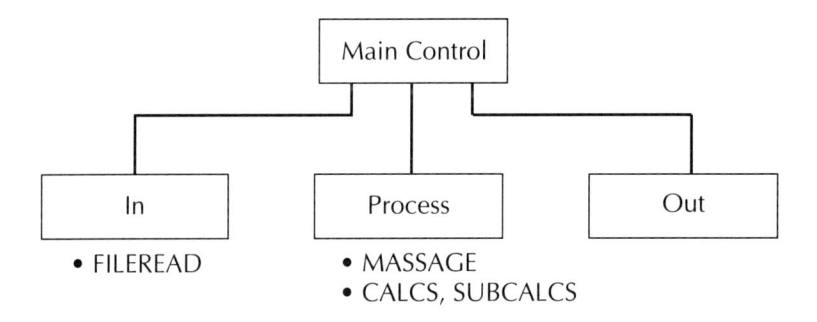

```
                    ┌──────────────┐
                    │ Main Control │
                    └──────┬───────┘
          ┌────────────────┼────────────────┐
     ┌────┴────┐      ┌────┴────┐      ┌────┴────┐
     │   In    │      │ Process │      │   Out   │
     └─────────┘      └─────────┘      └─────────┘
    • FILEREAD       • MASSAGE
                     • CALCS, SUBCALCS
```

Chapter 1 defined a report as output that is written to the screen, to the printer, or onto a disk. In your model program structure, you need to separate these report types. This gives you three subsections for the OUT part of your program:

- SCREENOUT (screen output)
- PRINTOUT (printed output)
- FILEOUT (disk file output)

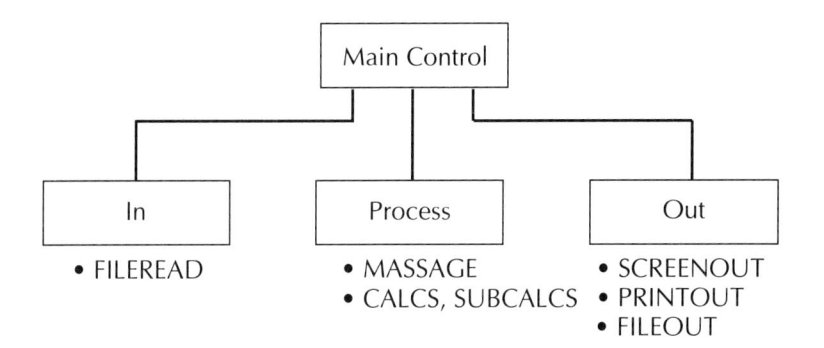

```
                    ┌──────────────┐
                    │ Main Control │
                    └──────┬───────┘
          ┌────────────────┼────────────────┐
     ┌────┴────┐      ┌────┴────┐      ┌────┴────┐
     │   In    │      │ Process │      │   Out   │
     └─────────┘      └─────────┘      └─────────┘
    • FILEREAD       • MASSAGE         • SCREENOUT
                     • CALCS, SUBCALCS • PRINTOUT
                                       • FILEOUT
```

The Stub

Finally, you need the STUB, which is a small series of statements at the beginning of the program needed to start the program.

The STUB does these things:

1. Gets today's date.
2. Enables the routine that OPENs the files that are going to be used.
3. Enables the MAIN CONTROL routine.
4. After MAIN CONTROL manages all the processing of data, it returns power to the STUB.
5. Closes all files and ends the program.

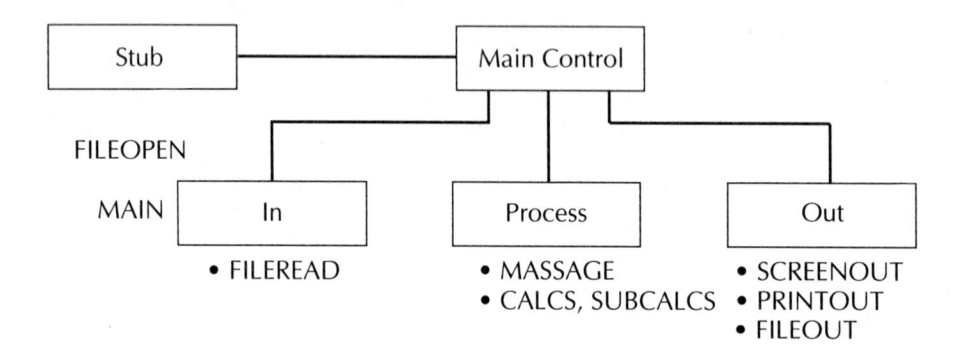

```
          ┌─────────┐        ┌──────────────┐
          │  Stub   │────────│ Main Control │
          └─────────┘        └──────────────┘
                                    │
FILEOPEN                            │
  MAIN    ┌─────────┐     ┌─────────┐     ┌─────────┐
          │   In    │     │ Process │     │   Out   │
          └─────────┘     └─────────┘     └─────────┘
          • FILEREAD      • MASSAGE       • SCREENOUT
                          • CALCS, SUBCALCS • PRINTOUT
                                          • FILEOUT
```

The End

The statement that ends a program resides in the STUB, not at the physical end of the program (very last statement). Instead, the END statement (which concludes the program) is the last statement of the STUB section.

The STUB passes control of the program to one of the routines. It does its work and returns control back again to the STUB. Then on to the next routine, and so on. Ultimately, control returns to the STUB, reads the END statement, and the program stops.

More powerful than the END is the CHAIN statement. Instead of simply ending the program, the CHAIN first ends the program that is running, then runs an entirely NEW PROGRAM. You will use CHAIN in all the programs that are selected and run from a menu.

Program Listing

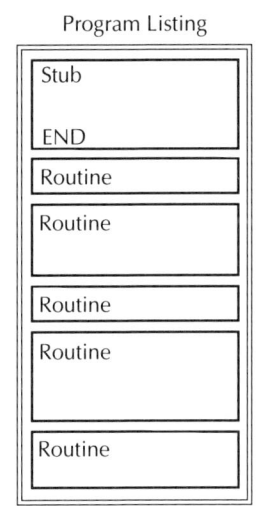

```
┌─────────────┐
│ Stub        │
│             │
│ END         │
├─────────────┤
│ Routine     │
├─────────────┤
│ Routine     │
│             │
├─────────────┤
│ Routine     │
├─────────────┤
│ Routine     │
│             │
├─────────────┤
│ Routine     │
│             │
└─────────────┘
```

The 10-part Model Program

Before you look more closely at each section (routine) of the model program, here are:

- The 10 routines
- How many of each are found within a program
- The routines that each controls (enables)

Now, for the functions of each routine:

1. STUB:
   - Directs program flow to:
     – FILEOPEN routine
     – MAIN routine
   - Includes CLOSE statement
   - Includes END statement
   - Usually CHAINs to another program

2. The FILEOPEN routine:
   - Opens all files
   - Establishes the layout of each file
3. The MAIN CONTROL routine enables FILEREAD, MASSAGE, CALC/SUBCALC, and OUT routines.
4. The FILEREAD routine:
   - Reads files
   - Unpacks information
5. The MASSAGE routines are any commonplace tasks that handle data, for example, errors, input, or date.
6. The CALC routine:
   - Changes data
   - Produces values to be saved or displayed
   - Optionally controls SUBCALC routines
7. The SUBCALC routines perform detailed calculations.
8. The SCREENOUT routine outputs information to the screen.
9. The PRINTOUT routine outputs information to the printer.
10. The FILEOUT routine outputs changed data back to the files.

Keep in mind that the names of these routines are not found in QBasic. I made them up. The names are used only to illustrate program organization.

Now here is the detail of each routine in the model program. Use this as an outline of the statements and concepts that are covered in this book. Take your best guess at the new terms and statements. Do not worry about not understanding the detail of each statement. They are explained in later chapters.

The STUB Routine

The STUB routine is a collection of statements like this:

```
REM - program "xxxxxxxx.bas" - created (date)
REM - data dictionary
```

```
REM - contains data item names and brief explanation of each
REM - data dictionary could be more than 400 REM statements!
REM -
GOSUB getdate: REM - enables (invokes) date setting routine
GOSUB openfiles: REM - enables routine that opens the files
GOSUB main: REM - enables (summons) main control routine
CLOSE: REM - closes all files
END: REM - stops the program
```

Every program you write should begin with a STUB of this form because:

1. A STUB puts descriptions (program name and date, names and explanations of all data items) at the beginning, where you can skim them at a glance.
2. A STUB begins your program with a building-block structure, as shown by the GOSUB statements in the STUB.

> **NOTE** The STUB is not main control, but it enables MAIN CONTROL. The STUB actually does little work, and it makes no decisions. Think of the STUB as an outline of the chapters in a book. It just points to the chapters.

A model STUB is shown above. Use it at the beginning of each new program, putting a REM in front of any statements that are not needed. (You should not need to add any statements.)

The FILEOPEN Routine

Three types of statements normally are in a FILEOPEN routine:

- OPEN is needed to make a file usable by the program.
- DIM defines the size of a table of data items stored in the file.
- FIELD defines the location of data items within a file.

The FILEOPEN routine places the definitions of all file data in one place.

The MAIN CONTROL Routine

This is the *air traffic controller* for the IN, PROCESS, and OUT routines. Actually, the MAIN routine controls everything except the STUB and its routines.

Most of the MAIN CONTROL routine is a loop (Chapter 10) that enables FILEREAD, SUBCALC, MASSAGE, and the three OUT routines. The loop enables these routines repeatedly, until all the data has been processed and sent to the OUT routines.

MAIN CONTROL is the focal point of your program, therefore, it's crucial to check and double-check the design of this routine. MAIN CONTROL is the routine where the more devastating errors are found. So, take the time to design your MAIN CONTROL thoughtfully.

MAIN CONTROL has the following statements:

- GOSUB enables a subroutine.
- CALL enables a procedure.
- GOTO redirects the program to a QBasic line within the MAIN CONTROL routine.
- IF...THEN tests if a condition is true, then does something.
- Statements that assign (give or calculate) values, such as:
    - maxlines% = 60.
    - partnum% = 1234.

These are also called formulas.

The FILEREAD Routine

Once a file is open, it can be read. However, some files have numeric data "packed" (compacted) to reduce storage space on disk. So the FILEREAD routine reads the files, then UNPACKs the numeric data so that it can be used.

Two statement types are in most FILEREAD routines:

- GET (to read a record from a random-access file.)
- unpack statements (which you'll see later on.)

The CALC and SUBCALC Routines

These are the routines that perform math calculations or data manipulation (move data from one file or data item to another). MAIN CONTROL calls the CALC routines, which then call SUBCALC routines if there are a lot of different calculations.

Your best bet is to group routines of this type in one part of the program for readability and ease of change.

Here are the statement types that are used in CALC or SUBCALC routines:

- CALL enables a procedure (a minor, repeated routine).
- GOTO redirects program flow to another program line within the CALC or SUBCALC routine.
- IF...THEN {calculate}/CALL/GOTO performs the indicated operation only when a condition is true.
- "Assign" statements manipulate, calculate, or move data.
- LSET (needed to compact data into disk files before they are written) works with the pack family of statements.
- The "pack" family of statements (MKI$, MKS$, MKD$, and MDL$) condenses numeric data to go into files.

The MASSAGE Routines

There can be any number of these small, data-manipulating, utility routines. When you find yourself needing a short routine that is called repeatedly during a program, write a MASSAGE routine. Assemble these small routines in one easy-to-read group, rather than scattering them throughout the program. That way you know where to look for any MASSAGE routine you need to change. You also know where to put a new one, so that you can easily find it later.

Here is a list of some MASSAGE routines:

- NUMERIC EDIT makes sure a number is valid (Is 12345z a valid number?).
- DATE EDIT makes sure a date is valid (Is 022994 a valid date?).

- DATE COMPARISON finds the earlier of two dates (Which is earlier, 043094 or 083193?).
- DAYS ELAPSED calculates the number of days between two dates (How many days elapse between 022893 and 060394?).
- DATE SWAP changes a date into date comparison format (Swap your standard format MMDDYY, into YYMMDD, for example, 061494 into 940614).
- ROUNDING rounds off dollars and cents to two decimals (33.63507 dollars = $33.64).

Appendix E contains a number of sample MASSAGE routines, ready for you to use in your programs.

MASSAGE routines can use most statement types, with the following exceptions:

- No file GETs and PUTs
- No GOSUBs (CALL is okay)
- No CLOSE
- No END

The SCREENOUT Routine

The SCREENOUT routine sends data to the screen. The statement types found in the SCREENOUT routine are:

- PRINT and PRINT USING.
- The "string" family of statements (such as CHR$, STR$, and MID$).
- LOCATE, which places the blinking cursor on the screen.
- CLS, which clears the screen.
- COLOR, which lets you use different colors on the screen.
- CSRLIN, which tells the program what line the cursor is on.
- POS, which tells the program what column the cursor is on.
- TAB, which positions the cursor at a specific column on the screen.
- "format" statements that are necessary for PRINT USING statements to work.

The PRINTOUT Routine

The PRINTOUT routine sends data to the printer. Statements used in the PRINTOUT routine are:

- LPRINT and LPRINT USING
- The "string" family of statements (see the previous list)
- TAB
- "format" statements

The FILEOUT Routine

The FILEOUT routine sends data to a disk file. The FILEOUT statements are:

- PUT
- LSET (needed for packing ALL data, not just numeric)
- The "pack" family of statements (MKI$, MKS$, MKD$, and MDL$), which outputs numeric data for files

Chapter 12 covers random files, data packing, and writing to them.

QBasic Routines

The use of the word "routine" until now has been as a general term of program structure. Now we can get specific. There are two types of routines in QBasic, the subroutine and the procedure. The next chapter discusses subroutines and procedures in detail.

Here is the difference between the two types:

- Subroutines are normally the major routines that control processing logic.
- Procedures accomplish a single task with some data, and control nothing else.

Here's another look at the 10 types of routines in the model program, and the choice between making each one a subroutine or a procedure:

Routine	Number of Occurrences	Routines that will be Enabled	Subroutine or Procedure?
1 STUB	1	All others	— neither —
2 FILEOPEN	1	None	Subroutine
3 FILEREAD	1 per file	None	Subroutine
4 MAIN CNTRL1		FILEREAD, PROCESS, SUBCALC, 3 OUTPUTS	Subroutine
5 CALC	0 to dozens	SUBCALC, MASSAGE	Subroutine
6 SUBCALC	0 to dozens	None	Either
7 MASSAGE	6 or more	Other MASSAGE	Procedure
8 SCREENOUT	0 to dozens	None	Either
9 PRINTOUT	0 to dozens	None	Either
10 FILEOUT	1 per file	None	Subroutine

You learn more on this distinction in Chapter 8.

NOTE Program organization is a routine process.

From Blueprint to Routines

The blueprint, which you learned about in Chapter 4, is a block diagram of your program. All you have to do is relate the steps in the blueprint to specific program routines (subroutines and procedures).

The rules are:

1. The STUB is the same for every program. No new control statements go into it. Only the data dictionary definitions of the variable names should ever be added. Other than that, do not change the STUB.

2. Every program contains one FILEOPEN routine, whether there are 16 files in the program or none. All OPENS go in this routine. If there are no files to be opened, then leave the subroutine itself with only a RETURN statement.

3. Each file that is read needs its own FILEREAD routine. This routine reads and unpacks one record each time it is invoked. If you have four files in one program, then you have four FILEREAD routines.

4. The MAIN CONTROL routine itself does no work. It serves only as the major loop that regulates getting data, processing it, and creating output. This routine controls all the reads, calcs, and writes (or prints). Therefore, do not assign tasks from your blueprint to MAIN CONTROL.

5. Put all print tasks in PRINTOUT routines, and all screen tasks in SCREENOUT routines. Use one master routine for each different screen layout or printed page layout. Each of the master routines may or may not control several other routines, depending on the complexity of the output.

6. Each file that is written to has its own FILEOUT routine, with minor routines, if needed.

7. The CALC routine controls calculations and the movement of data. It is invoked from MAIN CONTROL. The SUBCALCS do the actual calculations. SUBCALCS are enabled by either the CALC routine, or the OUT routines (SCREENOUT, PRINTOUT, or FILEOUT), whichever works better in your program. Put calculation and data movement tasks in the SUBCALCS, and do not worry about which routines manage the SUBCALCS until the very end. Then, do what fits more naturally in your program.

8. MASSAGE routines are usually procedures that do some specific operation (massaging) on a certain type of data. They are called many times in the same program, and are frequently saved for use in other programs. Most programmers build up a library of MASSAGE routines that they use over and over in their programs.

These are the steps for converting a blueprint into routines.

1. Write each step of your blueprint down the left side of a piece of paper.
2. Using rules 1 through 8 above, assign each task to a routine.

NOTE You always have one STUB, one FILEOPEN, one FILEREAD for each file read, one FILEOUT for each file written, and one MAIN CONTROL, so...

3. Get another sheet of paper, and group the other tasks by each type of SUBCALC, and OUT routines.
4. When you are all done, decide how many routines you want of each type, or whether you want to group several tasks into one routine.
5. Decide if you want the SUBCALCS controlled by one major CALC, or by the OUT routines.

You now have a program structure.

Summary

1. Program structure makes writing simpler because it breaks up the logic into small, workable blocks. This allows you to work on one block at a time and ignore the rest of the program. You also can test simply, one block at a time.
2. Every program has three major functions:
   - IN
   - PROCESS
   - OUT
3. The model program structure contains a STUB and nine (or fewer) other routine types.
   - FILEOPEN
   - MAIN CONTROL
   - FILEREAD
   - CALC
   - SUBCALC
   - MASSAGE
   - SCREENOUT
   - PRINTOUT
   - FILEOUT

4. Routines are the building blocks of program organization. Formulate program structure by specifying the tasks to be done, and assign each task to a routine.
5. Subroutines control program input, output, and major logic decisions.
6. Procedures perform small, frequently repeated, tasks on data.
7. Convert your blueprint into routines, then begin programming.

The Book in Review

1. Design and program thoughtfully.
2. To examine any QBasic program, break it up into blocks. Then study each block separately, and finally look at the logic that controls all the blocks.
3. QBasic gives you a complete working environment, which encourages writing programs in building-block fashion.
4. Blueprint your program *before* you write the first line of code.
5. Data names should be meaningful, short (but not cryptic), consistent, and clear.
6. The QBasic Editor is top shelf. Use the keys, rather than the menus, and you'll be productive.
7. **Program organization is crucial. Blueprint, assign the tasks to routines, then program each routine.**

Chapter 8

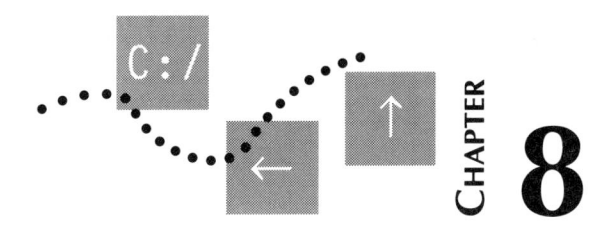

Control of Routines

This chapter teaches you about subroutines and procedures. The topics include:

- Routines
- Subroutines
- Procedures
- The Routine-selection test
- Global and local data
- Data into and out of Subroutines
- Data into and out of Procedures
- GOTO
- Routines in a program

Office Environment Analogy

WildWater Works has an *open* office environment, where people walk freely in and out of any office. When Chris goes somewhere to get a file folder, the folder is taken back to the work space. It's easy to get information. However, the system requires management (each of them tells the others what they are taking most of the time), or else no one knows where to find any of the file folders. If WWW had 50 employees, the open system would be unmanageable. Anyone in any office could use, abuse, or lose an original document from another office. Recovery from misuse of files could be time consuming or impossible.

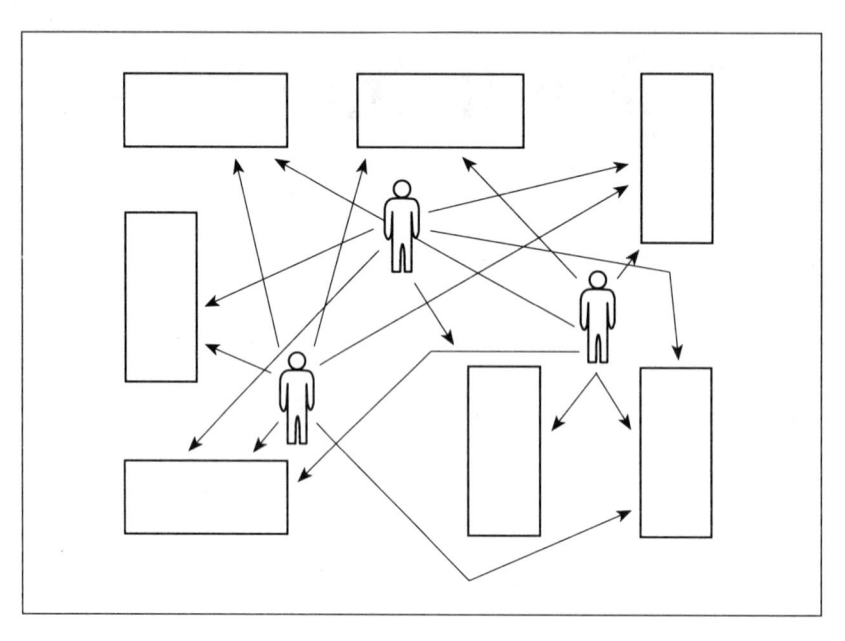

Figure 8.1   An open office.

Trippin Traveler Tips & Techniques, Inc. (TTTT) is a company that provides travelers with travel information in their own language, on every major country. A German can get information, written in German, on the Geisha theater in Kyoto. An American can get the scoop, written in English, on all the discos in Leningrad. Chris can get information in English on white water in Lithuania.

TTTT has a *closed* environment, where people can get and use information only in their own offices. Here, glass partitions separate one office from another. You exchange information in the files from one office to another through *translator slots* in the partitions like this:

1. You type your question (in the language of your office) into the *translator slot* machine.
2. Someone in the receiving office reads what you are asking for (in the language of their office).
3. The receiver of the question locates the information you want.
4. The receiver responds to you by typing a reply into the *translator slot*, which is printed out in the language of your office.

No one is permitted to carry the physical data out of an office. This method takes more effort to exchange information between offices, but everyone knows where the data is at all times. It's easier to control what belongs where in your own office—and no one from another office is going to lose any of your office's documents.

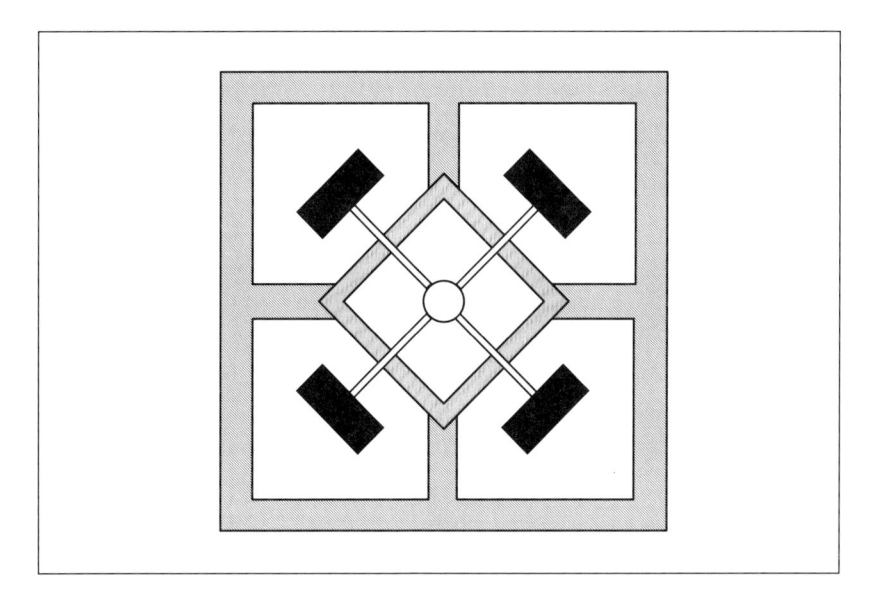

Figure 8.2 *A closed office.*

Each of these environments has advantages and disadvantages.

- An open office environment:
    - Is good for wide distribution and sharing of tasks. At WildWater Works, Chris, Pat, and Terry share all the work. When most of the work is in Pat's area of responsibility, both Chris and Terry pitch in to help.
    - Does not perform well in keeping original data intact, unless it is a small office like WWW.
- A closed office environment:
    - Works well for frequent processing of small amounts of information.
    - Has inflexible transfer of information in and out of offices.

Handling data in a program is like processing documents in an office with both open and closed environments. To accommodate this, QBasic gives you two routine types for processing information. In this discussion of subroutines and procedures, you also learn how data moves in and out of the routines in a QBasic program.

In this chapter, the word *enable* means to invoke, summon, or call another routine to do some work. ENABLE is used in place of the words CALL and PERFORM, to avoid mix-ups. (CALL and PERFORM are reserved words in computer language, so they are not used.)

Routines

A *routine* is a group of program lines treated as if they were all one huge statement. A *statement* is a single sentence in QBasic that does one simple task. (Refer to the sample programs in Chapter 2 and Chapter 3 for a look at some statements, or Chapter 7 for short explanations of some statements.) You name each routine, and that name defines the entire routine (statement group), which might include a hundred statements.

You work with two types of routines in QBasic, the subroutine and the procedure. The fundamental difference is that:

- *Subroutines* are usually the major routines that manage processing logic.

- *Procedures* are mostly routines that perform a single task (usually one that is used repeatedly in the program). They normally massage or calculate data directly rather than control anything else.

Subroutines

Subroutines are the blocks of the program that control the *detours*, *scenic overlooks*, and *pit stops* of program flow. Just as you can drive along an interstate highway and branch off occasionally to see a point of interest without really leaving the main route, so can the program follow its main logic while detouring for a specific purpose.

So you can say that a subroutine is the *gate keeper* of the main program flow. See what happens when you enable (summon) a subroutine (which is done with the GOSUB statement—explained later):

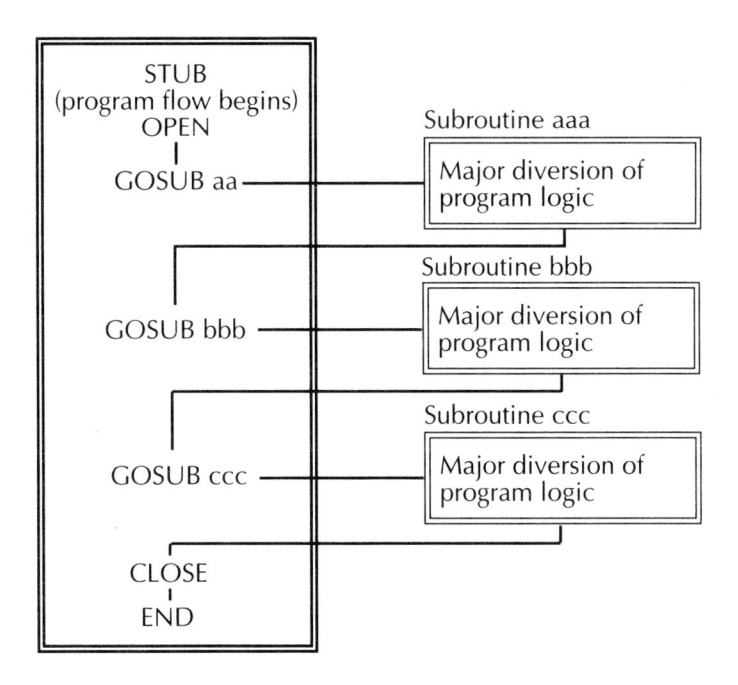

```
STUB
(program flow begins)
    OPEN                    Subroutine aaa
     |                      ┌──────────────────┐
    GOSUB aa ──────────────▶│ Major diversion of│
                            │ program logic    │
                            └──────────────────┘

                            Subroutine bbb
                            ┌──────────────────┐
    GOSUB bbb ─────────────▶│ Major diversion of│
                            │ program logic    │
                            └──────────────────┘

                            Subroutine ccc
                            ┌──────────────────┐
    GOSUB ccc ─────────────▶│ Major diversion of│
                            │ program logic    │
                            └──────────────────┘

    CLOSE
     |
    END
```

A subroutine cannot stand on its own because it is a subsection of the program in which it occurs. Therefore, think of a subroutine as a major redirection of your program logic to accomplish an important task.

Subroutine *aaa* in the previous diagram is conceptually one big statement made up of individual statement lines. Every time the statement *GOSUB aaa* is read by the program, the program branches directly to the routine named *aaa* and begins reading the statements in *aaa* as if they were the next ones in the program listing. (This is true for subroutines *bbb* and *ccc* as well.)

The syntax of the GOSUB and the subroutine it invokes are:

```
GOSUB {name of subroutine}
{intervening lines of program}
{name of subroutine}:
  .
  .
  .
RETURN
```

Notice that the statement lines of the subroutine do not directly follow the GOSUB in the program listing. The subroutine *must* be in a different part of the program from the GOSUB that invoked it. That way, the program does not *fall* into a routine in the normal downward progression of program flow. The subroutine must be enabled (branched to) only by a GOSUB statement.

Now look at how the program flows into and out of the GOSUB statement and the subroutine. The numbers in parentheses at the right show you the sequence of the flow process below:

```
{program begins}                      (sequence of
                                       execution)

GOSUB {name of subroutine}            (1)
{statement following GOSUB
(point RETURNed to)}                  (5)
  .
  .
  .
{ RETURN or END statement}            (6)
{name of subroutine}:                 (2)
  . {routine begins}                  (3)
  .
  .
RETURN                                (4)
```

Here's how the program flows:

1. The program flow reaches the GOSUB statement line, with the name of the subroutine being enabled.

2. The logic jumps to the program line beginning with that subroutine name. (A colon follows the subroutine name.)
3. The subroutine starts working. (Remember, a subroutine is treated as if it is one long statement.)
4. The subroutine's statements are executed sequentially up to the RETURN statement, at which time the program flows back to the statement immediately following the GOSUB.
5. Program flow continues at the statement after the GOSUB.
6. Just before the first line of the subroutine, there must be an END or RETURN which prevents the program from falling into the subroutine by mistake via the normal downward flow of logic.

A subroutine must only be entered (enabled) by the GOSUB statement.

Procedures

Much like little rest stops while traveling, small tasks are common in a program. You do not need to create a separate routine for every small task to be done. Sometimes it is better to write a line or two of code within a major subroutine instead. However, when a small task is performed repeatedly, you should consider writing a procedure. Also, if you are writing statements in different parts of the program that all do the same work, but use different values each time, then a single procedure is a good choice to replace all the statements.

To help you decide whether to use a procedure or a subroutine, here are two general guidelines:

1. Is it a stand-alone task? Does it perform a series of calculations giving one end result? Or does it change one number or string into a fancy print format? If so, make it a procedure. But if it makes any major processing decisions (decides which other routines to enable), then it's a major task, and should be a subroutine.
2. Is it a repeated task? Is it invoked by several other routines within the same program? Can it work with different kinds of data? If so, it's a procedure.

Ask yourself if the task is minor, repetitive, and unrelated to main program flow.

Procedures Stand Alone

Procedures are not integral parts of the programs in which you write them. A procedure can be saved separately from its original program, then later used in any other programs.

A procedure can stand alone. It is put easily into other programs.

This is the real merit of the procedure. If there is a task to be accomplished—one that applies to similar kinds of data with different names—then use a procedure.

The CALL statement enables a procedure, as shown below:

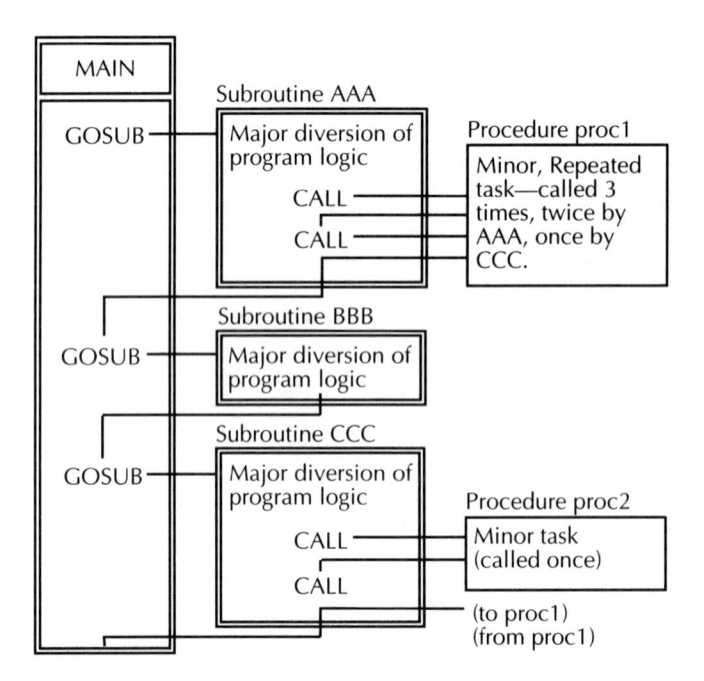

```
MAIN                Subroutine AAA
                    ┌──────────────────┐        Procedure proc1
GOSUB ──────────────│ Major diversion of│        ┌──────────────────┐
                    │ program logic     │        │ Minor, Repeated  │
                    │              CALL │────────│ task—called 3    │
                    │                   │        │ times, twice by  │
                    │              CALL │────────│ AAA, once by     │
                    └──────────────────┘        │ CCC.             │
                                                 └──────────────────┘
                    Subroutine BBB
                    ┌──────────────────┐
GOSUB ──────────────│ Major diversion of│
                    │ program logic     │
                    └──────────────────┘

                    Subroutine CCC
                    ┌──────────────────┐
GOSUB ──────────────│ Major diversion of│
                    │ program logic     │        Procedure proc2
                    │              CALL │────────┌──────────────────┐
                    │                   │        │ Minor task       │
                    │              CALL │        │ (called once)    │
                    └──────────────────┘        └──────────────────┘
                                                 (to proc1)
                                                 (from proc1)
```

The previous diagram shows repeated CALLing of procedures:

- One procedure, proc1, is CALLed twice by the same subroutine (AAA) to do a task (probably with two different sets of data). It is then called again by subroutine CCC.
- Another procedure, proc2, is CALLed once from subroutine CCC. In your programs, you create procedures that might be called 50 or 100 times.

The CALL statement and the procedure have the following syntax:

```
CALL {name of procedure (global data)}
.
{other program statements}
.
SUB {name of procedure (local data)}
.
.
.
END SUB
```

Here is the CALL statement and the procedure in a program:

```
REM shircost 6/15/94
INPUT "Enter a value for the rate of interest"; rate
INPUT "Enter the dollar amount invested in one_
shirt";costshirt
INPUT "Enter the number of months in the period"; months
INPUT "Enter the average number of shirts on hand"; onhand
CALL prindol (rate, costshirt, months, onhand)
END
SUB prindol (n1, n2, n3, n4)
dols = n1 * n2 * n3 * n4
PRINT "cost"; TAB(10); "interest"; TAB(20); "shirt_
cost";TAB(30); "months"; TAB(40); "num shirts" <Enter>
PRINT dols; TAB(10); n1; TAB(20); n2; TAB(30); n3; TAB(40);_
n4
END SUB
```

You can see that the procedure has a pattern similar to that of the subroutine. Like the subroutine, it should never be entered by way of the natural downward flow of logic.

A procedure must only be enabled (entered) by a CALL statement.

The Routine-selection Test

Remember the model program structure from the last chapter? There are three routines that can be either subroutines or procedures. How do you decide whether to write a specific SUBCALC, SCREENOUT, or PRINTOUT routine as a subroutine or procedure? There is not one fixed rule. It's your judgment call, and in most cases, either choice works. So here's a simple test to help you decide whether a new block of QBasic statements should be a subroutine or a procedure. (Don't worry. Your judgment gets better as you gain experience in designing and writing programs.) Read the following test like a program: make a yes-or-no choice at each step, and then follow that choice to the next block.

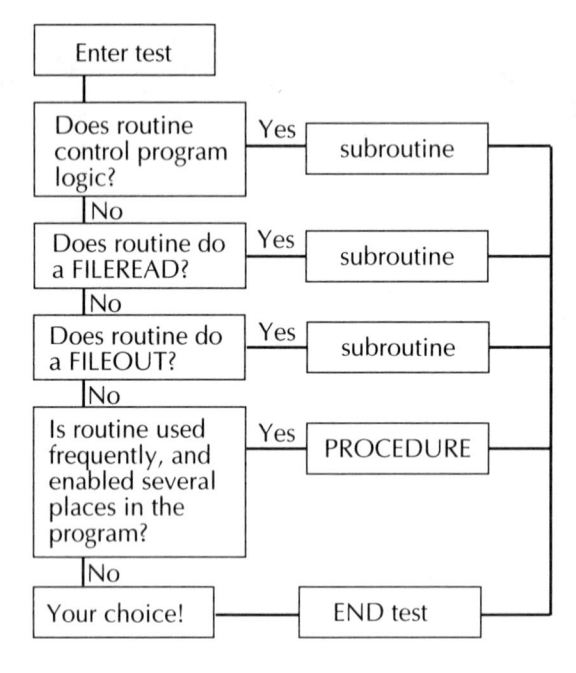

```
                    Enter test
                         |
            Does routine          Yes
            control program      -------> subroutine
            logic?
                 | No
            Does routine do       Yes
            a FILEREAD?          -------> subroutine
                 | No
            Does routine do       Yes
            a FILEOUT?           -------> subroutine
                 | No
            Is routine used       Yes
            frequently, and      -------> PROCEDURE
            enabled several
            places in the
            program?
                 | No
            Your choice!  --------------- END test
```

Even if you change your mind after having written the routine, the similarity of subroutine and procedure means that you can switch over easily. The differences in syntax (format) are slight, apart from adding (or removing) the *slot* through which data moves. Before you look at the translator slot of the procedure, look at data program-wide.

NOTE There are more complex methods of using procedures and their data. This book shows the simpler methods because the more difficult ones can mess up even veteran programmers.

Global and Local Data

Remember the rule in Chapter 5 that each data name must be unique? That's because data names are usually *global* throughout an entire program (including all the subroutines). When a variable name is given a value, that value is contained in that name throughout the entire program, and its subroutines. When the variable data name is assigned another value, that new value is carried into and out of every subroutine, until it is reassigned by any statement in any subroutine. Any data name can have its value changed by any subroutine of the program. A mistake in data names here can cause problems.

The procedure does not share the same attributes or concerns. It is blind to all the rest of the data in the program. The procedure is aware of only its own data. Variable names within a procedure are *local*. The only way that a procedure can get values from the program is through the *slot*, and a procedure can only pass values through the slot out to the program.

Inside a *procedure*, data names are *local*. Only the data names passed to the procedure can be changed.

Before you look further at data movement in both types of routines, here are three rules for global versus local data names:

1. Global: Inside the STUB and all subroutines, use unique, meaningful names.
2. Local: In procedures, you can use simpler data names such as a#, b, x$, y%, or wk1%. (Especially since procedures typically work on a class of data, rather than dealing with a specific data name.)
3. The safe bet is to avoid all duplication of both local and global data names in a program if possible.

Creating a Data Dictionary for your programs is the best way to check your data names. That is when you spot duplications. Trying to find it later on will cost you a lot of time.

Data Into and Out of Subroutines

Subroutines and procedures are not equivalent. The major difference is how each handles data.

Only the procedure requires special data treatment. For a subroutine, any data name anywhere in the program can be given a new value by any subroutine.

Like WWW's office at the beginning of this chapter, the subroutine is completely open to information exchange. If the subroutine reads in or assigns a value to a data name, then the changed value is kept by the program upon returning from the subroutine.

Every value assigned within any subroutine gets carried outside.

Data In and Out of Procedures

A procedure is a peripheral part of the program. It is connected to the rest of the program only by a slot. Remember the closed office (TTTT) at the beginning of this chapter? People in one office had to send data through the slot to get information from another office. That's just how a procedure works.

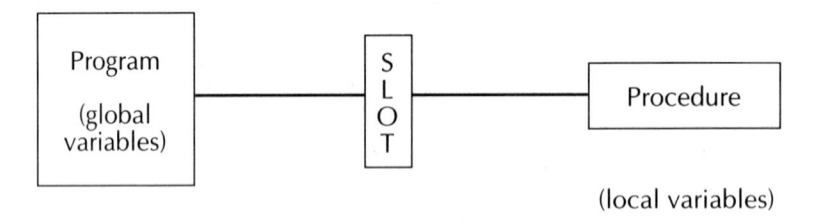

```
┌──────────┐           ┌─┐           ┌──────────┐
│ Program  │           │S│           │          │
│          │           │L│           │Procedure │
│ (global  ├───────────┤O├───────────┤          │
│variables)│           │T│           │          │
└──────────┘           └─┘           └──────────┘
                                     (local variables)
```

The format for writing the line, which enables a procedure is:

```
CALL {procedure name (global variables)}
```

The procedure itself has this syntax:

```
SUB {procedure name (local variables)}
 .
 .
 .
END SUB
```

The slot machine process (the conversion of global variables into local variables) is a simple one. Read on.

The Data "SLOT"

Suppose you are writing a program that has a procedure called *tripdisc*. In the procedure, you are going to calculate a discount for good customers who book a large trip.

1. Select the variables to be brought in from the program:
    - totaltrip
    - custrating%

totaltrip is the dollar total of the trip being booked. *custrating%* is an integer value ranging from 0 to 3, the number of raft trips that this customer has taken with WWW. The higher the number, the better the customer. Since they come from the program world outside of the *tripdisc* procedure, *totaltrip* and *custrating%* are global data names. They have no value inside the *procedure tripdisc*. So the CALL statement is needed to pass the value of the data names *totaltrip* and *custrating%* in through the data slot of the procedure as shown in the following illustration:

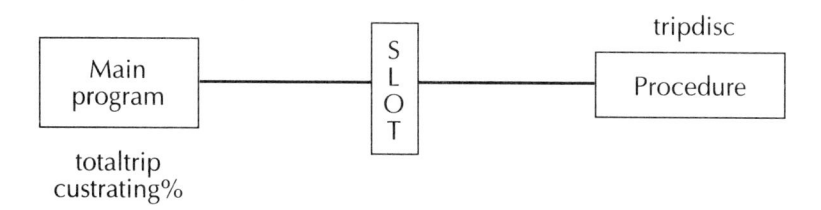

```
                                              tripdisc
  ┌──────────┐        S        ┌──────────┐
  │   Main   │────────L────────│          │
  │  program │        O        │ Procedure│
  │          │        T        │          │
  └──────────┘                 └──────────┘
   totaltrip
   custrating%
```

2. Now you need to add a variable for the discount that is calculated, then sent back to the program from the procedure. Use an imaginative global data name, *discount*. The value stored in this data name is the end result of *tripdisc*'s markdown calculation. It is the output of the procedure. (If no discount is given, then discount has a value of 0.)

So three global variables are passed through the data slot:

```
CALL tripdisc (totaltrip, custrating%, discount)
```

3. Create an equal number of local variables, using unique, different names from the global variables:
    - amt

- rating%
- disc

amt is the data name that the procedure *tripdisc* uses for the total, undiscounted amount of the trip. *rating%* is the value you can test to see if the customer qualifies for a reduction (suppose two trips or more denotes a good customer). *disc* is the discount resulting from the calculation.

So your data slot uses six variables:

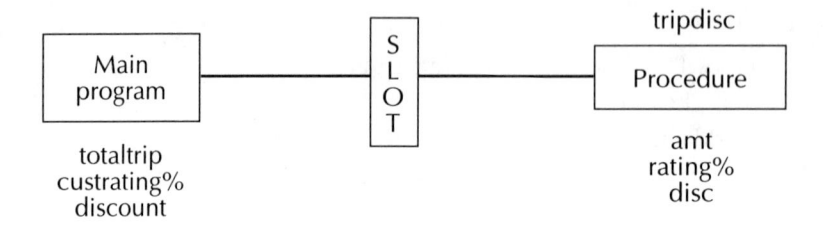

```
                                              tripdisc
     ┌─────────┐    ┌───┐    ┌──────────┐
     │  Main   │    │ S │    │          │
     │ program ├────┤ L ├────┤ Procedure│
     │         │    │ O │    │          │
     └─────────┘    │ T │    └──────────┘
                    └───┘
      totaltrip                  amt
     custrating%                rating%
      discount                   disc
```

The statements in the procedure itself look like this:

```
SUB tripdisc (amt, rating%, disc)
    IF rating% > 1 THEN disc = amt * .20
    IF rating% > 2 THEN disc = amt * .30
END SUB
```

4. The procedure creates a one-to-one correspondence between the data names in the two sets of parentheses in the order given:

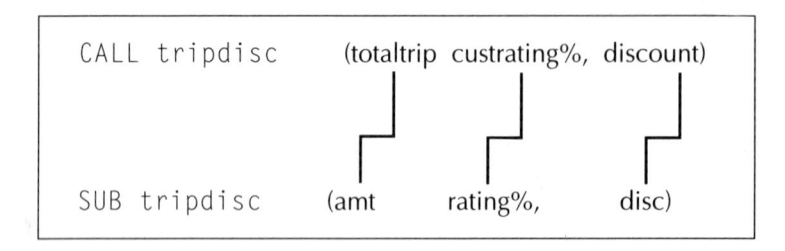

```
   ┌──────────────────────────────────────────────────────┐
   │ CALL tripdisc    (totaltrip  custrating%,  discount) │
   │                       │           │           │      │
   │                       │           │           │      │
   │                       ▼           ▼           ▼      │
   │ SUB tripdisc     (amt        rating%,      disc)     │
   └──────────────────────────────────────────────────────┘
```

- The first global (*totaltrip*) is linked to the first local (*amt*)
- The second pair is linked (*custrating%* and *rating%*)

- The third global (*discount*) is linked to third local (*disc*)

Note the two integer variables and four single-precision variables above. The local variables must be the same type as their corresponding global variables.

Through this linking, the procedure tripdisc equates:

- *amt* = totaltrip (meaning, "inside the procedure *amt* has the value of *totaltrip*)
- *rating%* = custrating% (meaning, "inside the procedure, *rating*% has the value of *custrating%*")
- *disc* = discount (meaning, "inside the procedure, *disc* and *discount* have the same value")

Meanwhile, what is happening outside the procedure? Only those data names in the slot can be modified by the procedure. All other variables in the program are not touched. The only global variables that potentially can be modified by the procedure *tripdisc* are *totaltrip*, *custrating%*, and *discount*. In this case, the only global data name that tripdisc changes is *discount*.

The GOTO Statement

Program logic is redirected by a GOSUB statement for subroutines and by a CALL statement for procedures. There is one other statement that redirects program flow.

The GOTO is the easiest (and most dangerous) of the three flow-redirecting statements to use. Here is the syntax:

```
GOTO {line name or number}
```

That's it. Simple. But what happens when flow moves to the line name that is in the GOTO? The program continues flowing downward from that point without ever going back. The critical distinction here is that, when the GOTO is used, the program flow does not return to the line immediately following the enabling statement (as it does with both GOSUB ... RETURN and CALL ... END SUB). The program moves to a new section and flows downward, until it is redirected again.

Here is a program example. At what point will the program print "Back to here?"

```
REM — program underway
```

```
.
.
GOTO newstate
PRINT "Back to here"
CLOSE
END
.
.
newstate:
PRINT "Now at new section in program"
REM — program continues from here on downward
.
.
```

Answer—never. The program never even reaches the CLOSE and END statements. Only another GOTO statement can get the program back to these statements.

Years ago, some *experts* decided that the GOTO statement was bad. They felt that programmers were abusing the GOTO and making a mess of their programs by jumping all around their programs and losing track of what was going on. In a lot of cases, the GOTO is misused. As a result, even some capable programmers avoid the GOTO.

You're not safe white water rafting just because you are wearing a life jacket. You have to know how to navigate white water. You are not a good driver just because you do not speed. You have to know how to drive. You are not a good programmer just because you do not use GOTO. You have to know how to program. Good programming, like good management, never really changes.

GOTOs simplify the redirection of program flow within the routine based on the outcome of some simple decision or condition. Prohibiting the GOTO means the programmer has to fabricate several (or many) IF... THEN statements to replace one simple GOTO statement. These IFs can get very complex. You might see 30 or 40 program lines for a single statement. In that situation, the program becomes unreadable.

The GOTO, properly and selectively used (it can only reference statements within the same routine), can make it easier to read statements that would otherwise be complex. Use a GOTO when it can simplify the logic of a program. Use GOTOs carefully, alone, or combined with simple IF... THEN statements.

Within the same routine, follow this absolute GOTO rule: Use GOTO only to go somewhere else within the same routine.

This brings to three the statements that control program logic:

- **GOSUB** enables a subroutine elsewhere in the program.
- **CALL** enables a procedure elsewhere in the program.
- **GOTO** redirects program execution to another statement in the *same* routine.

Remember that program control will not return automatically to the program line following the GOTO statement.

Routines in a Program

Here is a program with both a subroutine and a procedure. Go into QBasic and type it in, then run it.

```
REM shircost 6/01/94
GOSUB getinput
CALL prindol(rate, costshirt, months, onhand)
END
getinput:
INPUT "Enter a value for the rate of interest"; rate
INPUT "Enter the dollar amount invested in one_
shirt";costshirt
INPUT "Enter the number of months in the period"; months
INPUT "Enter the average number of shirts on hand"; onhand
RETURN
SUB prindol (n1, n2, n3, n4)    **** refer to note below ****
dols = n1 * n2 * n3 * n4
PRINT "cost"; TAB(10); "interest"; TAB(20); "shirt cost";_
TAB(30); "months"; TAB(40); "num shirts"
PRINT dols; TAB(10); n1; TAB(20); n2; TAB(30); n3; TAB(40);_
n4
END SUB
```

Notice that you are put into a separate screen right after you press **Enter** on the SUB statement. Keep on typing until you finish the END SUB.

Now press **F2**, and you see that you have two separate program parts: the main program, and the procedure *prindols*. You select the one that you want to work with by using the F2 feature. Use the Arrow keys to move to the one that you want, and

Press **Enter**.

Go back and forth a few times to get used to it. Then, save the program. Both the main program and its procedure are saved. Check this by exiting QBasic, then starting it up again, and opening up the program *shircost*. You see that both are there for your use.

Test the program by running it, then take a break—you are done.

Summary

1. Subroutines manage program input, output, and logic.
2. Procedures do stand-alone, repeated tasks.
3. GOSUB and CALL statements enable subroutines and procedures respectively.
4. Global and local variables, used with subroutines and procedures, give you flexibility in changing values program-wide or keeping them within a single procedure.
5. The data *slot* of the procedure passes values to those data names (variables) explicitly listed in the CALL and SUB statements, and no others.
6. The GOTO statement has a clear purpose but should be used only to go somewhere within the same routine. It is not a simple substitute for either GOSUB or CALL. Too many GOTOs can be hazardous to your program.

The Book In Review

1. Design and program thoughtfully.
2. To examine any QBasic program, break it up into blocks. Then study each block separately, and finally look at the logic that controls all the blocks.

3. QBasic gives you a complete working environment, which encourages writing programs in building-block fashion.
4. Blueprint your program *before* you write the first line of code.
5. Data names should be meaningful, short (but not cryptic), consistent, and clear.
6. The QBasic Editor is top shelf. Use the keys, rather than the menus, and you will be productive.
7. Program organization is crucial. Blueprint, assign the tasks to routines, then program each routine.
8. **GOSUB subroutines; CALL procedures. GOTO a line name that is within the same routine as the GOTO statement.**

CHAPTER 9

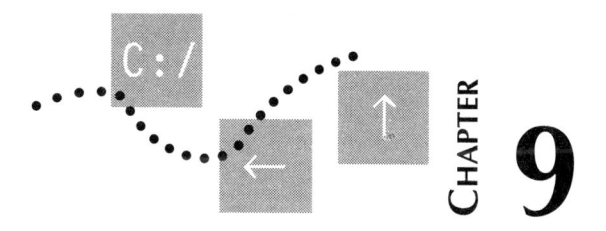

IF Statements

This chapter teaches you about IF...THEN statements and how to use them clearly in your QBasic programs. You also learn how to use ELSE and END IF statements. The topics include:

- Why use IF statements
- How IFs affect program flow
- Three types of IFs
- The ELSE statement
- Block IF statements
- Complex IF statements
- Two rules for IFs
- Why work hard
- Indenting IFs

Choices in Real Life

It is an autumn Tuesday evening, and rafting season is over. Pat is planning Saturday's activities and plans on sleeping late on Saturday. Pat has to take that into account in figuring out what to do Saturday. Pat is also unsure of the weather, since the meteorologists are talking about a 50% possibility of either a blizzard or a hurricane. But then, they are only right about 40 percent of the time, so Saturday could just as well turn out to be beautiful.

As a result, two conditions affect Pat's plans for Saturday:

1. The weather:
   - If it's nice, Pat can go mountain climbing at sunrise; otherwise a picnic would be nice later in the day.
   - If it's lousy, rafts can be repaired indoors or a book can be read, depending on when Pat wakes up.

2. What time Pat gets up:
   - If it's early, there are two options, mountain climbing or working in the WWW barn, depending on the weather.
   - If it's late, it is either a picnic in the sun or else read a book while some kind of storm rages outside.

Actually, there are four combinations affecting the decision, as these statements show:

1. IF Pat gets up early on Saturday, AND IF the weather is nice, THEN Pat will climb up one of the High Peaks.
2. IF Pat gets up early on Saturday, AND IF a storm hits, THEN Pat will patch some rafts.
3. IF Pat sleeps late, AND IF the weather is nice, THEN it will be a picnic at Indian Lake.
4. IF Pat sleeps late, AND IF the storm hits, THEN Pat will read a book.

In real life, decision-making is filled with "if" statements. They are also used when making decisions in QBasic programming. The IF statement is a precise way of expressing a decision, and it has to be exact so that a computer can work with it.

You can build IFs upon IFs. You can combine two or more IFs for a complex decision-making process. But, you can overdo it. If you combine too many IF conditions into one QBasic statement, the decision-making logic can be muddled.

Why Use IF Statements?

The purpose of an IF statement is to CHOOSE to do one or more things when a certain condition is true. Based on the test of a condition, the IF statement either permits or does not permit the program to:

- Read some data
- Write some data
- Perform a calculation
- GOTO some other statement in the routine and do something
- GOSUB to a subroutine elsewhere in the program
- CALL a procedure elsewhere in the program
- Examine another IF condition
- Do something with data

IF Syntax (Form)

An IF statement in QBasic has this syntax:

```
IF {some condition is true} THEN {execute the rest of this_
statement line}
```

The IF statement can be written in block form, so that the statement continues on one or more lines following the IF...THEN line:

```
IF {some condition is true} THEN
    {take an action}
END IF
```

The block form is easier to find in a program printout, easier to read and understand, and offers more flexibility than the single-line IF ... THEN statement.

How it Works

This is how an IF statement works.

After reading the IF, the program knows that it must test the condition that follows. The test finds the condition to be either true or false. For example, assume that today is February 15, 1994 and that it's 10:02:

```
1.  IF date$ = "021594" THEN
        {do something}
    END IF
2.  IF time$ <> "10:00" THEN
        {do something}  ( <> means "is unequal to")
    END IF
3.  IF shipdate < today THEN
        {do something}  ( < means "is less than")
    END IF
4.  IF custage > 99 THEN
        {do something}  ( > means "is greater than")
    END IF
```

NOTE >= means "greater than or equal to," and <= means "less than or equal to."

The condition in statement 1 tests true. So is the condition in statement 2 (the time is *not* equal to "10:00"). In the third statement, the condition will be true or false, depending on the value of the data name *shipdate* relative to today. Statement 4 could test true for a very advanced age. If any part of the condition is not true, then the program flows to the next line. The program ignores the THEN and everything following it in that IF construct.

How IFS Affect Program Flow

If the condition is true, then the computer reads and acts on the rest of the IF statement line. Data is read, written, calculated, or "massaged." Or, the flow is directed somewhere else in the program, if the rest of the statement is a GOTO, GOSUB, or CALL.

If any part of the condition is false, program control flows down to the next statement line. (Remember the stream-flow example of Chapter 4: water always flows downstream.)

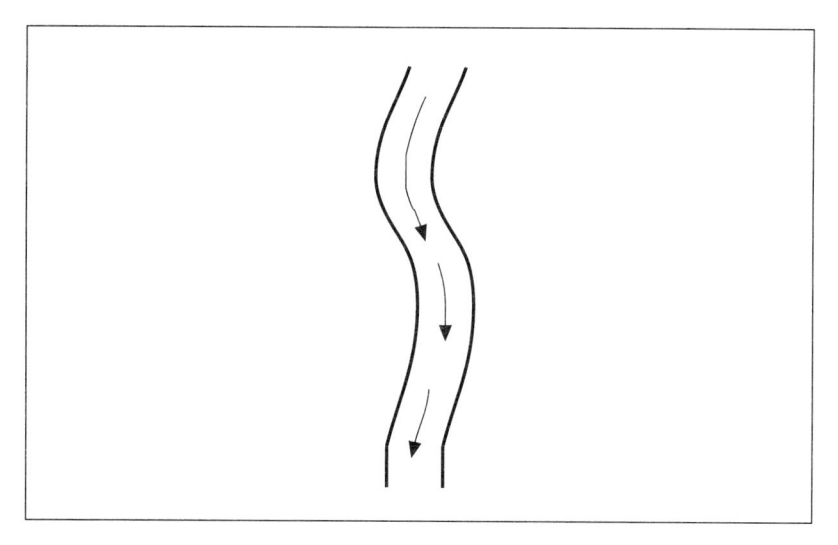

Figure 9.1   Water flowing downstream.

An IF statement works like a gate to an irrigation ditch, or some kind of gated channel off a river. If the alternative path is closed, then the water continues downstream. But if the gate is open, then the water is routed off to the side. The water passes through the gate and moves along the open path, doing whatever work it takes to get to the main stream and continue its downward flow.

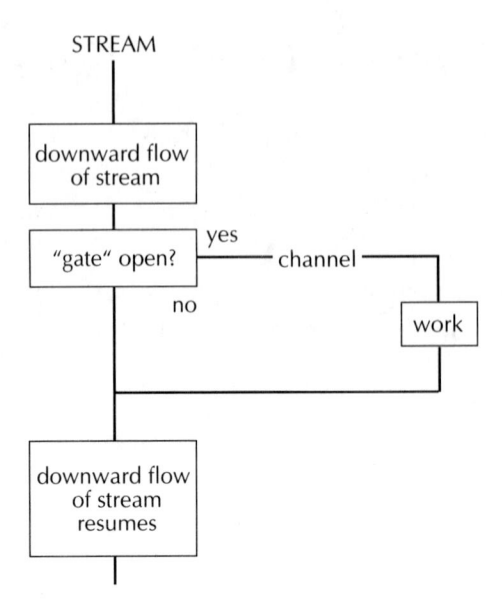

```
                    STREAM
                      │
              ┌───────────────┐
              │ downward flow │
              │   of stream   │
              └───────────────┘
                      │        yes
              ┌───────────────┐
              │ "gate" open?  ├──── channel ───┐
              └───────────────┘                │
                      │ no                     │
                                          ┌────────┐
                                          │  work  │
                                          └────────┘
                      │                        │
                      ├────────────────────────┘
              ┌───────────────┐
              │ downward flow │
              │   of stream   │
              │   resumes     │
              └───────────────┘
                      │
```

In QBasic, the "gate" is the condition of an IF statement that must be tested before the flow is diverted.

1. If the condition is met, then the "gate" opens, and the program continues reading the rest of that same statement line. At the end of the IF...THEN statement, the program flows down to the next statement line.
2. If the condition is not true, then control turns away from the closed "gate" to continue down the program like this:

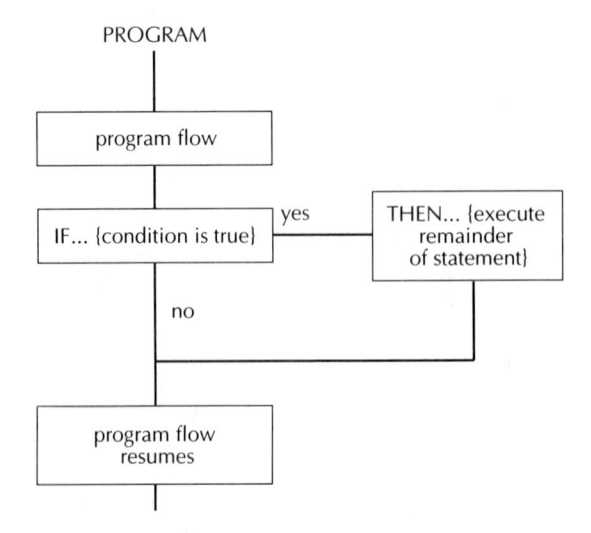

```
                    PROGRAM
                      │
              ┌───────────────┐
              │  program flow │
              └───────────────┘
                      │              yes        ┌──────────────────┐
              ┌─────────────────────┐           │ THEN... {execute │
              │ IF... {condition is true} ──────│    remainder     │
              └─────────────────────┘           │  of statement}   │
                      │ no                      └──────────────────┘
                                                         │
                      ├──────────────────────────────────┘
              ┌───────────────┐
              │  program flow │
              │    resumes    │
              └───────────────┘
                      │
```

The Three Types of IFs

You can reduce IF statements to three types that either:

1. Do something with data.

    ```
    IF {condition is true} THEN
        {do a read, write, display, or calculation/manipulation}
    END IF
    ```

    Examples:

    ```
    IF custtrips >2 THEN
         PRINT custname$
    END IF
    IF response$ = "yes" THEN
         PRINT custname$; " answered "; response$
    END IF
    IF custstat$ = "NY" THEN
         totpur = purprice * 1.07: REM — 7% NYS sales tax
    END IF
    ```

2. Alter the program flow.

    ```
    IF {condition is true} THEN
         {GOTO, CALL, OR GOSUB}
    END IF
    ```

    Examples:

    ```
    IF custtrips >2 THEN
         GOTO goodcust
    END IF
    IF response$ = "yes" THEN
         GOSUB printcust
    END IF
    ```

```
IF custstat$="NY" THEN
        CALL calctax(purprice,totput)
END IF
```

3. Test another condition.

```
IF {condition is true} THEN
        IF {another condition is true} THEN
            {do something}
        END IF
END IF
```

Example:

```
IF custstat$ = "NY" THEN
        IF custcity$ = "Albany" THEN
            PRINT city$
        END IF
END IF
```

The ELSE

There is an add-on, which makes the IF statement more flexible: an ELSE. Here is a sample IF...THEN...ELSE:

```
IF custtrips% > 1 THEN
    PRINT "2 or more trips"
    ELSE PRINT "1 or no trips"
END IF
```

The syntax for the ELSE statement is this:

```
IF {condition is true} THEN
    {do something}
    ELSE {do something different}
```

```
END IF
```

Notice that this is more than the IF...THEN... situation, where a false condition results in doing nothing. With the ELSE statement, you choose between two (or more) definite actions, depending on the results of the condition test.

Just as the with the IF you can reduce ELSE statements to three types:

1. Do something with data.

```
IF {condition is true} THEN
        {do a read, write, display, or calculation/_
manipulation}
        ELSE {do a read, write, display, or calculation/_
manipulation}
END IF
```

Examples:

```
IF custtrips >1 THEN
        PRINT custname$;"is a hot dog"
        ELSE PRINT custname$;" is a deadbeat"
END IF

IF response$ = "yes" THEN
        PRINT custname$; " answered "; response$
        ELSE PRINT custname$;" is a nerd"
END IF

IF custstat$ = "NY" THEN
        totpur = purprice * 1.07: REM—7% NYS sales tax
        ELSE totpur = purprice + 4.50: REM—shipping_
charge
END IF
```

2. Alter program flow.

```
IF {condition is true} THEN
        {GOTO, CALL, OR GOSUB}
```

```
        ELSE {GOTO, CALL, OR GOSUB}
END IF
```

Examples:

```
IF custtrips >2 THEN
        GOTO goodcust
        ELSO GOTO badcust
END IF
IF response$ = "yes" THEN
        GOSUB printcust
        ELSE GOSUB dropcust
END IF
IF custstat$="NY" THEN
        CALL calctax(purprice,totput)
        ELSE CALL calcship(purprice)
END IF
```

3. Test another condition.

```
IF {condition is true} THEN
        {do something}
        ELSEIF {another condition is true} THEN
            {do something}
END IF
```

Example:

```
IF custstat$ = "NY" THEN
        PRINT city$
        ELSEIF custstat$ = "MA" THEN
        PRINT city$, custstat$
END IF
```

Now compare the IF...ELSE combination with two simple IF statements. Think back to the opening discussion of what Pat will do if Saturday is nice. In order to hike up one of the High Peaks, Pat has to get up early. If Pat gets up late, then it will have to be a picnic.

1. IF Pat gets up early on Saturday, it will be climbing up one of the High Peaks.
2. IF Pat does not get up early on Saturday, it will be a picnic at Indian Lake.

Since the two conditions are mutually contradictory (Pat cannot get up both early and not early), the program is forced to select one action over the other. Consider the same situation when the condition has specific values. Use *rollout* as an integer representing an exact time with values between 1 and 12.

```
IF rollout < 7 THEN
    {climb a high peak}
END IF
IF rollout > 7 THEN
    {picnic}
END IF
```

Follow the logic for *rollout* = 7:

1. First condition tests FALSE (rollout equals 7, not <7):

    The program does not execute first THEN; reads END IF; goes to second IF...THEN

2. Second condition tests FALSE (rollout equals 7, not >7):

    The program does not execute second THEN; reads END IF; flow continues downward.

    Result: neither action is taken.

You can see that the only solution is an exact definition of the tests, that covers all three possible values of rollout (that is, <7, =7, and >7). The second test is more precise:

```
IF rollout < 7 THEN
```

```
        {climb a high peak}
    END IF
    IF rollout >= 7 THEN ( >= means "greater than or  equal to")
        {picnic}
    END IF
```

Now the ELSE statement can give the same results, and it can do so with less work.

```
    IF rollout < 7 THEN
        {climb a high peak}
    ELSE {picnic}
    END IF
```

For a wake-up time of 7 or later, Pat is off to Indian Lake for a picnic.

Block IF Statements

The block IF is easier to read because of its indenting. It also simplifies writing IFs when more than one action follows the THEN or the ELSE. Look at the following block-form IF.

```
    IF lasttripyr% < 94 THEN
        PRINT custname$, " (no trips this year)"
        PRINT "last trip was ";lasttripyr%
    ELSE PRINT custname$, " * * * (CURRENT TRIPPER) * * * "
        PRINT "number of trips is "; custtrips%
        END IF
```

Look at this figure to get the concept of the block IF:

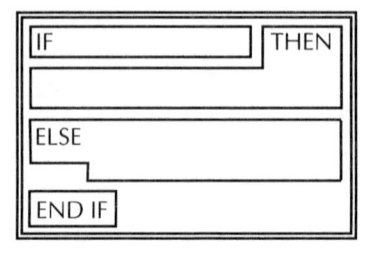

It illustrates that these lines are all one statement.

A single IF...THEN...ELSE statement in block form

> **NOTE:** An IF statement, no matter how long or complicated, is *always* just one statement.

Complex IF Statements

A complex IF statement contains two or more IF conditions. It tests the conditions, and, if all of them are true, the program picks an action. If any one of the conditions is false, then the program will skip the statement.

Like any other IF, a complex IF statement *is all one statement*. When ALL the IF conditions are true, the program acts upon the rest of the statement following the last THEN. When any one of the conditions is NOT true, the program stops at that failed condition test, SKIPS the rest of the complex IF statement, and flows down to the next program statement. This gives your programs a multi-level decision-making capability.

The syntax for complex IF statements is:

```
IF {first condition is true} THEN
    IF {second condition is true} THEN
        IF {third, etc., condition is true} THEN
            {take an action}
        END IF
    END IF
END IF
```

Examples:

You want to send a Christmas rafting greeting to your older rafters (50 or over) in New York.

```
IF custage% >= 50 THEN
    IF custstat$ = "NY" THEN
        GOSUB printgreetings
```

```
        END IF
    END IF
```

Here is another example. Follow the program logic through a test of several conditions: New York customer, 50 or over, more than two trips, and a customer since 1992.

```
IF custsinceyr% < 93 THEN
    IF custtrips% >2 THEN
        IF custage% >= 50
            IF custstat$ = "NY" THEN
                PRINT custname$;" top shelf - free_
T-shirt"
            END IF
        END IF
    END IF
END IF
```

The program reads in data from the record of customer Art Shane, who lives in Newton, Massachusetts, has just turned 50, and has been on 4 trips since 1990. The program logic proceeds through this complex IF statement as follows:

1. Is he a customer prior to 1993? yes
2. More than 2 trips? yes
3. Is the customer over 50? yes
4. Does the customer live in New York? no

The program prints nothing; one condition has tested false.

Now look at the program flow through the parts of the same complex IF statement in the case of Kate Anderson (a New Yorker, age 30, who has been rafting five times in 1993):

1. Was she a customer prior to 1993? no

The program found the first condition false, so it left the complex IF. It flows down to the next program statement. The output for this customer is nothing; one condition has tested false.

Two Rules for IF

Use these two rules to make your IF statements clear, consistent, and easy to write.

1. Limit a complex IF statement to four levels (like the examples above).

    When five or more tests have to be conducted, write them in two or more IF statements.

    Another problem is the use of an ELSE statement in complex IFs. You can easily get lost in logic if you do so. With this in mind, here is rule number two:

2. Use the ELSE statement only with a simple IF statement (one IF, one ELSE).

Why Work Hard?

So far you have seen some fairly simple processes to be executed following THENs and ELSEs. Here are some tips on writing more complicated IF statements.

- *Test first for the conditions that are more likely to be false.*

It is hard to make complicated decision-making easy. But decision-making should not waste computer time, or more important, your time. This means that you test each condition as few times as you can. You don't want unnecessary retesting of conditions or repetitious rewriting of programming statements.

There are countless variations that exist in decision-making. Therefore this book cannot provide you with an instruction manual on how to design the IF statements.

NOTE My recommendation based on experience is to try to set up program logic to test first for the condition that is most likely to be false.

Figure out which condition is most likely to be false, and test for that one first. Then, which of the remaining conditions is the next-most-likely false, and so on. For example:

Find rafters with more than two trips;
in New York;
age 50 or over;
female.

Suppose you know that:

- Rafters with two or fewer trips outnumber those with more than two trips about four to one.
- Rafters are fairly evenly distributed among seven states.
- Only six in 100 rafters are older than 50.
- Male and female rafters are roughly equal in number.

You can summarize the decision-making odds by ranking those least likely to be true down to the ones most likely to be true:

1. age   very few older customers
2. trips   25 percent are >2
3. state   balanced among seven
4. sex   50 - 50

To minimize testing, use the condition most likely to be false as the first.

```
IF custage >= 50 THEN
```

Then add the other conditions in increasing order of likely truth:

```
IF custage >= 50 THEN                        6 in 100
    IF custstate = "NY" THEN                 1 in 7
        IF custtrips% > 2 THEN               1 in 4
            IF custsex$ = "f" THEN           1 in 2
                CALL princust (custnum)
```

There is much less testing with this sequence than if every one of the records were tested first for the 50-50 sex condition.

- By starting with age, the program eliminates all but a few records (the over-50 customers).

- The next test (the second-level IF statement) eliminates all but about one-seventh of the records passing the first test, and so on.

This is a short example, so you might not notice the increase in processing speed. But if you were testing hundreds of conditions on a file with thousands of records, you would see a difference in program run time. Besides making the computer work faster, this method also encourages clear thinking and clean programming.

- *Keep your IF statements uncluttered and simple-to-read.*

Whenever there are three or more actions to be performed as the result of an IF condition, do the actions by invoking a routine, not within the IF itself.

Compare the readability of two versions of the same IF...THEN...ELSE.

1. All actions performed within the IF block:

```
{program begins}
    .
    .
    .
IF custtripyr% < 94 THEN
    PRINT custname$, " (no trips this year)"
    PRINT "last trip was ";custtripyr%
    PRINT "number of trips is ";custtrips%
    PRINT "send cust a 'We miss you' greeting card"
    PRINT custlastname$;"   ";custfirstname$
    PRINT custstreet$
    PRINT custcity$;" ";custstat$;" ";custzip
                    .
            {several other statements}
                    .
ELSE PRINT custname$, " * * * (CURRENT TRIPS) * * * "
    PRINT "number of trips is ";custtrips%
    PRINT "send cust a 'We appreciate your business'_
    greeting card"
```

```
    PRINT "send cust a Santa Rafting calendar"
    PRINT custlastname$;"  ";custfirstname$
    PRINT custstreet$
    PRINT custcity$;" ";custstat$;" ";custzip
                    .
            {several other statements}
                    .
END IF
{program continues}
```

2. All actions performed elsewhere:

```
    {program begins}
    IF custtripyr% < 94 THEN
            GOSUB notcurrent
    ELSE GOSUB current
    END IF
    {program continues}
        .
        .
        .
    notcurrent:
    PRINT custname$, " (no trips this year)"
    PRINT "last trip was ";custtripyr%
    PRINT "number of trips is ";custtrips%
    PRINT "send cust a 'We miss you' greeting card"
    PRINT custlastname$;"  ";custfirstname$
    PRINT custstreet$
    PRINT custcity$;" ";custstat$;" ";custzip
                    .
            {several other statements}
```

```
RETURN
current:
        PRINT custname$, " * * * (CURRENT TRIPS) * * * "
        PRINT "number of trips is ";custtrips%
        PRINT "send cust a 'We appreciate your business'_
greeting card"
        PRINT "send cust a Santa Rafting calendar"
        PRINT custlastname$;"   ";custfirstname$
        PRINT custstreet$
        PRINT custcity$;" ";custstat$;" ";custzip

            {several other statements}

RETURN
```

Indenting IFs

Indent each level of an IF statement two to four spaces. Your programs will be more legible, and the decision-making process will be clearer.

Rules on Indenting

Remember these rules for indenting IF statements:

1. Indent each IF to show every level of the decision.
2. If the action to be taken (whatever follows the THEN) is brief and uncomplicated, write it on the line after the IF.
   OR,
3. If the action requires three or more statements, put the action in a routine and have the IF statement enable the routine.

For example:

```
IF custage% < 25 THEN PRINT custname$
IF custtripyr% >= 93 THEN
    IF custtrips> 2 THEN
        IF custstat$ = "NY" THEN
            PRINT "new frequent rafter from New York"
        END IF
    END IF
END IF
```

Summary

1. The purpose of an IF statement is to make decisions to:
   - Read data
   - Write data
   - Perform calculations or manipulate data
   - GOSUB to a subroutine elsewhere in the program
   - CALL a procedure elsewhere in the program
   - GOTO somewhere else in the program
   - Make another decision

2. When the IF condition is true, the program executes the rest of the statement.

   When the condition is false, the program goes down to the next statement following the IF construct.

3. The three types of IF statements are:
   - IF {condition is true} THEN
     {do something with data}
   - IF {condition is true} THEN
     {alter program flow with CALL, GOSUB, or GOTO}
   - IF {condition is true} THEN
     {test another IF condition}

("complex if")

4. The ELSE is an extension of the IF statement. Instead of an "if true, then act; if not, then skip," the ELSE creates an "if true then do action-1 else do action-2" type decision. It has the same three types as the IF in number 3 above.
5. Use block form unless the IF is a simple statement (one IF). Finish each block with an END IF.
6. A complex IF statement is one with two or more conditions. When all conditions are true, the statement following the last THEN is executed. If any condition tests false, the program drops down to the next program line following the END IF.
7. Limit complex IFs to four levels (four IFs). When testing more than four levels, write two or more IF constructions.
8. Use an ELSE statement only with a simple (one IF) IF statement.
9. Test a condition as few times as possible. With complex IFs, test the condition least likely to be true first, then the rest, ranked in "least-likely sequence."
10. Write easy-to-read IFs; when there are three or more actions to be executed, put them in routines. Indent your IFs for ease of reading the program.
11. Keep IFs simple.

The Book in Review

1. Design and program thoughtfully.
2. To examine any QBasic program, break it up into blocks. Then study each block separately, and finally look at the logic that controls all the blocks.
3. QBasic gives you a complete working environment, which encourages writing programs in building-block fashion.
4. Blueprint your program *before* you write the first line of code.
5. Data names should be meaningful, short (but not cryptic), consistent, and clear.
6. The QBasic Editor is top shelf. Use the keys, rather than the menus, and you will be productive.

7. Program organization is crucial. Blueprint, assign the tasks to routines, then program each routine.
8. GOSUB subroutines; CALL procedures. GOTO a line name that is within the same routine as the GOTO statement.
9. **Keep your IFs simple, and easy to read.**

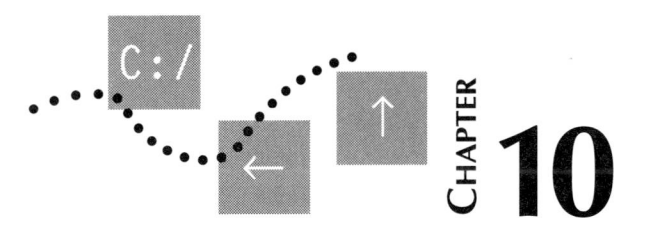

Loops

This chapter teaches you about loops and how to use them. You learn how to use the GOTO statement to make your programs perform loops. The topics include:

- The loop is the heart (pump) of every program
- Three loops
- The main routine loop
- Dangerous GOTOs

Non-Computer Loops

Terry is collating the WildWater Works quarterly newsletter as a favor to Chris. The newsletter is four pages, going out to WildWater Work's 2,000 customers. On a long table, Terry has four piles of paper. Each pile has 2,000 copies of one of the pages. Terry starts at one end of the table, gets the top sheet off each pile, staples each complete newsletter, then piles it on the floor. This is repeated 2,000 times.

Work is being performed similar to a computer program that is processing 2,000 customer transactions. Terry goes through the same loop—pick up four separate sheets, staple, stack; then walk back to the start, and do it all over again.

A QBasic program reads one portion of data at a time, operates on it, outputs it, and goes back to read another piece. This procedure is called a *loop*. Remember the water fountain from Chapter 4? Its water flow is like a loop in QBasic.

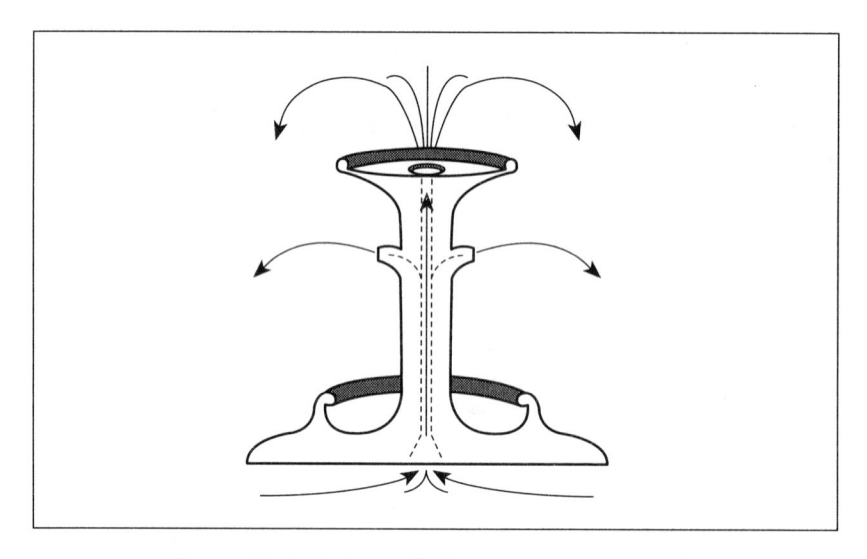

Figure 10.1 *A fountain flowing water upwards.*

The Loop is the Heart (Pump) of Every Program

A computer program does *one* thing at a time. To print 2,000 name and address labels, the computer:

1. Reads one customer's data
2. Prints one customer's name and address onto a label
3. Goes back to 1 again, then 2, and repeats this until 2,000 labels are printed.

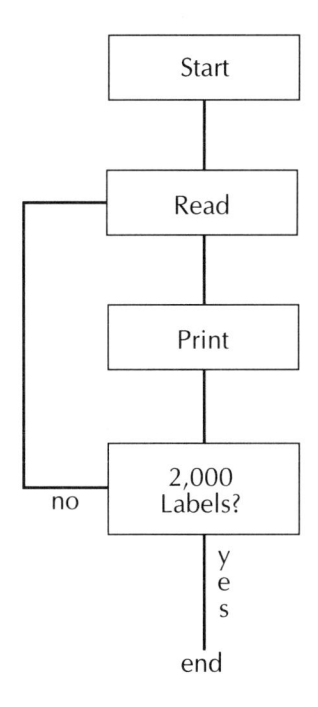

```
          Start
            |
          Read  ←──┐
            |      │
          Print    │
            |      │
         2,000    no
         Labels? ──┘
            |
           yes
            |
           end
```

The real strength of a computer program is its ability to process 1,000,000 pieces of data as easily as it processes one, by using loops.

The loop is the heart (pump) of a program because without it, data would be processed only once (only one label would be printed). Computers would be worthless without loops, because each piece of data would require its own series of program statements. That is, a program that processes 100,000 labels without using loops would have 1,000 times more statements than a program that processes 100 labels. Using loops, the program that prints 100 labels is exactly the same size as one that prints 100,000, or even 100,000,000 labels.

Figure 10.2 illustrates a program for printing 100 labels.

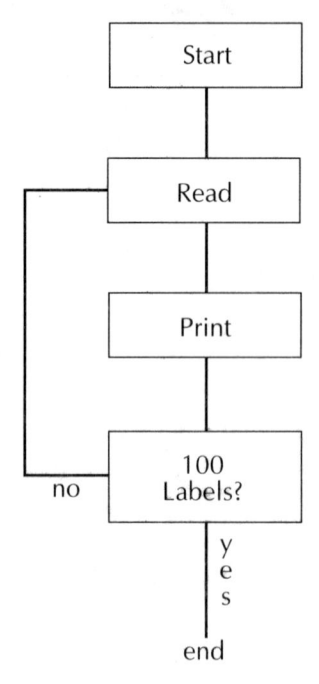

```
         ┌──────────┐
         │  Start   │
         └────┬─────┘
              │
    ┌────►┌──────────┐
    │     │   Read   │
    │     └────┬─────┘
    │          │
    │     ┌──────────┐
    │     │  Print   │
    │     └────┬─────┘
    │          │
    │     ┌──────────┐
    └─ no ┤   100    │
          │  Labels? │
          └────┬─────┘
               │ yes
               │
              end
```

Figure 10.2 *Label printing program.*

Figure 10.3 illustrates a program to print 100,000,000 labels.

```
                    Start
                      |
         ┌────────  Read
         │            |
         │          Print
         │            |
         │      100,000,000
         │         Labels?
         └─no─────────
                      |
                     yes
                      |
                     end
```

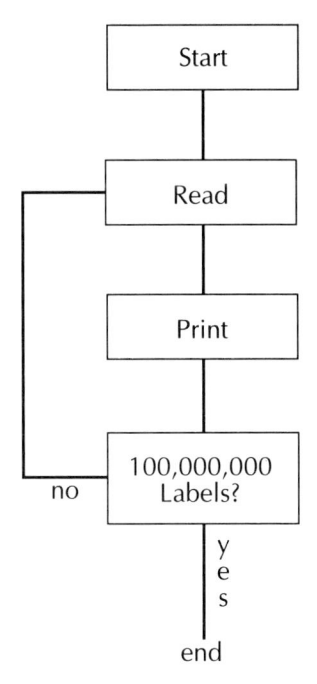

Figure 10.3 *Label printing program.*

Note that the only difference between the two programs is the one conditional IF statement, which tests to see how many labels have been printed.

Figure 10.4 on the next page shows an example of two programs that reach exactly the same result, one with a loop, and one with no loops.

The program with the loop prints five labels, if there were only five customer records in the file. If the file contained 50,000 records, it would print 50,000 labels, and so forth.

The program without the loop never prints more than five labels, no matter how many records are contained in the file. To print 50,000 labels, the program on the left would have to have an additional (49995 times), or 99,990 program steps (boxes).

Without Loops

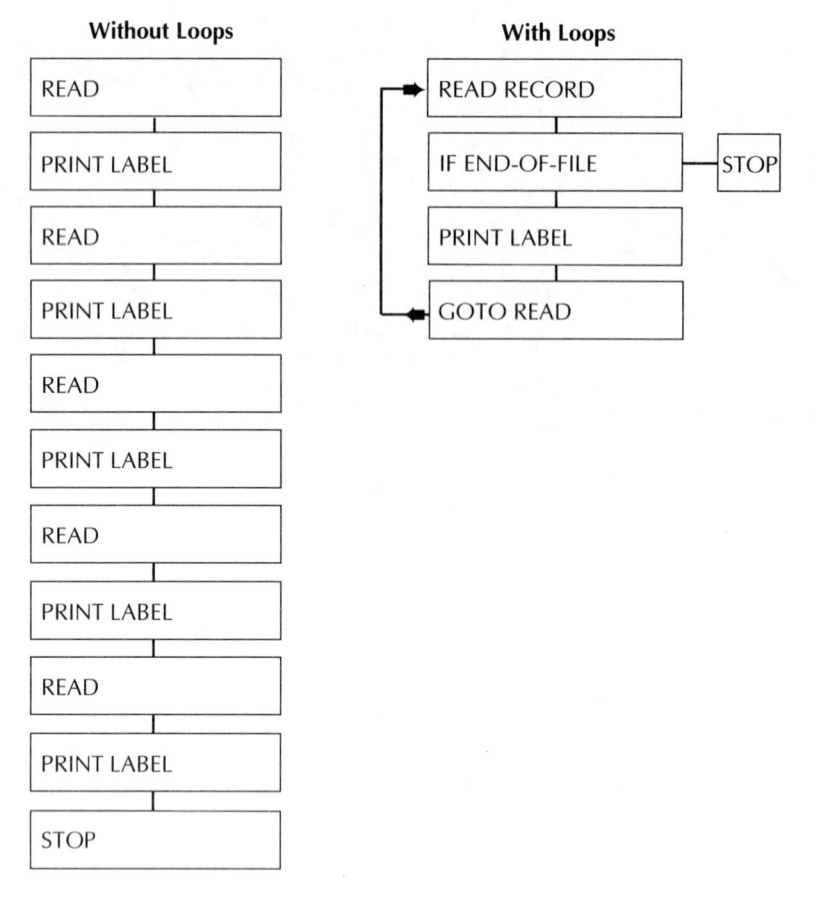

```
READ
PRINT LABEL
READ
PRINT LABEL
READ
PRINT LABEL
READ
PRINT LABEL
READ
PRINT LABEL
STOP
```

With Loops

```
READ RECORD
IF END-OF-FILE ─ STOP
PRINT LABEL
GOTO READ
```

Figure 10.4 *Two programs with the same result.*

Three Loops

The three types of loops are:

1. FOR...TO —— NEXT
   (Fixed loop)
2. DO UNTIL... —— LOOP
   (Conditional loop)
3. IF EOF —— GOTO
   (Read until end loop)

FOR...TO — NEXT

Use loop 1 to do something a fixed number of times, like 10, 10,000, 8,371,946, or any concrete number. This number could be a variable data name with a value; the point is that the loop is rigid. It will loop that specified number of times, then continue down the program.

Some uses might include:

- Summing the deductions on your paycheck.
- Totaling the expenses on your expense voucher.
- Adding up sales for a specific number of hours, days, weeks, or months.
- Summing the extended sales on the lines of an invoice.
- Totaling the hours on a payroll time card.

The syntax for this first type of loop is:

```
FOR {variable name 1} = {variable name 2, number or
expression}
    TO {variable name 3, number or expression}
    .
    .
    {several (or many) program statements}
    .
    .
    NEXT {variable name 1}
    .
{rest of the program}
```

FOR...TO — NEXT examples

This first piece of QBasic code totals 12 months of sales into a variable named *thisyrsales#*: (Look at *sales(i%)* as sales for each month of the year—you learn about tables and arrays in Chapter 18, so do not be concerned with the (i%) right now.)

```
thisyrsales# = 0
FOR i% = 1 to 12
```

```
        thisyrsales# = thisyrsales# + sales(i%)
NEXT i%
```

The next segment of code totals 100 entries of expenses into a variable named *totexpense*: (Look at *expns(i%)* as 100 different expense entries.)

```
totexpense = 0
numexpns%=100
FOR i = 1 to numexpns%
        totexpense = totexpense + expns(i%)
NEXT i%
```

DO UNTIL — LOOP

Use this loop form to do something until a particular condition becomes true. The condition can be of any form that can be put in an IF statement. (You learned about conditions from Chapter 9). The test might be something such as a data name having the same value as another data name, a value being less than 0, or the state changing from MA to VT. With this form, the loop has no fixed number of times to repeat. The computer keeps looping until the specified condition is true, then it exits the loop.

Some uses of this loop form might include:

- Doing one kind of calculation until a variable changes, then performing a different calculation.
- Printing until the number of print lines exceeds a page, then going to the next page.
- Printing until the value of a variable changes, then printing a subtotal, and going on to the next page.
- Adding to a total until the value of a variable changes.

This is the syntax for this second loop:

```
DO UNTIL {expression}
```

```
A group of program statements
    .
    .
    .
LOOP
```

DO UNTIL examples

The first section of QBasic program code below totals 12 months of sales into a variable named *thisyrsales#*:

```
thisyrsales# = 0
i% = 0
DO UNTIL i%=12
    i% = i% +1
    thisyrsales# = thisyrsales# + sales(i%)
LOOP
```

The next series of program statements totals 100 entries of expenses into a variable named *totexpenses*:

```
totexpenses = 0
i% = 0
DO UNTIL i% = 100
    i% = i% + 1
    totexpenses = totexpenses + expns(i%)
LOOP
```

This section of a program prints lines to the printer until the number of lines is equal to 56:

```
n%=0
DO UNTIL n%=56
    LPRINT {some data}: n% = n% + 1
    LPRINT {some more data} : n% = n% + 1
LOOP
```

The statements below add to a total until the value of *custstat*$ changes:

```
totstatepurch# = 0
f1 = 1
GET #1, f1
prevstat$ = custstat$
DO UNTIL custstat$ <> prevstat$
    totstatepurch# = totstatepurch# + custpurch
    prevstate$ = custstate$
    f1 = f1 +1
    GET 1, f1: REM — read another customer record
LOOP
```

Take the time to understand the loops in the examples above. You use this kind of logic regularly in printing and totaling.

IF EOF THEN GOTO

Use this last loop to read a file and process a record until there are no more data records to process because the computer has reached the end of the file (EOF). This construct is never found in our procedures. It is the essence of the loop in MAIN CONTROL. (Do not concern yourself with the detail of the EOF statement—it is just another type of IF. The same with the GET statement. You learn about this in Chapter 12.) Concentrate on the workings of the loop; that's what is important.

The IF EOF statement is a special version of the IF statement. The condition that is tested in an IF EOF statement is an end-of-file on the file specified. When the end-of-file is found, the condition tests as true, and the computer processes the statement following the THEN.

The use of the EOF file is to stop processing a file when it has reached the end.

The syntax for this loop is:

```
{line label 1}
        {some file read (usually a GET) statement}
    IF EOF( {a file number, from 1-32} ) THEN GOTO {line_
label 2}
```

```
        |
      {several program statements}
        |
   GOTO {line label 1 (the start of the IF EOF loop)}
{line label 2}
   {rest of program}
```

IF EOF THEN GOTO example

This is an example for using IF EOF THEN GOTO:

```
readcust:
    GET 1, f1 : REM—read a record from the customer file
    IF EOF(1) THEN GOTO endcust
    GOSUB PRINTCUST : REM—print a customer record
    GOTO readcust
endcust:
    {rest of program}
```

The Main Routine Loop

The *main* routine is a loop that controls all the processing logic of the program. The routine reads the most important file of the program, the one upon which all the calculations, data operations, printing, and disk writing are based.

Most every program that you write in QBasic bases the processing on one file, no matter how many files are used in the program. This one file controls the program—processing begins when the first record of this file is read, and ends when the end-of-file condition is found.

This is an example of a main routine loop:

```
main:
    CLS: REM—clear the screen
getcus:
    f1 = f1 + 1
```

```
    IF EOF(1) THEN GOTO endcus: REM—if end-of-file, get out
    GET 1, f1: REM—read the customer file
    GOSUB printcus: REM—print a customer record
    GOTO getcus: REM—go back and get another customer record
endcus:
    RETURN
```

This main routine reads and prints the records in the customer file until no more are left. The EOF statement tests file number 1 (in this case, the customer file) before every read. When the EOF condition is true (the end-of-file is reached), the main routine exits.

Dangerous GOTOs

If you use the GOTO inside a loop, never alter the program flow outside of the loop. If you break this rule, you break the program.

The GOTO is normally used inside a loop to skip forward over a statement within the loop. However, in the read loop (type 3), it is used only to go back to the EOF test. The GOTO should never jump backwards otherwise, and it should never jump outside of the loop. The use for the GOTO is to skip forward past some program statements that you do not want to run because of an IF condition.

These are examples for using GOTO:

- We want to add up all of the sales for the year, except for the month of April. The code below totals 11 months of sales into a variable named *thisyrsales#*:

```
thisyrsales# = 0
FOR i% = 1 to 12
   IF i% = 4 THEN GOTO skipsales
   thisyrsales# = thisyrsales# + sales(i%)
skipsales:
NEXT i%
```

- The next group of QBasic code totals 60 entries of expenses into a variable named *totexpenses*. Use the GOTO to skip the entries between 43 and 50.

```
    totexpenses = 0
FOR i% = 1 to 60
    IF i% > 42 THEN
            IF i% < 51 THEN
            GOTO skipexp
            END IF
    END IF
            totexpenses = totexpenses + expens(i%)
    skipexp:
NEXT i%
```

Use GOTO statements wisely within loops, and follow the rules. You will never be sorry when you do. You will always be sorry when you do not.

Summary

1. The computer does *one thing at a time*. The loop is the base logic that makes your program do the work.
2. The three types of loops that you use are:
   - FOR...TO — NEXT
     (The fixed loop, which repeats a specific number of times.)
   - DO UNTIL... — LOOP
     (The conditional loop, which keeps working until the condition is true.)
   - IF EOF — GOTO
     (The read-until-end-of-file loop.)
3. The MAIN routine is the read-until-end-of-file loop, which controls all processing logic for the program.
4. GOTOs are dangerous inside of a loop.
   - Never GOTO somewhere outside of the loop.
   - Except for jumping back to the EOF test, use the GOTO to jump forward to skip some statements within the loop.

The Book in Review

1. Design and program thoughtfully.
2. To examine any QBasic program, break it up into blocks. Then study each block separately, and finally look at the logic that controls all the blocks.
3. QBasic gives you a complete working environment, which encourages writing programs in building-block fashion.
4. Blueprint your program *before* you write the first line of code.
5. Data names should be meaningful, short (but not cryptic), consistent, and clear.
6. The QBasic Editor is top shelf. Use the keys, rather than the menus, and you will be productive.
7. Program organization is crucial. Blueprint, assign the tasks to routines, then program each routine.
8. GOSUB subroutines; CALL procedures. GOTO a line name that is within the same routine as the GOTO statement.
9. Keep your IFs simple, and easy to read.
10. **Loops are critical for good programming. You can destroy their structure with the wrong GOTO. Never GOTO somewhere outside the loop.**

CHAPTER 11

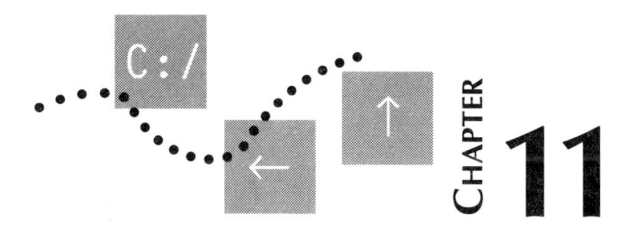

The Concept of Files

This chapter teaches you about files and how to use them in conjunction with your QBasic programs. You also learn about fields and records. The topics include:

- Data file definition
- File examples
- Record definition
- Record examples
- Field definition
- Field examples
- File structures
- File subject categories (and designing them)
- File layouts

Manual File Search

Chris is trying to find the receipt for the automatic beer bottle opener that was bought for the Steak-and-Beer dinner that WildWater Works serves all the guests. The opener does not work right; instead of just taking off the cap, it breaks off the neck of the bottle. Chris files all miscellaneous receipts in the bottom drawer of a desk. Now it is a hassle looking through each receipt as it is pulled out of the pile, trying to find the one for the automatic opener.

Chris is working with a data *file*.

Data File Definition

A *file* is a collection of similar things. In the case of computers, a *data file* is a collection of similar data. There are other kinds of computer files, such as program files and text files, but those are not topics for this book, which uses only data files.

File Examples

These are some examples of files that you may have around your house:

- A shoe box of old, unpaid bills
- The appointments in your personal calendar
- The work in your briefcase
- The compact discs in your disc case
- The tax forms in your file cabinet
- A shoe box of old, paid bills

And, after second thought:

- A stack of love letters
- The contents of your backpack
- The coins in your coin purse
- The food in your cupboards
- The clothing in your closet

- The tools in your toolbox
- The telephone book

Record Definition

A *record* is one of the like (similar) objects in your file.

Record Examples

These are some examples of records that you probably have.

- A copy of *War and Peace* in your bookcase
- One love letter—that sizzling one
- The 1988 tax form in your file cabinet
- One unpaid bill in your shoe box (from your company's collection agency)
- One of the job offer letters in your briefcase

And some others:

- The lucky penny in your wallet
- One name, address, and phone number—Software Factory, Inc. 9999 RT 9, Indian Lake 999-1234
- The foot powder from your backpack
- That ugly tie your mother-in-law gave you

Field Definition

A *field* is a recognizable unit within a record. A field is a data item that is read from and written to a disk file. The name given to a field is the variable name for the data in that part of the record. A field is the smallest part of a record that you normally work with. You can do these things to fields in QBasic:

- Add
- Subtract

- Multiply
- Divide
- Display
- Print
- Move
- Perform complex calculations
- Manipulate

Field Examples

These are examples of fields in your files and records mentioned previously:

- One sentence in that love letter
- That nonperformance clause in that big contract
- The definition of *programming* in the dictionary
- Tax OWED on the 1993 tax form
- One item on an unpaid bill (the one you are disputing)
- The broken item on a cash register receipt

And others:

- One kernel in an ear of corn
- One socket from the set in your toolbox
- The phone number 999-1234
- One line on an expense receipt

Figure 11.1 shows a picture of files, records and fields.

Now that you have a good conceptual grasp of files, records, and fields, you can explore file structures.

A Computer Data File (Parts file)	A Computer Data Record (Part record 1)
Record 1	Part Description
Record 2	Part Retail Price
Record 3	Part Wholesale Price
Record 4	Part Cost
Record 5	Part Quantity on Hand
Record 6	Part Quantity Sold
Record 7	Part Quantity on Order
Record 8	Part Quantity Returned
Record 9	Etc.

Figure 11.1 *Files, records, and fields.*

File Structures

While there are dozens of file structures, this discussion keeps it basic by explaining four of them:

- Sequential
- Random
- Indexed
- Linked

Sequential

A *sequential file* is one in which the records are read in order, one after the other. First you read record one, then record two, then record three, then record four, and so on, until you find the record you want, or until you reach the end of the file. In a sequential file, all the records that precede the sought-after record must be read to get to the record you want. To get to record 1234, the computer has to read the first 1233 records in the file, then read number 1234. It is similar to a cassette or VCR tape. The only way to get to the middle is to read through the first half of the tape. The only way to get to something that is at the end is to read through almost the entire file.

Sequential files are normally chosen by beginning programmers because they are easy to use. This book does not explain them because their limitations (especially the one in the previous paragraph) inhibit good programming and systems. They are just too restrictive. Figure 11.2 shows a sequential parts file.

Record 1
Record 2
Record 3
Record 4
Record 5
Record 6
Record 7
Record 8
Record 9
Record 10

Figure 11.2 *A sequential parts file.*

Random Files

A *random file* is one that you can read either sequentially, one after the other, or randomly (directly read any one record in the file). A random file is similar to your compact disc player. Just as you can go to any location on the disc, so can you go directly go to *any* record in a random file. You can also sequentially read the entire file, one record right after the other. Figure 11.3 shows a random parts file.

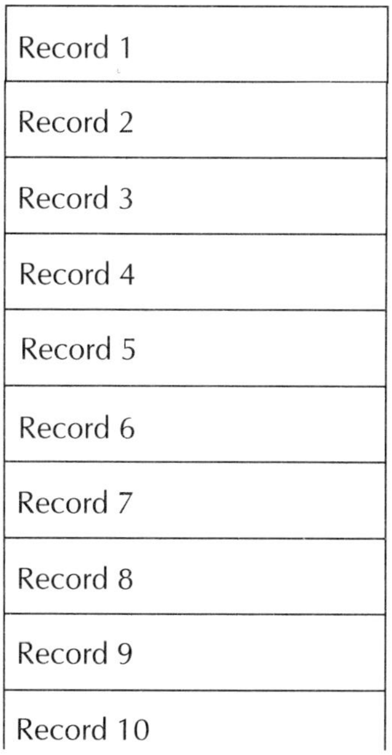

Record 1
Record 2
Record 3
Record 4
Record 5
Record 6
Record 7
Record 8
Record 9
Record 10

Figure 11.3 *A random parts file.*

Note that the random file looks the same as the sequential file on the previous page. There are many technical differences in using them, but there is only one practical difference (to you, the programmer) between a sequential file and a random file. *You can read any record of a random file without having to look at any of the other records.*

The next chapter works entirely with random files, which you use for all your QBasic applications in this book.

Indexed Files

An *indexed file* is a random file with a separate index by some name or number, which makes it easier to locate a record. The file works like the index in a book, which tells you on what page a certain topic is found.

To back up a little, a record in a random file can only be located by specifying the record number. That works, if you know the record number of that customer, vendor, part, or service. But what if you only know the part name, like *helmet*? If the file is indexed by part name, then the computer can:

1. Search the index.
2. Find the part name (HELMET).
3. Get the record number for HELMET.
4. Read the record containing the data for HELMET.

Indexed files are nice to have in your system, but they are too complex to cover at this level of learning. Figure 11.4 shows an indexed parts file.

Part	Index Pointer (to the record)	File itself
boots	(rec 9)	Record 1 (lifejacket)
gloves	(rec 3)	Record 2 (raft)
helmet	(rec 5)	Record 3 (gloves)
lifejacket	(rec 1)	Record 4 (rope)
paddle	(rec 7)	Record 5 (helmet)
raft	(rec 2)	Record 6 (T-shirt)
rope	(rec 4)	Record 7 (paddle)
sandals	(rec 10)	Record 8 (wetsuit)
T-shirt	(rec 6)	Record 9 (boots)
wetsuit	(rec 8)	Record 10 (sandals)

Figure 11.4 *An indexed parts file.*

Linked Files

A *linked file* is one in which each record has a pointer (a coupling, a reference), or LINK to a previous record. This file type is used to link together all of the transactions for a particular customer, vendor or corporation. A *transaction* is normally some form of sale or purchase. This is how a link in a transaction file works:

1. The first link (in the customer/vendor/corporation record) points to the latest (most current) transaction.
2. The link in the most current transaction record points to the previous transaction record.
3. The link in the second transaction record points to the transaction prior to that, the third transaction record for that customer/vendor/corporation.
4. This continues until there are no more transaction records for that customer/vendor/corporation.

Linked files are useful for connecting the transactions of customers/vendors, especially when a lot of transactions are involved. However, they are too complex for the scope of this book; so this description is for your understanding of files, not for your immediate use. Chapter 13 explains the concept of linked files, and Appendix F contains linked routines, if you want to learn how to use them.

The example in Figure 11.5 on the next page shows a linked file of sales transactions that have been recorded in the order as they occurred (chronologically). The most current sales record for each customer has a pointer, or *link*, to the previous sale for that customer, which in turn points to the third sale, and so on. As an exercise, follow the sales history, as shown in Figure 11.5, from the most current to the least current, for each customer by using the links.

Record Number	Name	Date of Sale	Pointer to Previous Record
112	Butkus	06/10/94	108
111	Richard	06/09/94	107
110	Neal	06/07/94	109
109	Neal	06/06/94	98
108	Butkus	06/04/94	105
107	Richard	06/04/94	102
106	Anderson	06/03/94	101
105	Butkus	06/03/94	104
104	Butkus	06/02/94	103
103	Butkus	06/01/94	91
102	Richard	06/01/94	83
101	Anderson	06/01/94	99

(Records 100 through 1 are not shown)

Figure 11.5 *Sales transactions in a linked file.*

File Subject Categories (and How to Design Them)

These are just a few tips for grouping data into files.

When you are designing a file to store data, it helps to know which file to put each data item in. Often it is hard to know where to put the fields. This section tries to show you some of the general kinds of files existing on computer systems, and what data items or fields go into each type of file.

When you design a file, you should try to group data items, or fields by the subject matter like this:

Customer/Vendor/Corporation file
Item or service file
Transaction files

Customer/Vendor/Corporation file contains (for example):

Customer/Vendor/Corporation number
Name
Address
Phone
Customer type
Notes
Credit limit
Purchases (by year, month or week)
Payment history
Billto/payto address
Shipto address
Balance
Contact names and phone numbers
Sales tax information
Total business
Discount information
Customer/Vendor since date

Item/service file contains (for example):

Item/service number
Description
Category
Supplier
Prices
Costs
Weight/time
For items, onhand, onorder, min, max, order quantities, etc.

Location
Sales by year, month, week or day
Receipts by year, month, week, or day

Transaction file contains (for example):

Transaction number
Transaction type
Transaction date
Transaction amount
Tax, if any
Shipping/travel, if any
Payment, if any
Pay type, if any
Description, if applicable
Discounts, if applicable

File Layouts

A *file layout* is a description of the fields in each record such as:

- Field name
- Field type
- Field length
- Position of the field in the record

The *field name* is the variable name that you give to the field. Chapter 5, *Data Names and Data Types*, recommends that the field name be 12 or fewer characters long, and be meaningful, so that any programmer, especially you, will understand what the field is, just by its name.

The field types that you work with are either:

numeric
alphanumeric
or a date

Numeric types consist of the integer, single precision, double precision, and large integer types that you found in Chapter 5.

Alphanumeric types are composed of letters, numbers, and other printable characters.

A *date* can be a single precision number with this format: MMDDYY, where:

MM is a two-digit month
DD a two-digit day
YY a two-digit year

Field length is the maximum number of letters or digits that are stored in the field as its value.

The positions in the record are the actual segment of record space (locations within the record) that the field takes up. Integers use two-character positions (bytes), and long integers take up four characters. Single-precision numbers employ four character positions and double-precision numbers use eight characters (rather than taking up a character for each digit).

Sample Customer File Layout

A simple record layout for a customer file might look like this:

Field name	Type	Length	Position
CUSNUM	S	5	1-4
CUSNAME	A	30	5-34
CUSADDR1	A	30	35-64
CUSCITY	A	20	65-84
CUSST	A	2	85-86
CUSZIP	L	4	87-90
CUSTYPE	I	2	91-92
CUSBAL	B	8	93-100

Where the types are:

A = Alpha   S = Small (single-precision) number
I = Integer B = Big (double-precision) number

Do not worry about understanding the detail in this last part—the next chapter glues data into files. Just get the *big picture*, and realize that you use files subconsciously every day. As a programmer, you work with them in a more precise fashion.

Summary

1. A *file* is a collection of similar things. A computer data file is a collection of like data.
2. A *record* is one of the like data objects in your file.
3. A *field* is an identifiable segment of a record, the smallest piece of data with which you normally work.
4. Four types of file structures are:
   - Sequential
   - Random
   - Indexed
   - Linked
5. Files can be classified by subject matter, such as:
   - Customer/vendor/corporation
   - Item or service
   - Transactions
6. A *file layout* is a description of the fields (data items) in a record:
   - Field name
   - Field type
   - Field length
   - Position within the record

The Book in Review

1. Design and program thoughtfully.
2. To examine any QBasic program, break it up into blocks. Then study each block separately, and finally look at the logic that controls all the blocks.
3. QBasic gives you a complete working environment that encourages writing programs in building-block fashion.
4. Blueprint your program *before* you write the first line of code.
5. Data names should be meaningful, short (but not cryptic), consistent, and clear.
6. The QBasic Editor is top shelf. Use the keys, rather than the menus, and you will be productive.
7. Program organization is crucial. Blueprint, assign the tasks to routines, then program each routine.
8. GOSUB subroutines; CALL procedures. GOTO a line name that is within the same routine as the GOTO statement.
9. Keep your IFs simple and easy to read.
10. Loops are critical to good programming. You can destroy their structure with the wrong GOTO. Never GOTO somewhere outside the loop.
11. **Group like items together, describe them, and you have the start of a file.**

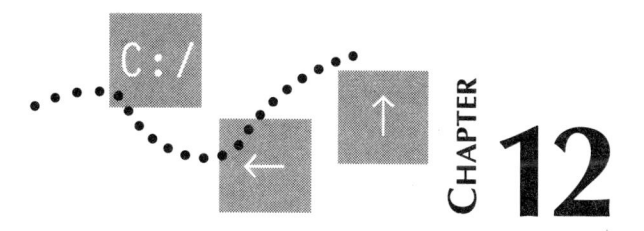

Random Files

This chapter teaches you about random files and how you can quickly access their records. You also learn how to use the OPEN, GET, and FIELD statements. The topics include:

- Random file definition
- Opening a random file
- Locating a record
- Reading and writing
- Record layout
- Packing and unpacking
- Creating a random file
- Determining the end of the file

A Frustrating File Search

Pat is trying to find a particular series of songs on a tape. The customers had a special request for particular songs to be played as they have their barbecue after the raft trip. The problem is, Pat is not sure exactly where the first song of that group is located. It is near the end of the tape, so Pat keeps fast forwarding, playing a little bit, then fast forwarding, then playing. *&%$@!%^*#@& (censored). The start of the song was just missed. The slow rewind does not work, so Pat rewinds a lot, then starts the searching process over.

Pat is working with a sequential file. Whether on a tape player, or on a computer, all sequential files have the same drawback. The only way to get to a particular location on the file is to first go through every bit of information that is in front of it. If Pat had the song on a compact disc, it could be directed to go directly to the right song. She would be working with a *random* file. A random file lets you go directly to any location on the file.

Sequential files are inconvenient (like Pat's tape player). Therefore, it may be best not to use them for all business-related programming. It's easier to declare every file as a random file, and then read it either sequentially, or randomly, depending on the program needs.

This whole chapter is about random files.

Random File Definition

A *random* file is a data file in which any one record can be accessed about as quickly as any other record.

Assume a file of 100,000 records. If that file is a random file, the amount of time to get the data in record 1 is roughly equal to the time it takes to get the data in record 100,000.

Opening a Random File

Before you can read from or write to any data file, you must first open it. You have to pull open a file cabinet before you can get at a case folder, you have to flip open your personal calendar to find an appointment, and you have to untie the stack of love letters to find a certain letter. In that same way, you must use an OPEN statement to open a random file in a QBasic computer program.

The syntax for an OPEN statement is:

```
OPEN "R", #{file number}, {file name}, {record length}
```

where:

- "R" states that the file is opened in Random mode.
- The *file number* is a number from 1 to 255. This number is used later in the read and write (GET and PUT) statements to tell the computer which file to read or write. Once a file name is mated to a file number by an OPEN statement, all GETs and PUTs use that number. Each file number must be unique, or the computer mixes up the files.

  Number your data files in every program sequentially, starting with 1 for the file that is used first. The first file number (1) should normally refer to the file whose reading and processing is contained in the Main Control loop. That's because the first file read normally controls the reading of all other files.

- The *file name* is the identifier (up to eight letters plus the .DAT extension), encased in quotes, of the file on disk. When you create a data file (the very first time an OPEN statement with that file name is run), QBasic writes that file name into a directory index onto the computer disk. Thereafter, each time the file is OPENed, the computer goes to the directory index to search for the file name, then gets its location on the disk and prepares to read data.

- The *record length* is the number of character positions (bytes) that each record of the file takes up on disk.

Remember that:

- Integers use two bytes.
- Long integers take up four bytes.
- Single-precision numbers employ four bytes.
- Double-precision (big) numbers take up eight bytes.

When designing a file, leave 20 to 30 bytes free for future expansion. It is also a good idea to make the record size of random files a multiple of 128 bytes (for technical reasons), and provide for expansion by going to the next higher multiple of 128. (For example, if the record size of a file added up to 211, make the record size equal to 256, allowing 45 characters for expansion.) If you do this, you normally have record sizes of 128, 256, 384, 512, 640, 768, 896, 1024, and so on. Because a disk is so inexpensive today, allow for expansion early on. It is better to waste a little space, and know that you can accommodate add-ons rather than being frustrated trying to fit additional data items into a small file later on.

File OPEN examples

Suppose that you had to use four files in one program:

> Customers (Assume that the file name is *cust.dat*, and the record length is 512.)
>
> Vendors (The file name is *vend.dat*, and the record is 256 bytes.)
>
> Parts (The file name is *part.dat*, and the record size is 256.)
>
> Service (The file name is *serv.dat*, and the record size is 128.)

The OPENs in the FILEOPEN routine would be:

```
OPEN "R", #1, "cust.dat", 512
OPEN "R", #2, "vend.dat", 256
OPEN "R", #3, "part.dat", 256
OPEN "R", #4, "serv.dat", 128
```

Locating a Record

Each record on a random file has a number. The first record is number 1, the second record is number 2, and so on. You read a random file by specifying the record number as the *key* of the record you want in QBasic. This record number can be any value from 1 to the number of records in the file. The record number is specified in the GET statement, which is explained later in this chapter.

The problem is, you might not want to assign the same numbers to customers, vendors, parts, and services. If each of these begins with the same number (1), you have a customer number 1, a vendor number 1, a part number 1, and a service number 1. By just looking at the number, you would not be able to distinguish between a customer and a vendor, or between a part and a service. So, in the design stage you can assign different numbers to each of these groups. For instance, you might want to number your customers from 1 to 6000, your vendors from 6001 to 7000, your parts from 7001 to 9000, and your services from 9001 to 10000. This gives you unique numbers for everything, for example:

- The number 100 must be a customer.
- The number 6100 has to be a vendor.
- The number 7100 can only be a part number.
- The number 9100 must be a service.

Then, to locate each record:

File Name	Record Number	Key Values	Formula
CUST	1-6000	1-6000	f1 = {key}
VEND	1-1000	6001-7000	f1 = {key - 6000}
PART	1-2000	7001-9000	f1 = {key - 7000}
SERV	1-1000	9001-10000	f1 = {key - 9000}

Customers

You locate a record in the customer file by specifying the customer number (1 to 6000) as the key. This key goes into the GET statement to read the customer record.

Vendors

Your vendors are numbered 6001 to 7000, which gives you 1000 vendors. The record numbers on your vendor file are numbered from 1 to 1000. Vendor number 6001 occupies record number 1, vendor 6002 has record number 2, and so on. Therefore, you find a record in the vendor file by calculating the record number (vendor number - 6000), and making it the key in the GET statement. This reads the vendor that you want.

Parts

Your part numbers range between 7001 and 9000, which means that you have 2000 parts. So the record numbers on your parts file are from 1 to 2000. Part number 7001 has record location 1, part number 7002 has record location 2, and so on. You identify a record in the parts file by calculating the record number (part number - 7000), and using it in the GET statement.

Services

Your service numbers are 9001 to 10000, so you have 1000 services. Record numbers on your service file are from 1 to 1000, with service number 9001 in location 1, 9002 in location 2, and so on. You read a record in the service file by specifying the record number (service number - 9000) as the key in the GET statement.

You can set up records in a random file by using any formula that works to calculate the record number (key), then specifying that key in a GET statement. If the formula gets you to the right record, use it.

Reading and Writing

Use a GET statement to read from a random file. Use a PUT statement to write to a random file.

GET Statement

The GET statement reads a record of the random file whose file number is contained in the statement. The syntax is:

```
GET {file number},{record number}
```

GET examples

```
GET 1,100    -   read record 100 of the file OPENed as #1

GET 2,2000   -   read record 2000 of the file OPENed as #2

GET 6,f6     -   read the record (determined by the value of f6) of the
                 file OPENed as #6. If f6 has a value of 69, the 69th
                 record of the file opened as #6 is read.
```

For the customer, vendor, part, and service files in the previous discussion, let's get record number 101 for each file:

Customer

Assume that the Customer Number variable name is *custno*, the file number is 1, and the file key is named *f1*.

```
REM - custno has a value of 101
f1=custno
GET #1, f1
```

Vendor

The Vendor number is called *vendno*, the file number is 2, and the file key is *f2*.

```
REM - vendno has a value of 6101
f2= vendno - 6000
GET #2, f2
```

Part

The part number name is *partno*, the file number is 3, and the part key is *f3*.

```
REM - partno has a value of 7101
f3 = partno - 7000
GET #3, f3
```

Service

The service number is *servno*, the file number is 4, and the service key is *f4*.

```
REM - servno has a value of 9101
f4 = servno - 9000
GET #4, f4
```

PUT Statement

The PUT statement writes a record onto the random file whose number is specified in the statement. The syntax is:

```
PUT {file number},{record number}
```

PUT examples

PUT 1,100 — write record 100 of the file OPENed as #1

PUT 2,2000 — write record 2000 of the file OPENed as #2

PUT 6,f6 — write the record (determined by the value of f6) of the file OPENed as #6. If f6 had a value of 69, the 69th record of the file opened as #6 would be written.

For the customer, vendor, part, and service files in the previous discussion, to write record number 101 for each file:

Customer

The Customer Number is *custno*, the file number is 1, and the file key is *f1*.

```
REM - custno has a value of 101
f1=custno
PUT #1, f1
```

Vendor

The Vendor key is *vendno*, the file number is 2, and the file key is *f2*.

```
REM - vendno has a value of 6101
f2= vendno - 6000
PUT #2, f2
```

Part

The part number is *partno*, the file number is 3, and the part key is *f3*.

```
REM - partno has a value of 7101
f3 = partno - 7000
PUT #3, f3
```

Service

The service number is *servno*, the file number is 4, and the service key is *f4*.

```
REM - servno has a value of 9101
```

```
f4 = servno - 9000
PUT #4, f4
```

Record Layout

In Chapter 11, you saw a sample customer record layout. The record layout below is an extension of that. The record has one more column to show the packed size of the numeric data fields:

Field name	Type	Length	Packed length	Position
custnum	S	5	4	1-4
custname$	A	30	30	5-34
custaddr1$	A	30	30	35-64
custcity$	A	20	20	65-84
custst$	A	2	2	85-86
custzip#	L	9	4	87-90
custtype	I	3	2	91-92
custbal#	B	12	8	93-100

Data types are:

A = Alphanumeric

I = Integer

S = Small number (single precision)

B = Big number (double precision)

L = Long integer (up to 16 digits)

QBasic uses a FIELD statement to specify the layout of a random record to the computer. This FIELD statement identifies the name and length of each field in the record. Since the fields are described in the same order in which they occur on the record, the FIELD statement is a complete definition of every position in a record.

The syntax for a FIELD statement is:

```
FIELD #{file number}, {packed length of 1st field} AS {name_
```

of 1st field}$, {packed length of 2nd field} AS {name of_
2nd field}$, {packed length of 3rd field} AS {name of 3rd_
field}$, etc.

FIELD example

```
FIELD #1, 4 AS custnum$, 30 AS custname$, 30 AS custaddr1$,_
20 AS custcity$, 2 AS custst$, 4 AS custzip$, 2 AS_
custtype$, 8 AS custbal$
```

So the FILEOPEN routine for a program that uses only this file is:

```
FILEOPEN:
    OPEN "R", #1, "cust.dat", 128
    FIELD #1, 4 AS custnum$, 30 AS custname$, 30 AS_
custaddr1$, 20 AS custcity$,2 AS custst$,4AS_
custzip$,2AScusttype$, 8 AS custbal$
    RETURN
```

Packing and Unpacking

Numeric variables are packed before being put into a random file to save disk space. Integers are packed into a two-character space, single-precision numbers pack into four bytes, double-precision numbers pack into eight bytes, and long integers pack into four characters. While alphanumeric variables are not packed, just stored, numeric variables *must* be packed in order to write them onto a random file.

Also, when you read a record from a random file, you must unpack a numeric variable before using it in a calculation, move, or display.

The syntax for the packing commands is:

```
LSET {variable name}$ = MK{type of data indicator} {variable
name}
```

where:

LSET does the packing, and

MKI, MKS, MKL and MKD determine the type of data being packed.

The packing commands are:

- MKI$ - packs integer variables
- MKS$ - packs single-precision variables
- MKD$ - packs double-precision variables
- MKL$ - packs long integer variables

Packing Examples

These packing examples use the customer file discussed previously:

- LSET custtype$ = MKI$(custtype%)
- LSET custnum$ = MKS$(custnum)
- LSET custbal$ = MKD$(custbal#)
- LSET custzip$ = MKL$(custzip&)

Note that all packing statements are preceded by the word LSET. The LSET is required in QBasic to store a data item onto a record, even if the item is not being packed. So, you need to add four more statements to finish storing data onto the customer record like this:

LSET custname$={customer's name}
LSET custaddr1$={customer's address}
LSET custcity$={customer's city}
LSET custst$={customer's state}.

Next, we try unpacking. The syntax for unpacking is:

```
{variable name}$ = CV{type of data indicator} ({variable_name}$
```

where:

CVI, CVS, CVL, and CVD show the type of data being unpacked.

The unpacking commands are:

- CVI - unpacks integer variables
- CVS - unpacks single-precision variables

- CVD - unpacks double-precision variables
- CVL - unpacks long integer variables

Unpacking examples

Using the Customer file again, here are some unpacking examples:

- custtype% = CVI(custtype$)
- custnum = CVS(custnum$)
- custbal# = CVD(custbal$)
- custzip& = CVL(custzip$)

The FILEOPEN and FILEREAD routines for the Customer file look like this (The FILEREAD routine is *custread*):

```
fileopen:
    OPEN "R", #1, "cust.dat", 128
    FIELD #1, 4 AS custnum$, 30 AS custname$, 30 AS_
custaddr1$, 20 AS custcity$, 2 AS custst$, 4 AS custzip$, 2_
AS custtype$, 8 AS custbal$
RETURN
custread:
    GET #1, f1
    custnum = CVS(custnum$)
    custzip& = CVL(custzip$)
    custtype% = CVI(custtype$)
    custbal# = CVD(custbal$)
RETURN
```

Type.... End Type Method

Most Basics programs use a FIELD statement to specify the layout of a random record to the computer. This FIELD statement identifies the name and length of each data element in the record. Because the data elements are described in the same order in which they occur on the record, the FIELD statement is a complete definition of every position in a record.

While you can use the FIELD statement in QBasic, the TYPE... END TYPE construct available in QBasic is simpler. It describes each data element in the record on a separate line. To come up with the exact positions of each data element, accumulate the packed length of all the previous data, then add in the packed size of the current data element. This completes the right column in the customer record table of the positions on the random file record.

The record layout of the above Customer file using Type...End Type in a program is:

```
TYPE cusdef
    custnum AS SINGLE
    custname AS STRING * 30
    custaddr1 AS STRING * 30
    custcity AS STRING * 30
    custst AS STRING * 2
    custzip AS LONG
    custtype AS INTEGER
    custbal AS DOUBLE
END TYPE
GLOBAL cusrec AS cusdef
```

Packing and Unpacking

When FIELD statements are used, numeric variables are packed before being put into a random file. When you read a record from a random file, you must unpack a numeric variable before using it in a calculation, move, or display.

When you use the TYPE.. END TYPE statement, packing and unpacking are unnecessary. This is another good reason to use it. However, the GET statement now has to include the recordname. So the GET would look like:

```
GET 1, f1, cusrec
```

If this method appeals to you, use it instead of the FIELD and pack/unpack approach. I suggest you first write the program using the FIELD method, make sure it works, then change to the TYPE...END TYPE.

Creating a Random File

As mentioned in *Opening a Random File*, the first time that a random file is OPENed, the file name is recorded on the disk directory, and the file is created.

Most programmers create a random file by OPENing it, writing a few records, then closing the file. However, the best way is to write a separate program to create every random file. This program initializes every numeric field to 0, using one of these statements:

LSET {fieldname}$ = MKI$(0)
LSET {fieldname}$ = MK$$(0)
LSET {fieldname}$ = MKL$(0)
LSET {fieldname}$ = MKD$(0)

The program then sets every alphanumeric field to spaces, and writes "blank" records to the file. Create this "blank" file with the maximum number of records that you expect the file to contain. This eliminates performance delays in the future, and avoids expanding files later on.

Random File Creation Program

This program creates a blank customer file for your sample customer file. The program creates a random access file of 6000 records, with record numbers of 1 through 6000, and customer numbers of 1 to 6000. You have over 30 characters free in each record for future expansion. The program looks like this:

```
REM crcust 060194
GOSUB fileopen
GOSUB main
CLOSE
END
fileopen:
OPEN "r", 1, "cust.dat", 128
    FIELD 1, 4 AS custnum$, 30 AS custname$, 30 AS_
custaddr1$
    FIELD 1, 64 AS fill1$, 20 AS custcity$, 2 AS custst$
```

```
    FIELD 1, 86 AS fill2$, 4 AS custzip$, 2 AS custtype$
    FIELD 1, 92 AS fill3$, 8 AS custbal$
RETURN
main:
    GOSUB clearcust
        FOR f1 = 1 TO 6000: REM — loop to write 6000_
blank cust REM — records
        LSET custnum$ = MKS$(f1)
        PUT 1, f1
        PRINT f1
    NEXT f1
RETURN

clearcust: REM — set up a blank record
    LSET custname$ = "         "
    LSET custaddr1$ = "        "
    LSET custcity$ = "       "
    LSET custst$ = "   "
    LSET custzip$ = MKL$(0)
    LSET custtype$ = MKI$(0)
    LSET custbal$ = MKD$(0)
RETURN
```

Determining the End of the File

When you are reading a random file sequentially, add one to the record number each time to get to the next record. However, if you do not stop this process in time, the computer goes past the last record of the file, and can read bad data that belongs to another file. To prevent this, here are two methods:

1. Use an IF statement to test if the record number is greater than the number of records you have specified for that file.
2. Use an IF EOF statement to test for reading beyond the end-of-file.

IF Statement Method

The syntax of the IF statement for testing the record number to be greater than the maximum is:

```
IF {record number} > {maximum number of records} THEN GOTO _
{line label}
```

where

{record number} is the current record number, which is_
about to be read,

{maximum number of records} is the total number of records_
(including blanks) in the file, and

{line label} is a label to go to after all reading is done.

IF Examples

These are some examples of using the IF statement:

```
IF f1 > 6000 THEN GOTO quitcust
IF recnum1 > 50000 THEN GOTO tranend
```

IF EOF Method

The syntax of the IF EOF statement for end-of-file testing is:

```
IF EOF( {file number} ) THEN GOTO {line label}
```

where

{file number} is the number of the file in the OPEN_
statement,

and

{line label} is a label to go to after the reading is done.

IF EOF Examples

These are some examples of using IF EOF:

```
IF EOF(1) THEN GOTO quit1
```

```
    IF EOF(3) THEN GOTO ender
```

The EOF test must be performed after the file is read.

A program that prints out the Customer file has a MAIN routine (major processing loop from Chapter 7), which looks like this, using IF:

```
main:
    f1 = f1 + 1
    IF f1 > 6000 THEN GOTO ENDMAIN
    GOSUB getcust: REM — reads a customer record
    GOSUB princust: REM — prints a customer record
    GOTO main
endmain:
    RETURN
```

For using IF EOF:

```
main:
    f1 = f1 + 1
    GOSUB getcust: REM — reads a customer record
    IF EOF(1) THEN GOTO ENDMAIN
    GOSUB princust: REM — prints a customer record
    GOTO main
endmain:
    RETURN
```

As you can see, with the exception of the end-of-file test, the main routines are identical.

Summary

1. A *random file* is one in which any record can be accessed about as quickly as any other.
2. Before you use a random file, OPEN it.

3. The *record number* is the sequence number of the record in a random file. Use the record number as the key to read a particular piece of data. You may have to perform a calculation to get the record number.
4. Read a random file with GET, write a random file with PUT.
5. A FIELD statement is the record layout for a random file.
6. The TYPE....END TYPE statements also show the record layout for a random file.
7. Numbers must be packed before they are written to random files. Unpack them after reading, before they are used.
8. Create a "blank" random file first. Then store data in it.
9. Test for an end-of-file condition (no more records left to be read), using:

   IF {record number} > {the number of records in the file}

   or

   IF EOF({file number})

The Book in Review

1. Design and program thoughtfully.
2. To examine any QBasic program, break it up into blocks. Then study each block separately, and finally look at the logic that controls all the blocks.
3. QBasic gives you a complete working environment, which encourages writing programs in building-block fashion.
4. Blueprint your program before you write the first line of code.
5. Data names should be meaningful, short (but not cryptic), consistent and clear.
6. The QBasic Editor is top shelf. Use the keys, rather than the menus, and you will be productive.
7. Program organization is crucial. Blueprint, assign the tasks to routines, then program each routine.
8. GOSUB subroutines; CALL procedures. GOTO a line name that is within the same routine as the GOTO statement.

9. Keep your IFs simple, and easy to read.
10. Loops are critical to good programming. You can destroy their structure with the wrong GOTO. Never GOTO somewhere outside the loop.
11. Group like items together, describe them, and you have the start of a file.
12. **Learn random files well; they are the foundation of all file work.**

CHAPTER 13

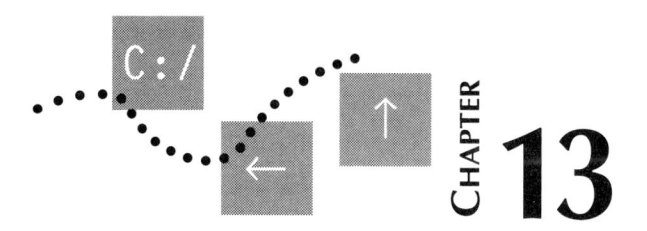

Linked File Concepts

This chapter introduces you to the idea of linked files. When files are linked, each record acts as an important piece of the information chain, referring you to the next link until you find the data you are looking for. The topics in this chapter include:

- How a linked file works
- Linked file examples
- The innards of a linked file
- Linking backward
- Linking forward
- Linking forward and backward
- Link to the master
- Linking to a document
- The last used record is critical
- The master link in the chain
- Linking the links

Remember the buried treasure game you used to play at camp when you were a kid? There were several groups of kids playing the game. Each group was given a different first clue. Solving the first clue guided you to a second one. The second got you to a third, and so on, until you were led to the *treasure*.

Linked list files work in a similar fashion.

How a Linked File Works

A linked list file is a data structure in which there are many *groups*—like the groups of kids in the game above. Each group has its own series of *clues* (records and pointers within each record) that directly lead from one record or *clue* to the next in that specific group. All the records for one group are *chained* together, and each pointer that leads to another record is a *link* within that chain. That is where the name *Linked List* comes from. In a linked list file, the first record of a group has a pointer that is the *key* to the second record. Once this pointer is used to read the second record of the group, the pointer in record 2 is available as the key to the third record of the group. Now the second pointer is used to read the third record, and the third pointer becomes available. The third pointer can read the fourth record, and so on. The process continues until you find the record you are looking for, or until you find a pointer of zero. A *zero pointer* means that there are no more records in the group to be read.

A linked list file could have thousands of groups, each with its own chain. A single chain could be made up of thousands of links.

> **NOTE** In the next few chapters we use the words *transaction*, *transaction record* and *linked record* interchangeably.

Linked File Examples

A common linked file is the invoice transaction file for customers of a business. Each customer (equate every customer to a group of kids in the treasure game) has a chain, and its links include every invoice for that customer. The link to the first invoice in the chain is located in the Customer record itself. The customer record pointer (link) contains the key to the first invoice record in the linked file. The first invoice in the chain has a link that is the key to the second, and so on, until the link has a value of 0. This chain has *backward* linking. That is, the chain goes backward chronologically, from newest transaction to oldest transaction.

Record Number	Customer	Date of Sale	Pointer to Next Record
112	Butkus	06/10/93	108
111	Richard	06/09/93	107
110	Shane	06/07/93	109
109	Shane	06/06/93	98
108	Butkus	06/04/93	105
107	Richard	06/04/93	102
106	Anderson	06/03/93	101
105	Butkus	06/03/93	104
104	Butkus	06/02/93	103
103	Butkus	06/01/93	91
102	Richard	06/01/93	83
101	Anderson	06/01/93	99

(Records 100 through 1 are not shown)

Figure 13.1 *Invoice transactions linked (backwards) to a Customer file.*

Another linked file example is the vendor invoices file. This operates in the exact same fashion as the customer invoices file. Each vendor has a backward chain, with links to all of its invoices. The head link in the chain is in the vendor record. This points to the first (newest) invoice, and so on.

Record Number	Vendor	Date of Invoice	Pointer to Next Record
212	Acme	06/10/93	208
211	Bestest	06/09/93	207
210	Worstest	06/07/93	209
209	Worstest	06/06/93	198
208	Acme	06/04/93	205
207	Bestest	06/04/93	202
206	Breakall	06/03/93	201
205	Acme	06/03/93	204
204	Acme	06/02/93	203
203	Acme	06/01/93	191
202	Bestest	06/01/93	183
201	Breakall	06/01/93	199

(Records 200 through 1 are not shown)

Figure 13.2 *Invoice transactions linked (backwards) to a Vendor file.*

Payroll systems also use linked lists. In this case, the employee record holds the master link to the first (latest) paycheck. The first paycheck links to the second, and this continues until you run out of paychecks.

Record Number	Employee	Date of Pay	Pointer to Next Record
12	Butkus	06/10/93	8
11	Pratt	06/10/93	7
10	Hussey	06/10/93	9
9	Hussey	06/03/93	0
8	Butkus	06/03/93	5
7	Pratt	06/03/93	2
6	Neal	05/27/93	1
5	Butkus	05/27/93	4
4	Butkus	05/13/93	3
3	Butkus	05/13/93	0
2	Pratt	05/13/93	0
1	Neal	05/13/93	0

Figure 13.3 *Pay transactions linked (backwards) to an Employee file.*

General Ledger systems link transactions to a general ledger (GL) account. The first link is in the account record. That points to the first transaction for that account, which points to the next, until all transactions are linked.

Record Number	Account	Date of GL Transaction	Pointer to Next Record
112	Sales	06/10/93	108
111	Cash	06/09/93	107
110	Office	06/07/93	109
109	Office	06/06/93	98
108	Sales	06/04/93	105
107	Cash	06/04/93	102
106	Refunds	06/03/93	101
105	Sales	06/03/93	104
104	Sales	06/02/93	103
103	Sales	06/01/93	91
102	Cash	06/01/93	83
101	Refunds	06/01/93	99

(Records 100 through 1 are not shown)

Figure 13.4 *Transactions linked (backwards) to a GL Account file.*

The Innards of a Linked File

A linked list file is a random file where each record is written sequentially, one right after the other, as they occur chronologically. The links may go either forward or backward. Backward linkage, from newest to oldest link, is more common and easier to use. What distinguishes this file structure from others is the links that chain physically scattered records to form the data belonging to a specific person, company, account, or object.

Now we form a linked file from scratch. Assume that we have created a blank transaction file, where all the links start out as zero. Watch the employee pay file fill as the data of each pay transaction is saved. This is an overview without all the detail, so some processes won't be explained until later in this chapter.

The Pay transaction file is initially blank, with no transaction data at all. The first employee paid is Neal. The transaction goes into record 1. Since no other transactions exist for Neal, the pointer to the next record is 0, as displayed in Figure 13.5.

Record Number	Employee	Date of Pay	Pointer to Next Record
1	Neal	05/13/93	0

Figure 13.5 *Building the Pay file—Transaction 1.*

The second employee paid is Pratt, so the transaction goes into record 2. No other transactions exist for Pratt, so the pointer to Pratt's next record is 0, as displayed in Figure 13.6.

Record Number	Employee	Date of Pay	Pointer to Next Record
2	Pratt	05/13/93	0
1	Neal	05/13/93	0

Figure 13.6 *Building the Pay file—Transaction 2.*

The third employee paid is Butkus, with the transaction put into record 3. Because no other transactions exist for Butkus, the pointer to his next record is 0, as shown in Figure 13.7.

Record Number	Employee	Date of Pay	Pointer to Next Record
3	Butkus	05/13/93	0
2	Pratt	05/13/93	0
1	Neal	05/13/93	0

Figure 13.7 *Building the Pay file—Transaction 3.*

Butkus gets paid again and the transaction put into the fourth record. Because he has a previous transaction, the pointer to his next record becomes 3, as shown in Figure 13.8. He now has a chain with one link—record 4 links to record 3.

Record Number	Employee	Date of Pay	Pointer to Next Record
4	Butkus	05/20/93	3
3	Butkus	05/13/93	0
2	Pratt	05/13/93	0
1	Neal	05/13/93	0

Figure 13.8 *Building the Pay file—Transaction 4.*

Butkus, being a valuable employee, gets paid still again, and the transaction is saved in the fifth record. Because he has previous transactions, the pointer to his next record becomes 4, as shown in Figure 13.9. Butkus now has a chain with 2 links. Record 5 links to record 4, which links to record 3.

Record Number	Employee	Date of Pay	Pointer to Next Record
5	Butkus	05/27/93	4
4	Butkus	05/20/93	3
3	Butkus	05/13/93	0
2	Pratt	05/13/93	0
1	Neal	05/13/93	0

Figure 13.9 *Building the Pay file—Transaction 5.*

Neal gets paid for the second time and the transaction put into the sixth record. Because there is a previous transaction, the pointer to the next record becomes 1. There is now a chain with one link—record 6 links to record 1, as displayed in Figure 13.10.

CHAPTER THIRTEEN: LINKED FILE CONCEPTS • 229

Record Number	Employee	Date of Pay	Pointer to Next Record
6	Neal	06/03/93	1
5	Butkus	05/27/93	4
4	Butkus	05/20/93	3
3	Butkus	05/13/93	0
2	Pratt	05/13/93	0
1	Neal	05/13/93	0

Figure 13.10 *Building the Pay file—Transaction 6.*

Pratt gets paid for the second time and the transaction goes into the seventh record. There is a previous transaction, so the pointer to the next record becomes 2. Pratt has a chain with one link—record 7 links to record 2, as displayed in Figure 13.11.

Record Number	Employee	Date of Pay	Pointer to Next Record
7	Pratt	06/03/93	2
6	Neal	06/03/93	1
5	Butkus	05/27/93	4
4	Butkus	05/20/93	3
3	Butkus	05/13/93	0
2	Pratt	05/13/93	0
1	Neal	05/13/93	0

Figure 13.11 *Building the Pay file—Transaction 7.*

Butkus gets paid once more and the transaction saved in the eighth record. Because he has previous transactions, the pointer to his next record becomes 5, as shown in Figure 13.12. Butkus now has a chain with 3 links. Record 8 links to record 5. Record 5 links to record 4, which links to record 3.

Record Number	Employee	Date of Pay	Pointer to Next Record
8	Butkus	06/03/93	5
7	Pratt	06/03/93	2
6	Neal	06/03/93	1
5	Butkus	05/27/93	4
4	Butkus	05/20/93	3
3	Butkus	05/13/93	0
2	Pratt	05/13/93	0
1	Neal	05/13/93	0

Figure 13.12 *Building the Pay file—Transaction 8.*

Record Number	Employee	Date of Pay	Pointer to Next Record
12	Butkus	06/10/93	8
11	Pratt	06/10/93	7
10	Hussey	06/10/93	9
9	Hussey	06/03/93	0
8	Butkus	06/03/93	5
7	Pratt	06/03/93	2
6	Neal	06/03/93	1
5	Butkus	05/27/93	4
4	Butkus	05/20/93	3
3	Butkus	05/13/93	0
2	Pratt	05/13/93	0
1	Neal	05/13/93	0

Figure 13.13 *Pay transactions linked to an Employee file.*

The process continues as each employee is paid, until the file looks like the figure on the lower left page.

Linking Backward

Note that the examples above actually chained backward, rather than forward. The more current record is linked to one less current, which pointed to an older transaction, and so on, until no records were left. This backward linking is the most common chain type found in linked list files.

Backward linking reads the most current transactions first, then links to read less current ones. The odds are that most inquiries and processes involve current, rather than old transactions. So backward linking is more efficient. It does not have to read through all the oldest transactions before getting the more current ones because it reads current ones first.

Linking Forward

In some cases you may want to link forward, from the oldest to the newest transaction. This linkage type is used when you want to build a complete history (from the beginning) of a company, individual, or object every time the file is accessed. It might also be used, if for some reason, you normally access older records more often than newer records.

Linking Forward and Backward

For real versatility you can chain a file both forward and backward. This means that a linked file can be read first as a random file using the specific record number. You can then read backward or forward along the chain to which the linked record belongs.

Link to the Master

Remember that most linked list files do not stand by themselves, because they are transactions. They belong to some master group, company, person, object, or account. We are always working with at least two files in this section—one (company/person/object/account) master file and one transaction (linked) file. So it is important that each transaction record of a linked file contains the record key of the master file or files it works with. Every linked record must have at least one master file key. It could have several—one transaction could involve a customer, a part or service, a sales tax jurisdiction, a sales category, and a sales person.

Linking to a Document

A document (invoice, perhaps) might have several lines of data that are important to keep available for reference. Rather than keeping only one record for an invoice transaction, this linked file could have many lines (each line taking up one record) for that one billing document. So the usual backward links point from one document to the start of the previous document.

In addition, it is useful to have a link in each invoice line record that points to the start of that billing document.

Besides linking to the start of a document, you need to know where the document ends. This is accomplished by having yet another link within each line record.

A linked file that contains multi-line documents might have 4 separate chains linking the records, as follows:

1. The master record key
2. Links to the start of each document
3. Links to the end of each document
4. Links to the start of the previous document

The Last Record Used is Critical

In building the Pay Transaction File discussed earlier, we always read the next available record, then put the data and links in that record. We went through the same process for the next record and kept it up until we were done. In order to build a linked file, we have to know the next available record in the file at all times.

This is accomplished by keeping the *LastUsed* record number at the very end of the linked file, and updating it as the file is built. Each time a new transaction is needed, the last record of the linked file is read, the LastUsed value increased by

1, and written back. This LastUsed value is then used as the record number for the new transaction. Without maintenance of the LastUsed, linked list files cannot work.

The LastUsed has other worth. If the linked file is read in sequential order for some reason, the read can be set to stop at the LastUsed, rather than continuing through empty records.

The Master Link in the Chain

We kept our examples simple when building the linked Pay file. In most cases, a master file is needed to start the linking process. Unlike a continuous bicycle chain, a chain of a linked file has a beginning and an end. The beginning of the chain is stored in a master file of a company, person or object, and the end is found in the last transaction record of the linked list file.

Remember that most linked list files are transactions that belong to a master company/person/object file. Each record of that master file has a link to the first transaction record in the linked file, if it exists. To read the transactions for that master record, the master link is used to read the first transaction record, the first transaction has a link to the second, and so on, until all transactions are read.

Linking the Links

Now we return to the Pay File example from the beginning of this chapter and, in detail, show how the Employee Master file, the Pay Transaction file, and the LastUsed are updated, one record at a time.

Record Number	Employee Name	Date of Last Pay	Pointer to Pay Record
100	Butkus	00/00/00	0
200	Pratt	00/00/00	0
300	Hussey	00/00/00	0
400	Neal	00/00/00	0

Figure 13.14 *Employee file.*

The Pay Transaction file in this example has 5,000 records, so the LastUsed is saved in record 5000. We start out with a blank Pay Transaction file. The Employee Master file links begin with a value of 0, as shown in Figures 13.14 (on the previous page) and 13.15.

Record Number	Employee Record #	Date of Pay	Pointer to Next Record
5000	0	00/00/00	0
12	000	00/00/00	0
11	000	00/00/00	0
10	000	00/00/00	0
9	000	00/00/00	0
8	000	00/00/00	0
7	000	00/00/00	0
6	000	00/00/00	0
5	000	00/00/00	0
4	000	00/00/00	0
3	000	00/00/00	0
2	000	00/00/00	0
1	000	00/00/00	0

Figure 13.15 *Pay transactions linked to an Employee file.*

On 05/13/93, Neal (employee number 400) is paid. As displayed in Figures 13.16 and 13.17, LastUsed in Pay record number 5000 is incremented to 1. A Pay record is written with a master link of 400 and a link pointer of 0 (there are no further pay records for employee number 400). Neal's master record in the Employee file has a link with a value of 1 to the Pay transaction file.

CHAPTER THIRTEEN: LINKED FILE CONCEPTS • 235

Record Number	Employee Name	Date of Last Pay	Pointer to Pay Record
100	Butkus	00/00/00	0
200	Pratt	00/00/00	0
300	Hussey	00/00/00	0
400	Neal	05/13/93	1

Figure 13.16 *Employee file.*

Record Number	Employee Record #	Date of Pay	Pointer to Next Record
5000	0	00/00/00	1
12	000	00/00/00	0
11	000	00/00/00	0
10	000	00/00/00	0
9	000	00/00/00	0
8	000	00/00/00	0
7	000	00/00/00	0
6	000	00/00/00	0
5	000	00/00/00	0
4	000	00/00/00	0
3	000	00/00/00	0
2	000	00/00/00	0
1	400	05/13/93	0

Figure 13.17 *Pay transactions linked to an Employee file.*

Record Number	Employee Name	Date of Last Pay	Pointer to Pay Record
100	Butkus	00/00/00	0
200	Pratt	05/13/93	2
300	Hussey	00/00/00	0
400	Neal	00/00/00	0

Figure 13.18 *Employee file.*

Record Number	Employee Record #	Date of Pay	Pointer to Next Record
5000	0	00/00/00	2
12	000	00/00/00	0
11	000	00/00/00	0
10	000	00/00/00	0
9	000	00/00/00	0
8	000	00/00/00	0
7	000	00/00/00	0
6	000	00/00/00	0
5	000	00/00/00	0
4	000	00/00/00	0
3	000	00/00/00	0
2	200	05/13/93	0
1	400	05/13/93	0

Figure 13.19 *Pay transactions linked to an Employee file.*

On 05/13/93, Pratt (employee number 200) is also paid, as shown in Figures 13.18 and 13.19, shown on the left. LastUsed in Pay record number 5000 is changed to 2. Pay record number two is written with a master link of 200 and a link pointer of 0 (there are no further pay records for employee number 200). Pratt's master record in the Employee file has a link with a value of 2 to the Pay transaction file.

Butkus, employee number 100, is also paid on 05/13/93, as displayed in Figures 13.20 and 13.21. LastUsed in Pay record number 5000 becomes 3. Pay record three is written with a master link of 100 and a link pointer of 0 (there are no further pay records for employee number 100). Butkus' master record in the Employee file has a link with a value of 3 to the Pay transaction file.

Record Number	Employee Name	Date of Last Pay	Pointer to Pay Record
100	Butkus	05/13/93	3
200	Pratt	05/13/93	2
300	Hussey	00/00/00	0
400	Neal	05/13/93	1

Figure 13.20 *Employee file.*

Record Number	Employee Record #	Date of Pay	Pointer to Next Record
5000	0	00/00/00	3
12	000	00/00/00	0
11	000	00/00/00	0
10	000	00/00/00	0
9	000	00/00/00	0
8	000	00/00/00	0
7	000	00/00/00	0
6	000	00/00/00	0
5	000	00/00/00	0
4	000	05/13/93s	0
3	100	00/00/00	0
2	200	05/13/93	0
1	400	05/13/93	0

Figure 13.21 *Pay transactions linked to an Employee file.*

Butkus is paid again on 05/20/93, as shown in Figures 13.22 and 13.23. LastUsed in Pay record number 5000 now has a value of 4. Pay record four is written with a master link of 100 and a link pointer of 3 (there is another pay record for employee number 100). Butkus' master record in the Employee file has a link with a value of 4 to the Pay transaction file. So his chain now goes from the master file to record 4 of the Pay file, then to record 3 of the Pay file.

Record Number	Employee Name	Date of Last Pay	Pointer to Pay Record
100	Butkus	05/20/93	4
200	Pratt	05/13/93	2
300	Hussey	00/00/00	0
400	Neal	05/13/93	1

Figure 13.22 *Employee file.*

Record Number	Record #	Pay	Record
5000	0	00/00/00	4
12	000	00/00/00	0
11	000	00/00/00	0
10	000	00/00/00	0
9	000	00/00/00	0
8	000	00/00/00	0
7	000	00/00/00	0
6	000	00/00/00	0
5	000	00/00/00	0
4	100	05/20/93	3
3	100	05/13/93	0
2	200	05/13/93	0
1	400	05/13/93	0

Figure 13.23 *Pay transactions linked to an Employee file.*

Butkus is paid once more on 05/27/93, as shown in Figures 13.24 and 13.25 on the next page. LastUsed in Pay record number 5000 is changed to 5. Pay record five is written with a master link of 100 and a link pointer of 4. Butkus' master record in the Employee file has a link with a value of 5 to the Pay transaction file. So his chain now goes from the master file to record 5 of the Pay file, then to record 4 of the Pay file, finally to record 3 of the Pay file.

Record Number	Employee Name	Date of Last Pay	Pointer to Pay Record
100	Butkus	05/27/93	5
200	Pratt	05/13/93	2
300	Hussey	00/00/00	0
400	Neal	05/13/93	1

Figure 13.24 *Employee file.*

Record Number	Employee Record #	Date of Pay	Pointer to Next Record
5000	0	00/00/00	5
12	000	00/00/00	0
11	000	00/00/00	0
10	000	00/00/00	0
9	000	00/00/00	0
8	000	00/00/00	0
7	000	00/00/00	0
6	000	00/00/00	0
5	100	05/27/93	4
4	100	05/20/93	3
3	100	05/13/93	0
2	200	05/13/93	0
1	400	05/13/93	0

Figure 13.25 *Pay transactions linked to an Employee file.*

Neal, employee number 400, is paid once more on 06/03/93, as displayed in Figures 13.26 and 13.27 on the next page. LastUsed in Pay record number 5000 is 6. Pay record six is written with a master link of 400 and a link pointer of 1. Neal's master record in the Employee file has a link with a value of 6 to the Pay transaction file. So the chain now goes from the master file to record 6 of the Pay file, then to record 1 of the Pay file.

242 • TEACH YOURSELF... QBASIC

Record Number	Employee Name	Date of Last Pay	Pointer to Pay Record
100	Butkus	05/27/93	5
200	Pratt	05/13/93	2
300	Hussey	00/00/00	0
400	Neal	05/13/93	6

Figure 13.26 *Employee file.*

Record Number	Employee Record #	Date of Pay	Pointer to Next Record
5000	0	00/00/00	6
12	000	00/00/00	0
11	000	00/00/00	0
10	000	00/00/00	0
9	000	00/00/00	0
8	000	00/00/00	0
7	000	00/00/00	0
6	400	06/03/93	1
5	100	05/27/93	4
4	100	05/20/93	3
3	100	05/13/93	0
2	200	05/13/93	0
1	400	05/13/93	0

Figure 13.27 *Pay transactions linked to an Employee file.*

This procedure continues for the four employees until the files look like Figures 13.28 and 13.29. Work the rest of the transactions through, one at a time, until you come up with these final results.

Record Number	Employee Name	Date of Last Pay	Pointer to Pay Record
100	Butkus	06/10/93	12
200	Pratt	06/10/93	11
300	Hussey	06/10/93	10
400	Neal	06/03/93	6

Figure 13.28 *Employee file.*

Record Number	Employee Record #	Date of Pay	Pointer to Next Record
5000	0	00/00/00	12
12	100	06/10/93	8
11	200	06/10/93	7
10	300	06/10/93	9
9	300	06/03/93	0
8	100	06/03/93	5
7	200	06/03/93	2
6	400	06/03/93	1
5	100	05/27/93	4
4	100	05/20/93	3
3	100	05/13/93	0
2	200	05/13/93	0
1	400	05/13/93	0

Figure 13.29 *Pay transactions linked to an Employee file.*

Chapter Summary

1. Linked files are based upon chains that link physically scattered records. There may be thousands of these chains.
2. Customer invoice files, vendor invoice files, employee pay files, and general ledger transaction files are examples of linked files.
3. Linked file records are written one after the other as they occur, so the transactions for any one company/person/object can be sacttered all over a linked file. The chain connects the transactions belonging to a particular company/person/object.
4. Backward linking begins with most current and reads until the least current transaction is read. This is the most common form of linking.
5. Forward linking begins with the oldest and reads through the chain to the lastest transaction.
6. Backward and forward linking allows reading in either direction at any time.
7. All records in a linked file have a link back to the master record on the company/person/object file.
8. Documents can have start-of-document and end-of-document links as well as forward, backward, and links to the master file.
9. The LastUsed record number is needed to process a linked file.
10. The Master link is the first link in each chain. It is located in the Master (company/person/object) file.
11. Adding records to a linked file involves:
    - Updating the LastUsed
    - Updating the link(s) in the linked file
    - Writing the linked record
    - Updating the Master Link

The Book in Review

1. Design and program thoughtfully.
2. To examine any QBasic program, break it up into blocks. Then study each block separately, and finally look at the logic that controls all the blocks.
3. QBasic gives you a complete working environment, which encourages writing programs in building-block fashion.
4. Blueprint your program *before* you write the first line of code.
5. Data names should be meaningful, short (but not cryptic), consistent and clear.
6. The QBasic Editor is top shelf. Use the keys, rather than the menus, and you will be productive.
7. Program organization is crucial. Blueprint, assign the tasks to routines, then program each routine.
8. GOSUB subroutines; CALL procedures. GOTO a line name that is within the same routine as the GOTO statement.
9. Keep your IFs simple, and easy to read.
10. Loops are critical to good programming. You can destroy their structure with the wrong GOTO. Never GOTO somewhere outside the loop.
11. Group like items together, describe them, and you have the start of a file.
12. Learn random files well; they are the foundation of all file work.
13. **The linked list structure is for transaction-type files.**

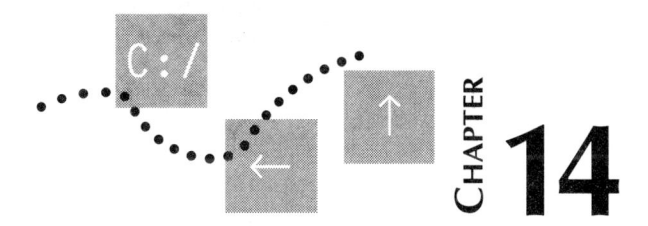

Keyboard Input

This chapter teaches you about the importance of editing incoming data to your programs. You learn how crucial it is to enter information correctly to receive the best results from your program. The topics include:

- Editing—it is critical
- Editing levels
- Error messages
- Screen neatness

Fast or Correct?

Pat offered to help Chris with the mailing list. They bought a list of 20,000 names from *River Rafter*, the rafting magazine. Chris needs to get the names into the computer as quickly as possible, so that the announcements for the spring flood raft trips can get out. So they hired the world's fastest keypuncher, Keyin' Kelly, to do the job. Kelly accomplished the task in just two days. Pat and Chris were thrilled.

One week later the announcements started coming back—"Return to Sender, No such address." Over 4,000 of them. They wasted over $1,600 in printing and mail costs.

After a quick study, they found that the addresses were typed wrong. They should have hired accurate Alex, who would have taken about a week, and done the job right.

Garbage in, garbage out. The most critical (and most overlooked) detail in computer processing is validation (editing) of data. Processing of bad data is more than a waste of time, it is the worst thing you can do. You can cause a bad sales projection, a failure to balance, and an accounting disaster. This chapter helps you prevent these problems.

Editing — It is Critical

In management school, you are taught to *nip the problem in the bud*. This means that you catch a problem before it becomes a catastrophe, requiring emergency measures.

In programming, you nip the problem in the bud by thoroughly testing every bit of data *before* it is accepted by a program, *before* it is written onto a file. You edit each entry for length, type, ranges and perhaps specific values.

If you do not do this with *every piece of data* coming in from the keyboard, and for *every file* that your programs did not create, you stand a chance of the program *blowing up* (stopping dead with no chance of continuing). This can put you in the situation where you have processed and written two-thirds of the records, and left one-third unprocessed—a real mess.

Programs blow up when:

- The program tries to divide by zero (remember elementary algebra?).
- It tries to read a record number of zero.
- It tries to read a negative record number.
- It tries to read a gigantic record number.

These are not the only reasons, but you can understand the idea.

Editing Levels

There are four levels of editing discussed in this book:

- Length
- Type
- Ranges
- Specific values

Length

Test the data item (variable name) for the maximum and minimum number of characters permitted for that field. If the length is greater than allowed, reject the data item. If the length is fewer than allowed, reject it.

Type

There are two types to consider:

1. *Numeric.* Test each character in the field to be a number between 0 and 9. If it is not, reject it.
2. *Date.* Ensure that the month has a value between 1 and 12, and that the number of days has a value between 1 and the maximum number of days allowable in that month. If it is not, reject the date.

Ranges

Test the data item for a maximum and minimum value, if applicable. If your customer numbers are 1 through 6000, for example, test for that range before accepting a customer number. If the customer types are 1 through 5, test the field for that range. Test everything that you can for proper ranges before accepting the data.

Specific Values

Test for one of a series of specific values for a field (variable name) before accepting an item. If the only acceptable categories of paddles are G (for guide) and P (for people), then reject anything else.

Editing Examples

The editing program statements are shown first, the explanation of the program follows it.

The LINE INPUT statement gets all the input. The syntax is:

```
LINE INPUT "{some prompt}";i$
```

where

`LINE INPUT` are QBasic reserved words that get data into a program through keyboard entry.

`{some prompt}` is any appropriate prompt that tells the person typing the input what data the program expects to be entered.

`i$` is the variable name that is given the data that is typed at the keyboard.

When the computer encounters a LINE INPUT statement, it:

Prints the prompt {some prompt}

Waits for data to be keyed in

When **Enter** is pressed, it continues with the next program statement.

> **NOTE** Work each of the next examples, one at a time. Read the first example, and try to guess at every statement's purpose. Then, get into QBasic, type in the first example, run the routine, and test it by typing valid data, then invalid data. Repeat the process for each example.

Before You Start — Some Review of QBasic

After typing the statements, run the program:

Press **F5**.

When you have finished with one example, and you are ready to type the next program statements, make sure that you save the previous example by performing these steps:

Press **Alt+F**.

Press **S**, then **Enter**.

When you are prompted for a name by QBasic, enter **EX** followed by the example number (no spaces), then,

Press **Enter**.

The example is then saved on disk with that name. Save the first seven examples as EX1, EX2, EX3 through EX7. Later in this chapter, you retrieve and improve them.

Ready? Here's the first set of statements.

Length Test Examples

LEN is a QBasic function that finds the length of an alphanumeric (string) variable. The next chapter explains it in detail.

Example 1

Save this as *EX1* when you are done.

```
getin:LINE INPUT "enter customer name";i$
    IF LEN(i$)>30 THEN GOTO getin
    IF LEN(i$)<2 THEN GOTO getin
    PRINT "OK"
```

Example 2

Save this as *EX2* when you are done

```
getin:LINE INPUT "enter customer state (2 characters)";i$
    IF LEN(i$)>2 THEN GOTO getin
```

```
    IF LEN(i$)<2 THEN GOTO getin
    PRINT "OK"
```

Example 3

Save this as *EX3* when you are done.

```
    getin:LINE INPUT "enter customer phone number";i$
        IF LEN(i$)>10 THEN GOTO getin
        IF LEN(i$)<5 THEN GOTO getin
        PRINT "OK"
```

The first example tested the length of *i$* (the customer name, in this instance) to be less than 2 or greater than 30. If either condition is true, the program goes back and asks for the name again.

The second example tested for the length of *i$* (the state) to be less than 2 or greater than 2. (All states are two characters.) If either condition is true, the program again asks for the state.

In the third example, you checked for a length less than 5 (a small phone number) or greater than 10. If either condition is found, the program again asks for the phone number.

Note that in each case, the LEN function detects the length of the input variable, *i$*. The LEN function finds the length of the variable inside the parentheses, and returns the number for the programmer's use.

Example 4: Type Test Example (Numeric Test)

Save this as *EX4* when you are done.

```
    getin:LINE INPUT "enter customer phone number";i$
       i1%=LEN(i$):REM — get the length of i$
       IF i1%>10 THEN GOTO getin
       IF i1%<5 THEN GOTO getin
       numtest%=0:REM — set a test flag to 0
       FOR i%=1 TO i1%:REM — set up a loop to check for numeric
       IF ASC(MID$(i$,i%,1))<48 THEN numtest%=1:REM — test for <0
```

```
        IF ASC(MID$(i$,i%,1))>57 THEN numtest%=1:REM - test for >9
        NEXT i%
        IF numtest%>0 THEN GOTO getin: REM—if any of the
                                       REM - characters were less
                                       REM - than 0 or greater_
than
                                       REM - 9, then go back to
                                       REM - getin
        PRINT "OK"
        REM - rest of program
```

In this numeric test example, the data is checked for acceptable length. If the length is wrong, there is no sense in checking further; it has to be re-entered.

The program then flows through a loop that selects each character of the item, and confirms it to be a number between 0 and 9. If the character is not a number, *numtest*% is set to 1.

After the loop is complete, test *numtest*% for a value >0. If it were greater than 0, it means that at least one non-numeric character is found. The program rejects the data and goes back to *getin* to ask for a valid numeric input.

Note that there are ASC and MID$ functions in the numeric test. ASC converts a character to its ASCII value (0 has an ASCII value of 48, 1 has a value of 49, and so on). MID$ selects a particular character within a string. (Look at each character, beginning with the leftmost one.) ASC and MID$ are explained in the next chapter. Please go over this example for general understanding; the detail comes later.

Example 5: Type Test Example (Date Test)

Save this as *EX5* when you are done.

```
getin:LINE INPUT "enter customer since date";i$
    i1%=LEN(i$):REM - get the length of i$
    IF i1%>6 THEN GOTO getin
    IF i1%<5 THEN GOTO getin
    numtest%=0:REM - set a test flag to 0
    FOR i%=1 TO i1%:REM - set up a loop to check for numeric
    IF ASC(MID$(i$,i%,1))<48 THEN numtest%=1:REM—test for <0
```

```
    IF ASC(MID$(i$,i%,1))>57 THEN numtest%=1:REM—test for >9
    NEXT i%
    IF numtest%>0 THEN GOTO getin: REM — if any of the
                                   REM — characters were less
                                   REM — than 0 or greater
                                   REM — than 9, then go back
                                   REM — to getin.
    IF i1%=5 THEN i$="0"+i$: REM — make it a six character
                             REM — field
    w1%=VAL(LEFT$(i$,2)):REM — get the value of the month
    IF w1%<1 THEN GOTO getin:REM — if month <1, goto getin
    IF w1%>12 THEN GOTO getin:REM — if month >12,goto getin
    w2%=VAL(MID$(i$,3,2)):REM — get the value of the day
    IF w2%<1 THEN GOTO getin:REM — if day <1, goto getin
    IF w2%>31 THEN GOTO getin:REM — if day >31, goto getin
    w3%=VAL(RIGHT$(i$,2)):REM — get the value of the year
    IF w3%>94 THEN GOTO getin:REM — if year >94, goto getin
    PRINT"OK"
    REM — rest of program
```

The date test example tests for a five- or six-character date with no slashes or dashes between month, day and year. The format that this routine expects is MMDDYY, where:

MM is a one or two character number (1-12) signifying month
DD is the two character number (01-31) of the day
YY is the two character number of the year

The program first tests for a valid length. If the length is wrong, the date is invalid, and must be re-entered. The next test is for numeric validity. If the entry is not numeric, it is wrong; it could not pass further testing, and has to be typed again. Then, the actual date testing begins. The month is isolated and tested for a value between 1 and 12. If this test fails, testing stops; the date is invalid and must be retyped. If the month test is passed, the day is separated, then tested for a value between 1 and 31, inclusive. If this test fails, the program goes back to request valid input. If the entry passes the day test, the computer gets the year, and tests for a value greater than 94. If greater, the routine rejects the date, and again asks for a valid date. If the year is 94 or less, the date is judged valid, and the program continues.

Example 6: Range Test Example

Save this as *EX6* when you are done.

```
getin:LINE INPUT "enter customer type";i$
  IF LEN(i$)>1 THEN GOTO getin:REM — if length >1, goto getin
  IF LEN(i$)<1 THEN GOTO getin:REM — if length <1, goto getin
  IF i$<"A" THEN GOTO getin:REM — if type < "A", goto getin
  IF i$>"C" THEN GOTO getin:REM — if type > "C", goto getin
  PRINT "OK"
  REM — continue with program
```

The range test example checks for length; if it's too long or too short, further testing is a waste. If the length is OK, it then checks for a value, "A" through "C" (A, B, or C would be acceptable). If the entry is less than A (not a letter) or more than C (any letter beyond C in the alphabet), it is rejected.

Example 7: Specific Value Test

Save this as *EX7* when you are done.

```
getin:LINE INPUT "enter customer type";i$
  IF LEN(i$)>1 THEN GOTO getin:REM — if length >1, goto getin
  IF LEN(i$)<1 THEN GOTO getin:REM — if length <1, goto getin
  IF i$="A" THEN GOTO goodtype:REM — if type = "A", leave_
test
  IF i$="C" THEN GOTO goodtype:REM — if type = "C", leave_
test
    GOTO getin:REM—go back and get a valid customer type
goodtype:
  PRINT "OK"
  REM — continue with program
```

The example test for specific values begins with the usual length test. If that test is passed, the data is then examined for the value, A. If that value is found, the entry is considered valid, and the routine exits. If not, the routine next looks for the value of C. If found, it exits. If not, the program goes back to get valid input. The program accepts A or C, but not B.

Error Messages

In the previous examples, when the program detected an error in a typed data item, it asked for the input data again. When you program in the business world, you should tell the key operators that an error is found, and what that error is. (So they do not repeat the type-in mistake.)

Since the operator may not be looking at the computer screen while typing, **RING THE BELL**. Type this into your computer and run it:

```
PRINT CHR$(7)
```

Then, try this:

```
FOR i%=1 TO 5
PRINT CHR$(7)
NEXT i%
```

The "bell" rings for a lot longer because you rang it five times. Do not use five rings for an error because one or two rings should make anyone notice an error.

Now that you have alerted the operator of an error, you should tell him or her the source of that error. Based on the tests above, you have six possible error messages. An example for each is:

- "Too long"
- "Too short"
- "Not numeric"
- "Bad date"
- "Out of range"
- "Not one of the acceptable values"

Following the examples below, add these messages to the same tests, and try each separately in QBasic on your machine. Type both valid and invalid data to test the error checking and messages.

Length Examples with Error Messages

Example 8 (First, retrieve *EX1*.)

    Press **Alt+F**.
    Press **O**, then **Enter**.
    Type **EX1**.
    Press **Enter**.

    Change the statements to look like this:

```
getin:LINE INPUT "enter customer name";i$
    IF LEN(i$)>30 THEN
        PRINT CHR$(7);"Too long"
        GOTO getin
    END IF
    IF LEN(i$)<2 THEN
        PRINT CHR$(7);"Too short"
        GOTO getin
    END IF
    PRINT "OK"
```

Run the test, then save it as *EX8*.

Example 9

First, retrieve *EX2*, then change it to look like this:

```
getin:LINE INPUT "enter customer state (2 characters)";i$
    IF LEN(i$)>2 THEN
        PRINT CHR$(7);"Too long"
        GOTO getin
    END IF
```

```
        IF LEN(i$)<2 THEN
                PRINT CHR$(7);"Too short"
                GOTO getin
        END IF
        PRINT "OK"
```

Run the test, then save it as *EX9*.

Example 10

First, retrieve *EX3*, then change it to look like this:

```
    getin:LINE INPUT "enter customer phone number";i$
        IF LEN(i$)>10 THEN
                PRINT CHR$(7);"Too long"
                GOTO getin
        END IF
        IF LEN (i$)<5 THEN
                PRINT CHR$(7);"Too short"
                GOTO getin
        END IF
        PRINT "OK"
```

Run the test, then save it as *EX10*.

Notice the special setup of the block IF statement. The IF condition is on one line with the corresponding THEN, followed by two indented statements, each on a separate line, and ends with END IF. If the condition is true, all statements up to the END IF are active.

Example 11: Type Example (Numeric Test) with Error Messages

Get *EX4* and make these changes:

```
    getin:LINE INPUT "enter customer phone number";i$
        i1%=LEN(i$):REM - get the length of i$
```

```
    IF i1%>10 THEN
        PRINT CHR$(7);"Too long"
        GOTO getin
    END IF
    IF i1%<5 THEN
        PRINT CHR$(7);"Too short"
        GOTO getin
    END IF
    numtest%=0:REM — set a test flag to 0
    FOR i%=1 TO i1%:REM — set up a loop to check for numeric
        IF ASC(MID$(i$,i%,1))<48 THEN numtest%=1:REM_
test for <0
        IF ASC(MID$(i$,i%,1))>57 THEN numtest%=1:REM_
test for >9
    NEXT i%
    IF numtest%>0 THEN
        PRINT CHR$(7);"Not numeric"
        GOTO getin
    END IF
    PRINT "OK"
```

Run the test, then save it as *EX11*.

Example 12: Type Example (Date Test) with Error Messages

Get *EX5* and make the following changes:

```
getin:LINE INPUT "enter customer since date";i$
    i1%=LEN(i$):REM — get the length of i$
    IF i1%>6 THEN
        PRINT CHR$(7);"Too long"
        GOTO getin
    END IF
```

```
    IF i1%<5 THEN
            PRINT CHR$(7);"Too short"
            GOTO getin
    END IF
    numtest%=0:REM — set a test flag to 0
    FOR i%=1 TO i1%:REM — set up a loop to check for numeric
            IF ASC(MID$(i$,i%,1))<48 THEN numtest%=1:REM_
test for <0
            IF ASC(MID$(i$,i%,1))>57 THEN numtest%=1:REM_
test for >9
    NEXT i%
    IF numtest%>0 THEN
            PRINT CHR$(7);"Not numeric"
            GOTO getin
    END IF
    IF i1%=5 THEN i$="0"+i$:REM — make it a six character_
field
    w1%=VAL(LEFT$(i$,2)):REM — get the month
    IF w1%<1 THEN
            PRINT CHR$(7);"Bad date"
            GOTO getin
    END IF
    IF w1%>12 THEN
            PRINT CHR$(7);"Bad date"
            GOTO getin
    END IF
    w2%=VAL(MID$(i$,3,2)):REM — get the day
    IF w2%<1 THEN
            PRINT CHR$(7);"Bad date"
            GOTO getin
    END IF
```

```
IF w2%>31 THEN
        PRINT CHR$(7);"Bad date"
        GOTO getin
    END IF
    w3%=VAL(RIGHT$(i$,2)):REM - get the year
    IF w3%>94 THEN
        PRINT CHR$(7);"Bad date"
        GOTO getin
    END IF
    PRINT "OK"
```

Run the test, then save it as *EX12*.

Example 13: Range Test Example

Open *EX6* and change it like this:

```
getin:LINE INPUT "enter customer type";i$
    IF LEN(i$)>1 THEN
        PRINT CHR$(7);"Too long"
        GOTO getin
    END IF
    IF LEN(i$)<1 THEN
        PRINT CHR$(7);"Too short"
        GOTO getin
    END IF
    IF i$<"A" THEN
        PRINT CHR$(7);"Out of range"
        GOTO getin
    END IF
    IF i$>"C" THEN
        PRINT CHR$(7);"Out of range"
        GOTO getin
```

```
        END IF
        PRINT "OK"
```

Run the test, then save it as *EX13*.

Example 14: Specific Values Test Example with Error Messages

Read in *EX7* and change it like this:

```
getin:LINE INPUT "enter customer type";i$
    IF LEN(i$)>1 THEN
            PRINT CHR$(7);"Too long"
            GOTO getin
    END IF
    IF LEN(i$)<1 THEN
            PRINT CHR$(7);"Too short"
            GOTO getin
    END IF
    IF i$="A" THEN GOTO goodtype:REM — if type = "A", leave_
test
    IF i$="C" THEN GOTO goodtype:REM — if type = "C", leave_
test
            PRINT CHR$(7);"Not 1 of the acceptable entries"
            GOTO getin
goodtype:
    PRINT "OK"
    REM — continue with program
```

Run the test, then save it as *EX14*.

You probably now have an appreciation for good editing.

Screen Neatness

The above routines are usable, but each time an entry is invalid, two more lines are printed on the screen. Just a few mistakes would cause the screen to fill, and scroll upward with each new line printed. Once the screen is filled, each time a line is printed to the bottom of the screen, the screen moves everything up one line, and the top line is lost. Screen layout is reserved for Chapter 16, but this section shows you how to go back to a specific location on the screen. This avoids a screen cluttered with old error messages and bad data that now are meaningless and confusing. When you find an error, you can go back to the screen location of the original data entry, and not have to scroll several lines upwards. Your screen shows only valid data instead of a muddle of bad data, good data, and error messages.

> **NOTE:** In this section, the *cursor* is the blinking underline (or blinking block, solid block, or solid underline) that shows you the current location on the screen.

In the examples below are three new QBasic commands. In brief, this is what they do:

- **POS**—gets the column position of the cursor.
- **CSRLIN**—gets the line position of the cursor.
- **LOCATE**—places the cursor in a specific spot on the screen.

Use the POS and CSRLIN to identify the point to return to in case of an error. If an error occurs, LOCATE the cursor back on that spot. The new data can then be keyed in on top of the old, invalid data.

The details of LOC, CSRLIN and POS are in Chapter 17. Follow the logic and the REM statements, and you will understand how it works.

Length Example with Error Messages and No Scrolling

Retrieve *EX8* and change it to look like the program below, then save this as *EX15*. Run it and see how it works.

```
    x%=POS(0):REM — get and save current column position
    y%=CSRLIN:REM — get and save current line
getin:LINE INPUT "enter customer name";i$
   IF LEN(i$)>30 THEN
        PRINT CHR$(7);"Too long";TAB(79);""
        LOCATE y%,x%:REM — go to original line & col
        GOTO getin
   END IF
   IF LEN(i$)<2 THEN
        PRINT CHR$(7);"Too short";TAB(79);""
        LOCATE y%,x%:REM — go to original line & col
        GOTO getin
   END IF
        PRINT TAB(79);"": REM — clear any previous error message_
by
                        REM — printing a blank line
    PRINT "OK"
```

Remember to save the program as *EX15*.

Type Example: (Numeric Test) with Error Messages and No Scrolling

Open *EX11*, make the changes, save it, and test it.

```
    x%=POS(0):REM — get and save current column position
    y%=CSRLIN:REM — get and save current line
getin:LINE INPUT "enter customer phone number";i$
    i1%=LEN(i$):REM — get the length of i$
```

```
IF i1%>10 THEN
    PRINT CHR$(7);"Too long";TAB(79);""
    LOCATE y%,x%:REM — goto original line & col
    GOTO getin
END IF
IF i1%<5 THEN
    PRINT CHR$(7);"Too short";TAB(79);""
    LOCATE y%,x%:REM — goto original line & col
    GOTO getin
END IF
numtest%=0:REM — set a test flag to 0
FOR i%=1 TO i1%:REM — set up a loop to check for numeric
IF ASC(MID$(i$,i%,1))<48 THEN numtest%=1:REM — test <0
IF ASC(MID$(i$,i%,1))>57 THEN numtest%=1:REM — test >9
NEXT i%
IF numtest%>0 THEN
    PRINT CHR$(7);PRINT"Not numeric";TAB(79);""
    locate y%,x%:REM — goto original line & col
    GOTO getin
END IF
PRINT TAB(79);"": REM — clear any previous error messages
                 REM — by printing a blank line
PRINT "OK"
```

Save the program as *EX16*.

Summary

1. No editing = bad results.
2. Your editing includes maximum and minimum lengths, numeric and date validation, range testing, and specific value confirmation.
3. Use short, clear error messages.

4. Keep the screen clear of unnecessary data and messages.

The Book in Review

1. Design and program thoughtfully.
2. To examine any QBasic program, break it up into blocks. Then study each block separately, and finally look at the logic that controls all the blocks.
3. QBasic gives you a complete working environment, which encourages writing programs in building-block fashion.
4. Blueprint your program before you write the first line of code.
5. Data names should be meaningful, short (but not cryptic), consistent and clear.
6. The QBasic Editor is top shelf. Use the keys, rather than the menus, and you will be productive.
7. Program organization is crucial. Blueprint, assign the tasks to routines, then program each routine.
8. GOSUB subroutines; CALL procedures. GOTO a line name that is within the same routine as the GOTO statement.
9. Keep your IFs simple, and easy to read.
10. Loops are critical to good programming. You can destroy their structure with the wrong GOTO. Never GOTO somewhere outside the loop.
11. Group like items together, describe them, and you have the start of a file.
12. Learn random files well; they are the foundation of all file work.
13. The linked list structure is for transaction-type files.
14. **Edit new data thoroughly or your program *dies*.**

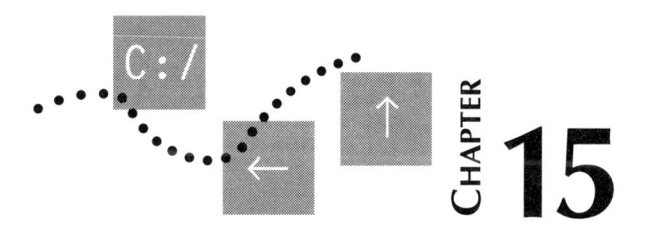

Reusing Edit Procedures

This chapter teaches you about the importance of forming and using standard edit procedures. You see examples that show you how to build these edit procedures. The topics include:

- Reusable edit procedures
- LINE INPUT statement
- LEN function
- String processing functions

No Two Alike

Picture a truly custom raft building firm. The employees consider themselves *artists*, building everything from scratch. They never use the same pattern twice because they are always improving things. They even make the air valves, ropes, and D-rings themselves. Their name is *Lightning Raft Builders*. True to their name, they never do produce the same raft twice.

Seem ridiculous? Sure, but that is what a lot of programmers do. They write each program from scratch, rather than building *patterns* and *molds* to reuse over and over. In this chapter, you are going to write procedures that you can reuse in your programs.

Reusable Edit Procedures

It may seem like editing is getting to be a pain, and a lot of work. You might as well get used to it. Thorough editing is a vital function of programming. But there are ways to reduce the tedium of writing edit code. You probably noticed a lot of repetition in the coding of these edits. To avoid this, you can use a procedure that is called repeatedly instead of retyping the same code for every edit.

Set up three procedures:

1. An error routine to ring the bell, print the error message, and locate the cursor at the original entry.
2. A numeric testing routine that checks each character to be between 0 and 9.
3. A date testing routine that checks for a valid month, day, and year.

These are simple, usable routines. Appendix E has more thorough editing routines for your use in future programming work. (Do not look ahead until you are done with this chapter.)

The Error Routine (It's a Procedure)

```
SUB printerr (e$,r%,c%): REM - e$ is the error message,
```

```
REM — r% is the line number,
REM — and c% is the column number,
REM — at which to locate.
   PRINT CHR$(7);e$;TAB(79);"":REM — ring the bell &
   REM — print error message.
LOCATE r%,c%:REM — set the cursor at the original location
END SUB
```

The error procedure has three arguments passed to it by the main program:

- *e$* is the error message which is displayed on the screen.
- *r%* is the line (row) on the screen where the cursor is placed to ask for input.
- *c%* is the column position on the screen where the cursor is placed to ask for input.

The error procedure gets the arguments, rings the bell, prints the error message, places the cursor at the designated location, then returns.

The Numeric Testing Routine (It's Also a Procedure)

```
SUB numtest (n$,lgth%,e%):REM — n$ is the data, lgth% is the
       REM — length of the data item, and
       REM — e% is an error flag (0=no
REM — error,1=error)
    e%=0:REM — set the error flag to 0 (no error)
    FOR i%=1 TO lgth%:REM — set up a loop to check for_
numeric
       IF ASC(MID$(n$,i%,1))<48 THEN e%=1:REM—test for <0
       IF ASC(MID$(n$,i%,1))>57 THEN e%=1:REM—test for >9
    NEXT i%
END SUB
```

The numeric test procedure has three arguments:

- *n$* is the data item exactly as it was input in the main program.

- *lgth%* is the length of the item, as determined in the main program.
- *e%* is the error flag that is returned to the main program. If a non-numeric character is found, e% has a value of 1. If the numeric test is passed, e% has a value of 0.

The numeric test routine gets the arguments, then uses a loop to check each character in the data item. If the character is found to be less than 0 or greater than 9, the error flag, e%, is set to 1. When the loop is done, the procedure exits.

The Date Testing Routine (Also a Procedure)

The following program code shows a date testing routine:

```
SUB datest (dat$,lgth%,e%): REM - dat$ is the date, lgth% is_
the
                            REM - length of the date, and
                            REM - e% is an error flag
                            REM - (0=no error, 1=error)
   e%=1: REM - set error flag to 1 (assuming that until the
         REM - date passes all the tests, that an error has_
been
         REM - found).
   IF lgth%<5 THEN GOTO quitdate: REM-if the length <5 then
                                  REM - leave the procedure_
with
                                  REM - the error flag e% set
                                  REM - to an error
   IF lgth%=5 THEN dat$="0"+dat$: REM - make it a six_
character
                                  REM - field
   w1%=VAL(LEFT$(dat$,2)):REM - get the month
   IF w1%<1 THEN   GOTO quitdate
   IF w1%>12 THEN   GOTO quitdate
   w2%=VAL(MID$(dat$,3,2)):REM - get the day
```

```
    IF w2%<1 THEN  GOTO quitdate
    IF w2%>31 THEN  GOTO quitdate
    w3%=VAL(RIGHT$(dat$,2)):REM — get the year
    IF w3%>94 THEN  GOTO quitdate
    e%=0:REM — reset error flag to 0 (no errors found)
quitdate:REM — just a label to go to
END SUB
```

The date test procedure gets three arguments:

- *dat$* is the date, passed from the main program.
- *lgth%* is length of the date, as found in the main program.
- *e%* is the error flag that is returned to the main program. If e% is zero, then no errors are found. If the date is incorrect, then e% is set to one.

When the *datest* procedure begins, it sets the error flag, e% to 1. This is based on the logic that if any errors are found, the procedure will immediately exit. (If all tests are passed, the flag is reset to 0 before exiting.)

Now *datest* checks the length for fewer than five characters. If this is true, the procedure exits. If not, the month is checked to be between 1 and 12; the day is examined for values between 1 and 31; and the year is tested for a value of 94 or less. If the item fails any of these tests, the procedure quickly exits with the error flag (e%) set to 1, showing an error. If the item passes every test, the procedure resets the error flag to 0, then flows back to the main program.

Try it. Get into QBasic. Type in each of the three routines above, and save them under their procedure names.

Retrieve the saved procedures, type in the additional code to complete each example below, then run and test each in QBasic. With this new set of routines, you minimize coding and standardize your editing.

Length Test with Editing Routines

This program code shows a length test with editing routines:

```
        y%=CSRLIN
        x%=POS(0)
```

```
getin:LINE INPUT"enter customer name";i$
   IF LEN(i$)>30 THEN
           CALL printerr("Too long",y%,x%)
           GOTO GETIN
   END IF
   IF LEN(i$)<2 THEN
           CALL printerr("Too short",y%,x%)
           GOTO GETIN
   END IF
   PRINT TAB (79);""
END : REM — end the program
SUB printerr (e$,r%,c%): REM — e$ is the error message
                        REM — r% is the line number, and
                        REM — c% is the column number
                        REM — at which to locate.
   PRINT CHR$(7);e$;TAB(79);"":REM — ring the bell &
   REM — print error message
   LOCATE r%,c%:REM — set the cursor at the original location
END SUB
```

Numeric Test with Editing Routines

```
      y%=CSRLIN
      x%=POS(0)
getin:LINE INPUT"enter customer phone number";i$
      i1%=LEN(i$)
   IF i1%>10 THEN
           CALL printerr("Too long",y%,x%)
           GOTO getin
   END IF
```

```
        IF i1%<5 THEN
                CALL printerr("Too short",y%,x%)
                GOTO getin
        END IF
        CALL numtest(i$,i1%,er%)
        IF er%>0 THEN
                CALL printerr("Not numeric",y%,x%)
                GOTO getin
        END IF
        PRINT TAB (79);""
END : REM end the program
SUB numtest (n$,lgth%,e%):REM — n$ is the data, lgth% is the
                          REM — length of the data item, and
                          REM — e% is an error flag (0=no
                          REM — error, 1=error)
        e%=0:REM — set the error flag to 0 (no error)
        FOR i%=1 TO lgth%:REM — set up a loop to check for_
numeric
                IF ASC(MID$(n$,i%,1))<48 THEN e%=1:REM—test for <0
                IF ASC(MID$(n$,i%,1))>57 THEN e%=1:REM—test for >9
        NEXT i%
END SUB
SUB printerr (e$,r%,c%):REM — e$ is the error message
                        REM — r% is the line number, and
                        REM — c% is the column number
                        REM — at which to locate.
PRINT CHR$(7);e$;TAB(79);"": REM — ring the bell &
                             REM — print error message
LOCATE r%,c%:REM — set the cursor at the original location
END SUB
```

Date Test with Editing Routines

The following program code shows a date test with editing routines:

```
        y%=CSRLIN
        x%=POS(0)
  getin:LINE INPUT"enter customer since date";i$
        i1%=LEN(i$)
        IF i1%>6  THEN
                CALL printerr("Too long",y%,x%)
                GOTO getin
        END IF
        IF i1%<5 THEN
                CALL printerr("Too short",y%,x%)
                GOTO getin
        END IF
        CALL numtest(i$,i1%,er%)
        IF er%>0 THEN
                CALL printerr("Not numeric",y%,x%)
                GOTO getin
        END IF
        CALL datest(i$,i1%,er%)
        IF er%>0 THEN
                CALL printerr("Bad date",y%,x%)
                GOTO getin
        END IF
        PRINT TAB (79);""
  END : REM end the program
  SUB numtest (n$,lgth%,e%):REM-n$ is the data, lgth% is the
                           REM - length of the data item, and
                           REM - e% is an error flag (0=no
```

CHAPTER FIFTEEN: REUSING EDIT PROCEDURES • 275

```
                        REM — error,1=error)
    e%=0:REM — set the error flag to 0 (no error)
    FOR i%=1 TO lgth%:REM — set up a loop to check for_
numeric
            IF ASC(MID$(n$,i%,1))<48 THEN e%=1:REM—test for <0
            IF ASC(MID$(n$,i%,1))>57 THEN e%=1:REM—test for >9
    NEXT i%
END SUB
SUB datest (dat$,lgth%,e%):REM — dat$ is the date, lgth% is
                        REM — the length of the date, and
                        REM — e% is an error flag
                        REM — (0=no error, 1=error)
    e%=1:REM - set error flag to 1 (we're assuming that_
until the
    REM — date passes all the tests, that an error has
    REM — been found).
    IF lgth%<5 THEN GOTO quitdate:REM — if the length <5_
then
                            REM — leave the procedure
                            REM — with the error flag_
e%
                            REM — set to an error
    IF lgth%=5 THEN dat$="0"+dat$: REM — make it a six_
character
                            REM — field
    w1%=VAL(LEFT$(dat$,2)):REM — get the month
    IF w1%<1 THEN  GOTO quitdate
    IF w1%>12 THEN  GOTO quitdate
    w2%=VAL(MID$(dat$,3,2)):REM — get the day
    IF w2%<1 THEN  GOTO quitdate
    IF w2%>31 THEN  GOTO quitdate
```

```
        w3%=VAL(RIGHT$(dat$,2)):REM — get the year
        IF w3%>94 THEN  GOTO quitdate
        e%=0:REM — reset error flag to 0 (no errors found)
quitdate:REM — just a label to go to
END SUB
SUB printerr (e$,r%,c%): REM — e$ is the error message
                        REM — r% is the line number, and
                        REM — c% is the column number
                        REM — at which to locate.
        PRINT CHR$(7);e$;TAB(79);"":  REM — ring the bell &
                                      REM — print error message
        LOCATE r%,c%:REM — set the cursor at the original_
location
END SUB
```

Now combine the three routines, and all of the data for a customer, even with a few typing mistakes, fits onto one input screen.

Next comes the routine that gets all the data for a new customer and writes it to the customer record on a disk file.

After analyzing the subroutine below, call up your three edit procedures, type the rest of the example into your computer and test it. First, be sure to clear your previous routines:

Press **Alt+F**.

Press **N**, then press **Enter**.

New Customer Routine

The following program code shows a new customer routine:

```
        GOSUB getnewcust
END
getnewcust
    y%=CSRLIN
```

```
        x%=POS(0)
getin1:LINE INPUT"enter customer last name";i$
    IF LEN(i$)>15 THEN
            CALL printerr("Too long",y%,x%)
            GOTO getin1
    END IF
    IF LEN(i$)<2 THEN
            CALL printerr("Too short",y%,x%)
            GOTO getin1
    END IF
    PRINT TAB (79);""
    LSET custlname$=i$
    y%=CSRLIN
    x%=POS(0)
getin2:LINE INPUT"enter customer first name";i$
    IF LEN(i$)>12 THEN
            CALL printerr("Too long",y%,x%)
            GOTO getin2
END IF
    IF LEN(i$)<1 THEN
            CALL printerr("Too short",y%,x%)
            GOTO getin2
    END IF
    PRINT TAB (79);""
    LSET custfname$=i$
    y%=CSRLIN
    x%=POS(0)
getin3:LINE INPUT"enter 1st customer address line";i$
    IF LEN(i$)>30 THEN
```

```
                CALL printerr("Too long",y%,x%)
                GOTO getin3
        END IF
        IF LEN(i$)<1 THEN
                CALL printerr("Too short",y%,x%)
                GOTO getin3
        END IF
        PRINT TAB (79);""
        LSET custaddr1$=i$
        y%=CSRLIN
        x%=POS(0)
getin4:LINE INPUT"enter 2nd customer address line";i$
        IF LEN(i$)>30 THEN
                CALL printerr("Too long",y%,x%)
                GOTO getin4
        END IF
        IF LEN(i$)<1 THEN
                CALL printerr("Too short",y%,x%)
                GOTO getin4
        END IF
        PRINT TAB(79);""
        LSET custaddr2$=i$
        y%=CSRLIN
        x%=POS(0)
getin5:LINE INPUT"enter customer city";i$
        IF LEN(i$)>20 THEN
                CALL printerr("Too long",y%,x%)
                GOTO getin5
        END IF
        IF LENi$)<1 THEN
```

```
                CALL printerr("Too short",y%,x%)
                GOTO getin5
        END IF
        PRINT TAB (79;""
        LSET custcity$=i$
        y%=CSRLIN
        x%=POS(0)
getin6:LINE INPUT"enter customer state";i$
        IF LEN(i$)>2
                THEN CALL printerr("Too long",y%,x%)
                GOTO getin6
        END IF
        IF LEN(i$)<2 THEN
                CALL printerr("Too short",y%,x%)
                GOTO getin6
        END IF
        PRINT TAB(79);"
        LSET custstat$=i$
        y%=CSRLIN
        x%=POS(0)
getin7:LINE INPUT"enter customer zip code";i$
        i1%=LEN(i$)
        IF i1%>9 THEN
                CALL printerr("Too long",y%,x%)
                GOTO getin7
        END IF
        IF i1%<5 THEN
                CALL printerr("Too short",y%,x%)
                GOTO getin7
        END IF
```

```
        CALL numtest(i$,i1%,er%)
        IF er%>0 THEN
                CALL printerr("Not numeric",y%,x%)
                GOTO getin7
        END IF
        PRINT TAB(79);""
        LSET custzip$=MKD$(VAL(i$))
        y%=CSRLIN
        x%=POS(0)
getin8:LINE INPUT"enter customer phone number";i$
        i1%=LEN(i$)
        IF i1%>10 THEN
                CALL printerr("Too long",y%,x%)
                GOTO getin8
        END IF
        IF LEN(i$)<5 THEN
                CALL printerr("Too short",y%,x%)
                GOTO getin8
        END IF
        CALL numtest(i$,i1%,er%)
        IF er%>0 THEN
                CALL printerr("Not numeric",y%,x%)
                GOTO getin8
        END IF
        PRINT TAB(79);""
        LSET custphone$=MKD$(VAL(i$))
        y%=CSRLIN
        x%=POS(0)
getin9:LINE INPUT "enter customer type";i$
        IF LEN(i$)>1 THEN
```

```
              CALL printerr("Too long",y%,x%)
                 GOTO getin9
         END IF
         IF LEN(i$)<1 THEN
                 CALL printerr("Too short",y%,x%)
                 GOTO getin9
         END IF
                  IF i$="A" THEN GOTO goodtype: REM — if type =_
"A",
                                              REM — get out
                  IF i$="C" THEN GOTO goodtype: REM — if type =_
"C",
                                              REM — get out
         CALL printerr("Not 1 of the acceptable entries",y%,x%)
         GOTO getin9
good type: PRINT TAB(79);""
         LSET custtype$=i$
         y%=CSRLIN
         x%=POS(0)
getin10:LINE INPUT"enter customer notes";i$
         IF LEN(i$)>60 THEN
                 CALL printerr("Too long",y%,x%)
                 GOTO getin10
         END IF
         PRINT TAB(79);""
         LSET custnotes$=i$
         y%=CSRLIN
         x%=POS(0)
getin11:LINE INPUT"enter customer since date";i$
         i1%=LEN(i$)
         IF i1%>6 THEN
```

```
                CALL printerr("Too long",y%,x%)
                GOTO getin11
        END IF
        IF LEN(i$)<5 THEN
                CALL printerr("Too short",y%,x%)
                GOTO getin11
        END IF
        CALL numtest(i$,i1%,er%)
        IF er%>0 THEN
                CALL printerr("Not numeric",y%,x%)
                GOTO getin11
        END IF
        CALL datest(i$,i1%,er%)
        IF er%>0 THEN
                CALL printerr("Bad date",y%,x%)
                GOTO getin11
        END IF
        PRINT TAB(79);""
        LSET custdate$=MKS$(VAL(i$))
        PUT 1,f1:REM — write the customer record
RETURN
SUB numtest (n$,lgth%,e%):  REM — n$ is the data, lgth%
                            REM — is the length of the
                            REM — data item, and e% is
                            REM — an error flag (0=no
                            REM — error,1=error)
        e%=0:REM — set the error flag to 0 (no error)
        FOR i%=1 TO lgth%:REM — set up a loop to check for_
        REM — numeric
            IF ASC(MID$(n$,i%,1))<48 THEN e%=1:REM - test for <0
```

```
            IF ASC(MID$(n$,i%,1))>57 THEN e%=1:REM - test for >9
        NEXT i%
END SUB
SUB datest (dat$,lgth%,e%): REM — dat$ is the date,
                            REM — lgth% is the length
                            REM — of the date, and e%
                            REM — is an error flag
                            REM — (0=no error, 1=error)
        e%=1: REM — set error flag to 1 (assuming that until
              REM — the date passes all the tests, that an
              REM — error has been found).
IF lgth%<5 THEN GOTO quitdate: REM — if the length
                               REM — <5 then leave
                               REM — the procedure
                               REM — with the error
                               REM — flag e% set to
                               REM — an error
IF lgth%=5 THEN dat$="0"+dat$: REM — make it a six-
                               REM — character field
        w1%=VAL(LEFT$(dat$,2)):REM — get the month
        IF w1%<1 THEN   GOTO quitdate
        IF w1%>12 THEN  GOTO quitdate
        w2%=VAL(MID$(dat$,3,2)):REM — get the day
        IF w2%<1 THEN   GOTO quitdate
        IF w2%>31 THEN  GOTO quitdate
        w3%=VAL(RIGHT$(dat$,2)):REM — get the year
        IF w3%>94 THEN  GOTO quitdate
        e%=0:REM - reset error flag to 0 (no errors found)
quitdate:REM — just a label to go to
END SUB
```

```
              PRINT CHR$(7);e$;TAB(79);"":  REM — ring the bell &
                                            REM — print error
                                            REM — message
        LOCATE r%,c%:  REM — set the cursor at the original
                       REM — location
   END SUB
```

Run this on your computer and see how it works. Enter all combinations of data, good and bad. Your customer routine should never have problems.

Now come and explore the new statement types in this chapter.

LINE INPUT Statement

The LINE INPUT statement is the only statement that you use to get data from the keyboard. This statement allows commas, quotes, semicolons and most anything as input without blowing up. After the data is entered, the editing is up to you.

The LINE INPUT statement has this syntax:

```
LINE INPUT "{some prompt}";{some string variable}
```

where

{some prompt} is any combination of letters, numbers, and special characters (except quotation marks because the prompt must have quotes at the beginning and the end), which the programmer uses to tell the person entering data what data item to enter.

{some string variable} is the string variable name into which the input is placed. A *string* is a group of letters, numbers. other characters, or a combination of the three. A *string variable* is a variable name that contains a string.

LINE INPUT Example

This is a LINE INPUT example:

```
LINE INPUT "Please enter customer name"; i$
```

The prompt also could be a string variable, rather than a character string encased by quotes. This next example uses a string variable to produce the same results as the previous one:

```
p$="Please enter customer name"
LINE INPUT p$;i$
```

In each case, the value entered is given to the string variable i$. Here are some conventions you can use for keyboard input:

- *i$* is any input.
- *i1%* is the length of the input data.
- *w1%,w2%,w3%* are work variables, used for testing data.

Use any convention that is clear to you, but establish standard names for your keyboard input variables now. Write them down, and always use them.

LEN Function

The LEN function determines the length of a string variable. The format is:

```
{variable name 1}=LEN({variable name 2})
```

where

`{variable name 1}` is a numeric variable which is given the value of the length of the string `{variable name 2}` within the parentheses.

LEN Function Example

This is a LEN function example:

```
i1%=LEN(i$)
```

The length of the string variable, *i$*, is found and given to the integer variable *i1%*.

String Processing Functions

String processing functions are used to:

1. Convert any single string character into the ASCII (a computer language number between 0 and 255) representation of that character.
2. Convert a string into a number.
3. Isolate one or more specific characters of a string so that these characters can be tested or manipulated.
4. Combine two or more strings, or parts of strings. The string processing functions give you the power to separate and convert or combine and convert any part of any string.

ASC Function

The ASC function gets the ASCII value of the first character in a string. The ASCII value of a character is a number between 0 and 255. The character 0 has an ASCII value of 48, the character *1* has a value of 49, the character *2* has an ASCII value of 50, the character *9* has a value of 57, the character *A* has a value of 65, and so on. (Refer to your QBasic book for ASCII character codes.) In the *numtest* procedure example discussed earlier, the ASC function tests for numeric characters between 0 and 9 (between ASCII values 48 and 57). The program flows through the string i$ and checks each character to confirm that it is a valid ASCII number.

The syntax for the ASC function is:

```
{variable name 1}=ASC({string variable name 2})
```

where

{variable name 1} contains the numeric ASCII value of the first character of {string variable name 2}.

The function ASC ({string variable name 2}) is also used in a calculation, an IF statement, or a PRINT statement.

ASC Function Examples

These are examples of the ASC function:

```
w1%=ASC(i$)
```

```
IF ASC(i$)<48 THEN PRINT"error"
PRINT ASC(i$)
```

VAL Function

The VAL function converts a string variable, or part of a string variable, into a numeric variable. This is commonly used for the editing of numeric data entered as a string (probably using the LINE INPUT statement).

The syntax for the VAL function is:

```
{variable name 1}=VAL({string variable name 2})
```

where

{variable name 1} is a numeric variable which is given the numeric value of {string variable name 2}.

The function VAL ({variable name 2}) can also be used as a number in a calculation, an IF statement, or PRINT statement.

VAL Function Examples

These are some examples of the VAL function:

```
i$="46"
w1%=VAL(i$):REM — w1% now has a value of 46
IF VAL (i$)> 99 THEN PRINT"error": REM — because VAL(i$) is
                                  REM — 46, the word"error"
                                  REM — would not be printed
PRINT VAL(i$):REM — would print 46
```

MID$, LEFT$, and RIGHT$ Functions

These functions are used to select a part of a string. Use the date editing in the procedure *datest* as an example. Assume that the date string is exactly six characters long. (Remember that you make it six characters long by adding a 0 if necessary.)

- MID$ extracts the day from the date.

- LEFT$ gets the month from the date.
- RIGHT$ gets the year from the date.

The syntax for these functions is:

```
MID$({data name 1},{starting position},{number of_
positions})

LEFT$({data name 1},{number of positions})

RIGHT$({data name 1},{number of positions})
```

where

{data name 1} is a string variable.

{starting position} is the location in the string of the 1st character you are extracting.

{number of positions} is the number of characters that are pulled out.

MID$, LEFT$, and RIGHT$ examples

The examples use *dat$* as a six-character string that represents a date:

```
w2$=MID$(dat$,3,2)
```

Here *w2$* is given the value of the two-character string that begins in position 3 in the string *dat$* and continues for two characters (positions 3 and 4). *w2$* is the string representation of the day of the month, when *dat$* is a date.

```
w1$=LEFT$(dat$,2)
```

*w1$* is given the value of the two-character string that begins in position 1 (the LEFTmost position in the string dat$) and continues for two characters (positions 1 and 2). *w1$* is the string representation for the month in the date *dat$*

```
w3$=RIGHT$(i$,2)
```

w3$* is given the value of the two-character string that begins in position 6 (the RIGHTmost position in the string *dat$) and continues to the left for two characters (positions 6 and 5). *w3$* is the string representation of the year in the date dat$.

Concatenating Strings

The concatenation (joining) of strings is not a special QBasic function. It is accomplished using the plus sign (+).

The syntax for joining two strings is:

    {string 1} = {string 2} + {string 3}

where

{string 1} is the string that is formed by placing {string 3} at the very end of {string 2}.

Concatenation Examples

These are some examples of concatenation:

    a$="ABC":REM — give value to a$
    b$="DEF":REM — give value to b$
    c$=a$ + b$: REM — c$ now has the value of "ABCDEF"
    d$="XYZ":REM — give value to d$
    e$=c$ + d$: REM — e$ now has the value of "ABCDEFXYZ"
    f$=a$ + b$ + d$: REM —f$ now has the value of "ABCDEFXYZ"

Combining String Functions

The numeric routine *numtest* used this combination of functions within a loop:

    ASC(MID$(n$,i%,1))

which means that it is extracting the *i*th character from the string *n$*, then finding the ASCII value for that character. This is done in a loop, once for each character in *n$*. Each character (of the field *n$*) is converted into ASCII, then tested for a value between 0 and 9 (ASCII values 48 and 57, respectively). In the date test routine, *datest*, there is this combination of functions:

    VAL(LEFT$(dat$,2))

```
VAL(MID$(dat$,3,2))
VAL(RIGHT$(dat$,2))
```

where the program extracted the:

- first two characters of the date (the month) and made them a number
- middle two characters of the date (the day) and made them a number
- last two characters of the date (the year) and made them a number

so that you could test the month, day, and year respectively.

```
        w1%=VAL(LEFT$(dat$,2)):REM — get the month
        IF w1%<1 THEN   GOTO quitdate
        IF w1%>12 THEN  GOTO quitdate
        w2%=VAL(MID$(dat$,3,2)):REM — get the day
        IF w2%<1 THEN   GOTO quitdate
        IF w2%>31 THEN  GOTO quitdate
        w3%=VAL(RIGHT$(dat$,2)):REM — get the year
        IF w3%>94 THEN  GOTO quitdate
        e%=0:REM — reset error flag to 0 (no errors found)
quitdate:REM — just a label to go to
END SUB
```

As you can see, the string processing functions give you the power to do whatever you want with any segment of a string.

Summary

1. Develop standard editing routines with error messages. Always use them; keep improving them.
2. Keep the screen uncluttered and avoid unnecessary text.
3. Use the LINE INPUT statement for all your input.
4. The LEN function finds the length of a string.
5. The ASC function gets the ASCII value of the first character in a string.

6. The VAL function converts a string into a number.
7. The MID$, LEFT$, and RIGHT$ functions isolate some part of a string.
8. The plus sign (+) tacks one string onto the end of another.

A better numeric test allows for decimal points and minus signs, and the date test should check each month for its own maximum number of days (for example, April not more than 30, February not more than 29). The routines in Appendix E have these features.

The Book in Review

1. Design and program thoughtfully.
2. To examine any QBasic program, break it up into blocks. Then, study each block separately, and finally look at the logic that controls all the blocks.
3. QBasic gives you a complete working environment, which encourages writing programs in building-block fashion.
4. Blueprint your program before you write the first line of code.
5. Data names should be meaningful, short (but not cryptic), consistent, and clear.
6. The QBasic Editor is top shelf. Use the keys, rather than the menus, and you will be productive.
7. Program organization is crucial. Blueprint, assign the tasks to routines, then program each routine.
8. GOSUB subroutines; CALL procedures. GOTO a line name that is within the same routine as the GOTO statement.
9. Keep your IFs simple, and easy to read.
10. Loops are critical to good programming. You can destroy their structure with the wrong GOTO. Never GOTO somewhere outside the loop.
11. Group like items together, describe them, and you have the start of a file.
12. Learn random files well; they are the foundation of all file work.
13. The linked list structure is for transaction-type files.
14. Edit new data thoroughly or your program dies.
15. **Set up standard edit procedures and use them.**

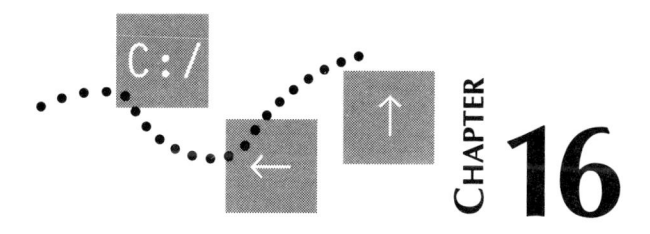

Print it Out

This chapter teaches you how to lay out information so that it is useful and meaningful when you print it. You can use examples in this chapter to build sample reports. The topics include:

- Start at the end
- The (lack of) value in printed output
- Types of page layouts
- Laying out a page
- Print formats
- FORMAT statement
- LPRINT and LPRINT USING statements
- TAB function
- CHR$ function
- Commas and semicolons
- WIDTH statement

The Unreadable Sales Report

Terry is trying to read a sales report sent by a T-shirt company from which WildWater Works buys their shirts. The report has all the sales data on every inventory item, but unfortunately, was poorly designed:

WILDWATER WORKS, INC. T-SHIRT SALES

INVENTORY NUMBER 123B DESCRIPTION PADDLE OR DIE!!

TYPE TANK COLOR BLACK RETAIL PRICE 14.99 DEALER PRICE 8.00

NUMBER BOUGHT THIS YEAR 371

JANUARY SALES 6 FEBRUARY SALES 11 MARCH SALES 119

APRIL SALES 157 MAY SALES 43 JUNE SALES 0 JULY SALES 0

AUGUST SALES 0 SEPTEMBER SALES 0 OCTOBER SALES 0

NOVEMBER SALES 0 DECEMBER SALES 0

INVENTORY NUMBER 202R DESCRIPTION I SURVIVED WILDWATER WORKS!!

TYPE SWEAT COLOR RED RETAIL PRICE 19.95 DEALER PRICE 10.00

NUMBER BOUGHT THIS YEAR 144

JANUARY SALES 0 FEBRUARY SALES 3 MARCH SALES 7

APRIL SALES 14 MAY SALES 14 JUNE SALES 0 JULY SALES 0

AUGUST SALES 0 SEPTEMBER SALES 0 OCTOBER SALES 0

NOVEMBER SALES 0 DECEMBER SALES 0

Is this report almost unreadable? Every bit of the data on every T-shirt is printed. There is so much information, that you have to look hard to figure out where each item is.

Here's a quick story about a similar report. There was an executive who insisted on a report with every bit of information on every item the company sold. The company had a lot of products, and the report was six inches thick. Each week the secretary put a new report on their desk, but they never used it! They could not figure it out—so they called people to get their numbers.

When designing a printed report, never print anything that is not essential—the simpler the better.

Start at the End

The report is the reason for the program. So the logical place to begin is with the design of the report. Once the report is fully defined, you work backwards to find the required data, and then design the program. (Refer to the section on program blueprints in Chapter 4.)

The (Lack of) Value in the Printed Output

Printed output has a value when three conditions are met:

1. The information is up to date.
2. The information is easily recognizable.
3. The report is instantly available to the people who need it.

Up-to-Date Output

Some large companies have extensive computer systems with hundreds of reports produced every week, on every facet of the company's operations. However, many of these reports have outdated information. By the time the data is entered by the Data Entry section, verified, processed, and reports printed and distributed, the information is four days old. Line managers who make decisions based on current information end up keeping their own manual updates to the information, or asking their employees for the real status. The value of the reports is more for historical purposes than for making decisions, making them worthless to line managers. Printed information must be current enough so that the people who use the report can depend on its information.

In the case of WildWater Works, Terry needs a new status report every day in order to sell T-shirts. There are a lot of phone and mail order requests, and if the report were not current, it would be worthless. Terry does not have the time to manage the office, take orders, and check the stock in the back room (they carry over 100 different shirts, caps, and river shorts).

However, Terry needs a report only once a week to review what is moving and what is not, for projecting their needs to the clothing suppliers.

Easily Recognizable Output

Look back at the supplier's report at the start of this chapter. It is hard to read, and you are only looking at two inventory items. How long would it take you to find a sales figure, when the full report crowds eight items onto every page?

A report must make the needed data leap out to the attention of the person who uses it. This means that both the purpose of each report and the data in it must be thoughtfully defined.

Terry knows that not one, but two purposes are involved in inventory reporting:

- Terry needs to know what WildWater Works has on hand with current pricing information.
- Sales history and on-hand information is needed to be able to project the silk-screening needs to WildWater Work's suppliers.

As a result, Terry designed the following two separate reports:

```
5/14/94                                                      page 3
                    WildWater Works Inventory status (daily)

         ITEM    COLOR   DESCR                DEALER  RETAIL  ONHND
  123B   SHIRT   BLACK   PADDLE OR DIE!!      8.00    14.95   35
  202R   SWEAT   RED     I SURVIVED WWW!!     10.00   19.95   106
```

and

```
5/18/94                                                     page 10
                    BIKES PEAK Inventory Movement (weekly)

  123B    SHIRT   BLACK   PADDLE OR DIE!!              our cost 8.00
          lyr   623    tyr   316   onhd 35
  Jan   Feb   Mar   Apr   May   Jun   Jul   Aug   Sep   Oct   Nov   Dec
  6     11    119   157   43    0     0     0     0     0     0     0

  202R    SWEAT   RED     I SURVIVED WWW!!!            our cost 10.00
          lyr   0      tyr   38    onhd 106
  Jan   Feb   Mar   Apr   May   Jun   Jul   Aug   Sep   Oct   Nov   Dec
  0     3     7     14    14    0     0     0     0     0     0     0
```

Note that Terry's first report is simple and gives only the numbers needed. That's important, because Terry needs quick answers in phone sales situations, and cannot waste time wading through a lot of numbers. The most important number, the on-hand quantity, is at the right margin where it can be seen instantly. Terry knows what shirts WildWater Works has too many of (probably should sell at a discount), and what items not to push to the customers (there are not any, or just a few left).

The weekly report is also more readable. Terry can easily see the inventory movement by month and look at last year's figure to project what to order over the next two months.

Terry has designed each report for ease of recognition, therefore, the job can be done quicker and better. This is even more important when Chris and Pat cover for Terry. Since they are not as familiar with the inventory as Terry is, the ease of report use is critical.

When each person has a different job, the minimum of information well presented is the most valuable.

Instantly Available Output

When you are in the field, in the warehouse, or on the production floor, the report on your desk is worthless. Terry often answers on the portable phone while helping blow up rafts for the next trip. There is always a current daily report in the pouch on Terry's belt. That's another reason the report has the minimum of data; it's got to be small enough to fit in that pouch. Since each page has a date and a page number, Terry never has missing or wrong information.

Types of Page Layouts

These are the two basic types of page layouts:

- Columnar
- Labeled data

Columnar Layout

Columnar layout is used in Terry's daily report. Each line has a different inventory item, and the data is lined up in columns for quick reading. Every page has headers, or titles to identify each piece of data.

This is the easiest report to lay out because it is so readable. Use it whenever you can fit all the data for one item on a single line.

Labeled Data

Labeled data is used for Terry's second (weekly) report. There are four lines of movement information on each inventory number because the data for each inventory item cannot fit on one line. Each piece of data is identified unless it is naturally obvious.

This type of report is tough to design because data is not in columns, and every line is different. It can look inconsistent. Ease of understanding is hard to effect. You will probably use a lot of trial and error at first, but it's worth it. Once you have a good format, the report is instantly usable to the reader.

The way to test for instant readability is to ask someone if you can put your report design in front of their face for 60 seconds. Then, ask them to tell you what the report says. Try this with different people. Never trust your judgment alone. You will be surprised at the good criticism and suggestions that you get.

Rules for Laying Out a Page

1. Keep it simple. Never report information that is not immediately useful to the person or persons for which it's designed. The report should be clear at a glance.
2. Make it purely columnar, if possible. Use smaller print, if you have to. It is better to fit everything for an item on one line than to have two lines per item.
3. If you cannot make the report completely columnar, and you have to use labeled data, then move data around the report, and use every means possible to line up some columns. This helps readability because the eye likes to view data in straight vertical lines.
4. Line up alphabetic information on the left.

5. Line up numbers on the right, or by decimal point.
6. Keep labels short, but not cryptic. You do not want to use more space for labels than data. Also, you need white space for a neat report.
7. Eliminate unneeded labels such as NAME, STREET, CITY, STATE, ZIP, PHONE, CUSTOMER NUMBER, ITEM NUMBER, and ITEM DESCRIPTION.

Print Formats

Lack of print formats was a shortcoming of BASIC. Originally, BASIC printed numbers in a format acceptable only to engineers and scientists. Today, using the FORMAT statement, you can produce the same report in QBasic as can be done in COBOL, the most common business language used on large computers. You can now present numbers in a business-like manner.

FORMAT Statement

The FORMAT statement is a layout of the line. It is not a special statement, exclusively used for printing. Rather, it is a string assignment statement (using special symbols encased in quotes) that works as a template for the LPRINT statement (which is explained in the next section). The format has windows through which data is printed onto paper. The windows are defined using special characters to specify the type and size of the data that is printed.

Where there is text in a FORMAT statement, that text is printed. The text in a FORMAT statement is the labels or titles in the line. The blank space in a FORMAT statement is the white (blank) space of the printed line.

The syntax for a FORMAT statement is:

```
{data name 1}$="{####    \ \    ! $$###.## $$#,###.##}"
```

where {data name 1} is a string variable,

#	denotes that a number is printed.
\ \	means that alphanumeric characters are printed.
!	specifies that a single alphanumeric character is printed.

$$###	means that a dollar sign is printed immediately before the first digit of the number.
###.##	indicates that a number is printed with a decimal point and 2 decimal places.
#,###	prints a number with a comma, if the number is large enough to need it. If not, only the number is printed.

FORMAT Example

```
LIN1$="####  \      \    $$#,###.##  !   $$###.##  !   #####"
```

The FORMAT statement is used by the LPRINT statement to output lines onto the printer. (Examples of the LPRINT using the FORMAT statement are in the next section.)

LPRINT, LPRINT Using Statements

LPRINT is the statement that prints onto the paper, in the layout defined by the FORMAT statement. LPRINT tells the computer what data to print in that format. There are variations of LPRINT, but here are two forms that can do everything:

The first form has this syntax:

```
LPRINT {data name 1}; TAB ({position 1}); {data name 2};_
TAB({position 2}); {data name 3}; ETC
```

where {data name 1}, {data name 2}, and {data name 3} are variable names to be printed, and {position 1} and {position 2} are columns that are moved ("tabbed") to before printing data names 2 and 3, respectively.

The second form has this syntax:

```
LPRINT USING {format name};{data name 1}; {data name 2};_
{data name 3}
```

where {format name} is the name of a previously defined FORMAT statement, and data names 1, 2, and 3 are variable names to be printed.

LPRINT Examples

(form 1)

```
LPRINT partnum;TAB(10);partdesc$;TAB(50);partcost
```

(form 2)

```
LPRINT USING LIN1$; partnum; partdesc$; partcost;_
partlistpr; partonhd
```

Below are the FORMAT and LPRINT statements, which produce the daily reports for Terry.

──────────────── LPRINTS & FORMATS (daily) ────────────────

FORMATS:

```
lin1$="\     \    page ###"
lin2$="    WildWater Women Inventory Status (Daily)"
lin3$="    ITEM   COLOR   DESCR  DEALER   RETAIL      ONHND"
LIN4$="\ \ \    \ \    \ \    \  ###.##   ###.##   ###.##"
```

LPRINTS:

```
LPRINT USING lin1$; dat$; pagnum: REM—prints date & page_
number
```

```
LPRINT lin2$: REM — prints the report title
```

```
LPRINT lin3$: REM — prints the column headers
```

```
LPRINT USING lin4$;invnum;invname$;invcolr; invdesc$;_
invcost; invretpr; invonhd :REM — this prints one item line
```

TAB Function

The TAB function positions the printer to a specific column before printing a variable or label. The format for the TAB function is:

```
TAB ({position})
```

where {position} is a number between 1 and 255 that represents the print column at which to stop. (TAB never stands alone, it must be used within an LPRINT statement.)

TAB Example

```
LPRINT TAB(10);partnum
```

CHR$ Function

The CHR$ function is used with LPRINT to:

- Print 1 or more blank lines.
- Start a new page.
- Give special print commands to your printer.

LPRINT prints one blank line.

LPRINT CHR$(10) prints two blank lines.

LPRINT CHR$(10);CHR$(10) prints three blank lines and so forth.

LPRINT CHR$(12) moves to a new page on the printer.

LPRINT CHR$({number 1});CHR$({number 2}); etc. with different values for {number 1} and {number 2} (which are ASCII numbers) instruct your printer to do different things, like:

- Change the font (type) style.
- Change the font (type) size.
- Print graphics.

There are other things that vary with the brand of printer. Because the commands are different for every printer, consult your printer manual for specifics.

Commas and Semicolons

This book does not include a discussion about the use of commas with LPRINT statements, because their use can result in poor printed output. Instead of using a comma in an LPRINT statement (not an LPRINT USING), follow it with a semicolon when you TAB to a position, and follow every variable name with a semicolon (except the last piece of data on the print line). This prevents the sloppiness that commas lend to an LPRINT statement. For the best quality printer output, use LPRINT USING combined with the FORMAT statement.

Width Statement

The WIDTH statement tells QBasic the size of the print line in characters. If no WIDTH is specified, then the line defaults to 80 characters wide.

The syntax is:

```
WIDTH "{printer port}",{number of characters}
```

where {printer port} is the port on your computer that is connected by a cable to the printer (usually LPT1:).

{number of characters} is the maximum number of characters for a print line (1-255). The number of characters you specify depends on the size of the print type and the maximum number of characters that your printer can print on one line with that size type.

WIDTH Example

```
WIDTH "LPT1:", 132
```

Place the WIDTH statement in the FILEOPEN routine. Since it is defining the size of one of your files (the print file), that is the right place for this statement.

Summary

1. Begin your program design with report layout.
2. Printed output is valuable when the information is:
   - Up-to-date
   - Easily recognizable
   - Instantly available
3. There are two basic types of page layouts:
   - Columnar
   - Labeled data
4. Rules for laying out a page:
   - Keep it simple.
   - Make it columnar, if possible.
   - If the layout is not columnar, line up as many columns as possible.
   - Line up alphabetic data on the left, numbers on the right, or by decimal point.
   - Keep labels short, but not cryptic.
   - Eliminate labels on obvious data.
5. The FORMAT statement is a template for the line.
6. The LPRINT statement provides the data for the FORMAT statement to produce printed output.
7. The TAB function positions to the specified column.
8. The CHR$ function is used with LPRINT to:
   - Print 1 or more blank lines
   - Start a new page
   - Give special commands to your printer
9. Do not use commas; use semicolons in your LPRINT statements.
10. The WIDTH statement sets the maximum of a print line.

The Book in Review

1. Design and program thoughtfully.
2. To examine any QBasic program, break it up into blocks. Then study each block separately, and finally look at the logic that controls all the blocks.
3. QBasic gives you a complete working environment, which encourages writing programs in building-block fashion.
4. Blueprint your program before you write the first line of code.
5. Data names should be meaningful, short (but not cryptic), consistent and clear.
6. The QBasic Editor is top shelf. Use the keys, rather than the menus, and you will be productive.
7. Program organization is crucial. Blueprint, assign the tasks to routines, then program each routine.
8. GOSUB subroutines; CALL procedures. GOTO a line name that is within the same routine as the GOTO statement.
9. Keep your IFs simple, and easy to read.
10. Loops are critical to good programming. You can destroy their structure with the wrong GOTO. Never GOTO somewhere outside the loop.
11. Group like items together, describe them, and you have the start of a file.
12. Learn random files well; they are the foundation of all file work.
13. The linked list structure is for transaction-type files.
14. Edit new data thoroughly or your program dies.
15. Set up standard edit procedures and use them.
16. **Design each report with the least amount of data to achieve its purpose.**

Chapter 17

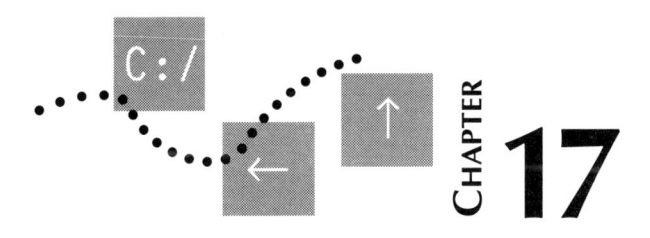

Screen it Out

This chapter teaches you how to lay out information on screens so that it is useful and meaningful to the person reading it. You learn what to use and what to avoid to design screens that are easy to use: The topics include:

- Begin at the end
- The (lack of) value of screen output
- Screen layout
- Color, underlining, and blinking
- Ten mistakes to avoid
- Keep it simple
- PRINT FORMATS
- FORMAT statement
- PRINT and PRINT USING statements
- The TAB function
- Commas and semicolons

- CHR$ function
- CLS statement
- Moving to a point on the screen
- The COLOR statement
- The only criterion

The Disoriented Customer Data Screen

This is the first layout of WildWater Work's corporate customer data screen. The screen is supposed to show all the information Chris needs when talking with a corporate executive on the phone.

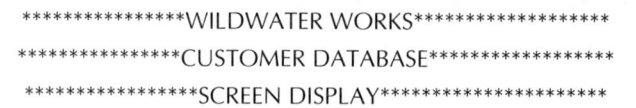

```
***************WILDWATER WORKS******************
***************CUSTOMER DATABASE*****************
***************SCREEN DISPLAY********************
CUSTOMER  MARINE MANAGERS, INC  CONTACT CHUCK BUTKUS NUMBER 12345
CUSTOMER ADDRESS 999 ROUTE 9       NORTHVILLE NY 54321
PHONE 1235551212                   LAST YEAR 1247.00
THIS YEAR 3241.50                  LAST TRIP 92194  8 PEOPLE
   NOTES: WILL BUY ANY NEW TEAM MANAGEMENT RAFTING COURSES
```

Does this look a little confusing to you? It did to everyone else, including Chris, who designed it in the first place. The staff at WildWater Works found, that when first getting on the computer to look up a customer, it took several minutes to figure out each data item. After working with the lookup for 20 minutes, they adjusted. However, the first few lookups took a while. So Chris asked for Terry's help. Terry, using the rules in this chapter, came up with this display:

```
                    CUSTOMER INFORMATION
   1234    MARINE MANAGERS        type C  phone       1235551212
           999 ROUTE 9                    cust since  21192
           NORTHVILLE NY 54321            last mail   101294
   contact: CHUCK BUTKUS                  last call   121294
```

WILL BUY ANY NEW MANAGEMENT RAFTING COURSES

		last raft trips	
		people	date
total purchases		8	92194
this year	3241.50	4	71494
last year	1247.00	6	42194

See the difference in the presentation of the same data? The methods for good screen layout are similar to a labeled text printout. This chapter is similar to the previous one. (This book does not cover screen graphics—it would take up several books by itself.)

Begin at the End

Just as a printed page is a report, so is a screen display of data. Since the screen display is the reason for the program, you begin with screen design. Once the screen layout is established, work backwards to find the sources of the data being displayed, and then define the program.

The (Lack of) Value of Screen Output

Screen displays, like any reports, are valuable when three conditions are met:

1. The information is up-to-date.
2. The information is easily recognizable.
3. The screen display is instantly available to the people who need it.

Up-to-Date Output

Screen displays generally have less chance of obsolete data than a printout because the data (in the computer) is the most current available. However, the most current data might be slow getting into the computer; then a screen lookup program might be misleading.

The information on the WWW computer is current because Terry sees to it. In this way a customer lookup screen is a big asset whenever they are on the phone with a customer.

Easily Recognizable Output

This requires the most work on a screen layout. Some people want to see all the information that can fit on one screen. However, it is a bad idea for different classes of employees with totally different job functions to share that same fully stuffed screen.

Where you have different job functions, you should design the screen with the *minimum* of information, just as you would a printed report. The screen is uncluttered, yet each person has the data to do their job. Since the screen has a minimum of data on it, it is easier to design, and the screen is more readable.

At WildWater Works, the same information on each customer is used by all. Chris, Pat, and Terry want to know all the information available on every customer. And they need to make a quick decision or answer a question based upon that data. So screen design is critical in presenting the data in an at-once recognizable fashion.

Instantly Available Output

Everyone knows that a computer screen always gives information instantly, right? Not always, and here are two reasons why:

- The screen may be physically in another part of the building, or in a different building.
- Several persons may be trying to use one screen.

If there are enough screens in the right physical location, the information should be instantly available. If not, reports should be printed on paper for some **people**, while others use the screens.

WildWater Works has only one Personal Computer, hence one screen. But there are only two phone lines, and only one person at a time needs screen **display** access. So the information is instant and available.

Screen Layout

Screen layout is still an art. It varies with each individual user and the screen report purpose. But there are some basic techniques:

1. Tailor the screen to the individuals that are to use it. Do not display information onto the screen unless it is absolutely necessary. Excessive data:
   - Clutters the screen.
   - Makes the necessary data hard to find.
   - Makes it more difficult to design the screen layout.

   So keep it simple.

2. Arrange the data into categories that the computer user wants to see arranged together, in one place. Then, break up the screen into sections that accommodate each category's data. In the example on the first page of this chapter, Terry set up the screen into three groups:
   - Name and address, phone, last contact
   - Dollars spent
   - Notes and trip dates

3. Line data up in columns as much as possible:
   - Line up alphabetic data on the left.
   - Align numbers on the right, or by decimal point.

4. Keep labels short, but not so short that they are unclear. You want a screen display to have more data than labels. By minimizing labels, you increase blank space, making the screen easier to focus on.

5. Eliminate unnecessary labels such as NAME, STREET, CITY, STATE, ZIP, PHONE, CUSTOMER NUMBER, VENDOR NUMBER, ITEM NUMBER, and ITEM DESCRIPTION.

6. Since most data is either numbers or uppercase letters, display your labels in lowercase letters.

Color, Underlining, and Blinking

Novices think that a lot of color, underlining, and blinking, really make data items stand out on a screen. However, that is not true. When color, underlining, and blinking are excessive, it numbs your vision, rather than focusing it. The screen is so busy (with no two things alike) that you cannot find the data you need. So here are three simple rules (based on painful experience) to follow for successful screening:

1. Use color sparingly—too much and you dazzle the eyes, and inhibit focus.
2. Underlining seems like a good way to draw attention to data. However, it only works when it is restricted to a few items. Underlining makes a screen *busy*; then data that is not underlined is hard to find. When all data is underlined, all you see is the horizontal lines.
3. A blinking screen is extremely distracting. Some programmers use this in the case of entry errors. It is infuriating to be reminded of a mistake you made by an unreadable blinking screen. That's what makes people want to punch out their computers. Forget using blink.

Ten Mistakes to Avoid

Avoid these things when you design the layout of a screen:

1. Poor data grouping, or none at all
2. Failure to align data items by column whenever possible
3. Unnecessary data
4. Too many labels
5. Multi-word and overly long labels
6. Cryptic labels
7. Not enough blank space
8. Underlining
9. Blinking
10. Too much color

Color is great, if you have it. However, 16 different colors is a blur. You can use color to make certain data items stand out. You might want to use color to separate different groups of data that are physically close on the screen. Use bright colors for the more important data. Use color to alert that a problem is about to happen with a particular customer, inventory item or order. But use it sparingly. Set up rules for color use, always use them, and keep upgrading them.

Keep it Simple

This means avoid the glitz, organize the screen, and present it so that anyone can comprehend the data quickly. It is the easiest way to avoid the above mistakes.

Print Formats

The print formats for a screen are *exactly* like those for a printer, discussed in Chapter 16.

FORMAT Statement

The FORMAT statement works as a template for the PRINT statement exactly like it works for the LPRINT in Chapter 16.

The syntax for a FORMAT statement is:

{data name 1}$="####   \   \   ! $$####.## $$#,###.##"

where {data name 1} is a string variable.

#	prints a number.
\ \	prints alphanumeric characters.
!	prints a single alphanumeric character.
$$###	puts a dollar sign immediately before the first digit of the number.
###.##	specifies a number with the decimal point and two decimal places.
#,###	prints a number, inserting a comma, if the number is large enough to need it.

FORMAT Example

```
LIN1$="####   \      \   $$#,###.##  !  $$####.##  !  #####"
```

The FORMAT statement is used by the PRINT statement to display data onto the screen. (Examples of PRINT using "formats" are in the next section.)

PRINT and PRINT USING Statements

PRINT is the statement that displays the data on the screen. You can reduce all the forms of PRINTs down to two:

The first form has this syntax:

```
PRINT {data name 1}; TAB ({position 1}); {data name 2}; TAB_
({position 2}); {data name 3}; ETC.
```

where

{data name 1}

{data name 2}

{data name 3}

are variable names to be printed, and

{position 1}

{position 2}

are columns that are moved (tabbed) to before printing data names 2 and 3, respectively.

The second form has this syntax:

```
PRINT USING {format name};{data name 1}; {data name 2};_
{data_ name 3}
```

where

{format name} is a previously defined FORMAT statement, and data names 1, 2 and 3 are variable names to be printed.

PRINT Examples

(form 1)

```
PRINT invnum;TAB(10);invdesc$;TAB(50);invcost
```

(form 2)

```
PRINT USING LIN1$; invnum; invdesc$; invcost; invsell;_
invonhd
```

Below are the FORMAT and PRINT statements that produce the screen display that Terry designed for Chris.

——————— PRINTS & FORMATS ———————

FORMATS:

```
lin1$="    CUSTOMER INFORMATION"
lin2$="####  \       \ type !    phone ##########"
lin3$="      \       \           cust since ######"
lin4$="      \       \  \\ \ \"  last mail  ######"
lin5$="contact: \ \              last phone ######"
lin6$="\              \"
lin7$="                          last raft trips"
lin8$="                          people date"
lin9$="total purchases     ###   ######"
lin10$="this year #####.##        ###   ######"
lin11$="last year #####.##        ###   ######"
```

PRINTS:

```
CLS
PRINT lin1$
PRINT
PRINT USING lin2$;custnum;custname$;custtype$;custphone
```

```
PRINT USING lin3$;custaddr$;custsince
PRINT USING lin4$;custcity$;custst$;custzip$;custlastmail
PRINT USING lin5$;custcontact$;custlastcall
PRINT
PRINT USING lin6$;custnotes$
PRINT lin7$
PRINT lin8$
PRINT USING lin9$;custpeopl%(1);custtripdat(1)
PRINT USING lin10$;custthisyr#;custpeopl%(2);custtripdat(2)
PRINT USING lin11$;custlastyr#;custpeopl%(3);custtripdat(3)
```

The TAB Function

The TAB function puts the cursor at a specific column before printing a variable or label. The format for the TAB function is:

```
TAB ({position})
```

where {position} is a number between 1 and 80 that represents the point at which to locate. (TAB never stands alone, it must be used within a PRINT statement):

TAB Example

```
PRINT TAB(10);partnum
```

Commas and Semicolons

The same rule applies for screen layout that applies for print layout in the last chapter. Do not use commas in a PRINT statement. When you TAB to a position, follow it with a semicolon, and follow every variable name with a semicolon (except for the last one on the print line).

(PRINT USING with "formats" provides the best quality screen output.)

CHR$ Function

The CHR$ function is used with PRINT to print one or more blank lines:

- PRINT prints one blank line.
- PRINT CHR$(10) prints two blank lines.
- PRINT CHR$(10);CHR$(10) prints three blank lines and so forth.

CLS Statement

The CLS statement clears the entire screen. It gives you a blank screen, then locates the cursor at line 1, column 1.

The syntax is:

```
CLS
```

Whenever you want to start a new "page" on the screen, use CLS.

Locating a Point on the Screen

LOCATE places the cursor in a specific spot on the computer screen. POS and CSRLIN find the current location of the cursor (on the screen). Since they often work together, they are described together.

In many cases, you can work with LOCATE alone. When your data goes on the same lines on every page (of the screen), you clear the screen with CLS, then LOCATE and PRINT every line.

When the data is not always in the same place on the screen, POS and CSRLIN are used to find out where the cursor is. Then, depending on cursor position, you LOCATE the start of the next display data in the right place.

The syntax for LOCATE is:

```
LOCATE {line number},{column number}
```

where {line number} is the value (1-24) of the text line where the cursor is to be placed; and {column number} is the value (1-80) of the column position to place the cursor. The values can be actual numbers, or numeric variables.

LOCATE Example

This is an example of how to use the LOCATE statement:

```
LOCATE 1,1:REM — places the cursor at line 1, column 1
LOCATE 24,80:REM — sets the cursor at line 24, position 80
LOCATE y%,x%:REM — puts the cursor at line y%, position x%
     REM — where y% is a variable with a value
     REM — between 1 and 24, and x% is a variable
     REM — having a value between 1 and 80
```

The syntax for CSRLIN is:

```
{variable name} = CSRLIN
```

where {variable name} is any numeric integer variable name.

CSRLIN Example:

```
y%=CSRLIN:REM — Get the line that the cursor is on
```

The syntax for POS is:

```
{variable name} = POS(0)
```

where {variable name} is any numeric integer variable name.

POS Example:

```
x%=POS(0):REM — get the column position of the cursor
```

The COLOR Statement

The COLOR statement sets the colors of the characters and the background on which the characters are printed. When the computer monitor has only one color, the COLOR statement can set degrees of brightness, or shades of the single color.

The syntax for the COLOR statement (on any monitor) is:

```
COLOR {character color number}, {background color number}
```

where

the {character color} is a number or variable with a value from 0-15,

the {background color number} is a number or variable with a value from 0-7,

In some cases, you can get more colors, but this is plenty to work with.

COLOR Example

```
COLOR 15,1:REM — sets bright white characters on a blue
     REM — background
```

It is hard to pick the right color combinations because the presentation varies with each screen's shading capabilities and the actual colors it produces. (A red, brown, or blue, on six different color screens are slightly different.) So here is a program for you to try (if you have a color monitor) to find which combinations you like best (or maybe which show up at all, if you only have a monochrome monitor). This is a color testing program:

```
*************** COLOR TESTING PROGRAM ****************
REM screen   010194
REM note on a piece of paper the color combinations that REM
look best
FOR j% = 0 TO 7
     FOR k% = 0 TO 15
          COLOR k%, j%
          PRINT"*****************************************"
          PRINT
          PRINT "Characters="; k%; TAB(25);"Background=";_
j%
          PRINT
          PRINT"*****************************************"
          COLOR 7, 0
          LINE INPUT "Press enter to continue"; i$
```

```
        NEXT k%
NEXT j%
************** END OF COLOR TESTING PROGRAM **************
```
Remember, a lot of different colors are pretty, but it blurs the data.

The Only Criterion

Ask yourself this question: Will this make the screen easier to read? If not, forget using color.

Summary

1. Begin a lookup program with screen design.
2. Screen output is valuable when the information is:
   - Up-to-date
   - Easily recognizable
   - Instantly available
3. REmember, for screen layout design:
   - Tailor the screen simply for the user.
   - Group the data into categories; have a separate section on the screen for each category.
   - Line up data in columns when you can.
   - Keep labels short, but recognizable.
   - Eliminate unnecessary labels.
   - Make labels lowercase.
4. Use color sparingly.
5. Do not underline.
6. Do not use blinking.
7. Keep it simple.
8. Formats are the templates for the screen lines.

9. PRINT USING statements work with the formats to produce a screen report.
10. The TAB function positions the cursor to a column on a line.
11. Do not use commas; use semicolons.
12. CHR$ is used with PRINT to print 1 or more blank lines.
13. LOCATE places the cursor at a specific point on the screen.
14. POS returns the current column position of the cursor.
15. CSRLIN returns the current line of the cursor.
16. The COLOR statement sets the colors of the characters, and background. Use COLOR thoughtfully.
17. The only question you need to ask when designing screens is: Will this make the screen easier to read?

The Book in Review

1. Design and program thoughtfully.
2. To examine any QBasic program, break it up into blocks. Then study each block separately, and finally look at the logic that controls all the blocks.
3. QBasic gives you a complete working environment, which encourages writing programs in building-block fashion.
4. Blueprint your program before you write the first line of code.
5. Data names should be meaningful, short (but not cryptic), consistent, and clear.
6. The QBasic Editor is top shelf. Use the keys, rather than the menus, and you will be productive.
7. Program organization is crucial. Blueprint, assign the tasks to routines, then program each routine.
8. GOSUB subroutines; CALL procedures. GOTO a line name that is within the same routine as the GOTO statement.
9. Keep your IFs simple and easy to read.
10. Loops are critical to good programming. You can destroy their structure with the wrong GOTO. Never GOTO somewhere outside the loop.

11. Group like items together, describe them, and you have the start of a file.
12. Learn random files well; they are the foundation of all file work.
13. The linked list structure is for transaction-type files.
14. Edit new data thoroughly or your program dies.
15. Set up standard edit procedures and use them.
16. Design each report with the least amount of data to achieve its purpose.
17. **Does this design make the screen easier to read? If not, forget it.**

… **CHAPTER 18**

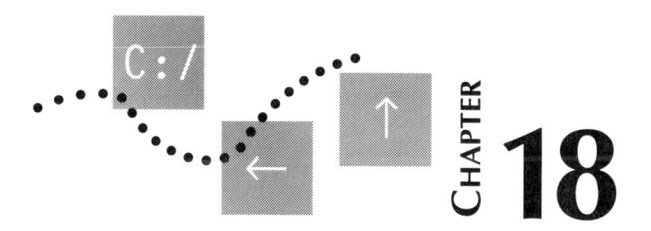

Calculations

This chapter teaches you how to use calculations in your QBasic programs. You learn how to use the operators and the functions that you need to get the correct answers. The topics include:

- Where computer calculations start
- Operators
- Combining strings
- Division by zero
- What is calculated first in a formula
- The use of parentheses
- Using the right data types to get the correct answer
- Rounding and presenting the answer
- CINT, INT, FIX, and CLNG functions
- Math functions
- String functions and calculations
- Date calculations

The Cost of Service

After a year in business, Chris, Pat, and Terry had taken over 1,500 people down the Upper Hudson River. However, they realized that they did not know what it cost them to send each person down the river. That is not unusual; many companies do not know the real cost of their services. So they got out their calculator, a pad, and pen, and began itemizing the cost of their least expensive trip.

It may seem easy, but this procedure involves dozens of calculations, which eventually go into a computer program. So in this chapter, you can see how they figured their costs to show what goes into this kind of program.

This is the conversation they had:

Chris: "We have to include our fixed costs—insurance, rent, phone, and utilities."

Pat: "We also need to add our pay and my travel expenses."

Terry: "And besides actual food costs, we also need to add the cost of using each raft, paddle, wet suit, and life jacket based on its useful life."

This chapter explores how to convert these thoughts into formulas for a computer program. You can start with the formulas themselves.

Where Computer Calculations Start

Calculations on computers are based on formulas that were first worked out with a paper and pencil. Computers can do repetitive calculations better than people most of the time. So once the formula is worked out by hand and proven correct, it is written into a computer program.

WildWater Works has to add up all their overhead (insurance, rent, phone, utilities, payroll, travel expenses, and interest expense), then apply these costs to each person they send down the river. They could do this by:

1. Dividing the total overhead by the number of people they host.
2. Dividing the overhead number by the number of square feet in the barn that they rent. This produces the overhead cost per square foot of space.

They can then find the number of square feet of space that each activity requires, such as:
- Raft storage
- Changing rooms
- T-shirt display
- Office

They can then multiply these things by the overhead cost per square foot, or any one of a dozen methods. But ultimately, they have to find the correct formulas, then apply them using the computer.

Operators

These are the operators:

+   is the addition operator.
−   is the subtraction operator.
*   is the multiplication operator.
/   is the division operator.
^   is the exponentiation operator (raises a number to a power).

Operator Examples

These are examples of using operators:

```
a=b+c:REM — add b to c, place the result into a
a=a+b:REM — add b to a, place the result into a
a=b-c:REM — subtract c from b, place the result into a
a=a-b:REM — subtract b from a, place the result into a
a=b*c:REM — multiply b by c, place the result into a
a=a*b:REM — multiply a by b, place the result into a
a=b/c:REM — divide b by c, place the result into a
```

```
a=a/b:REM - divide a by b, place the result into a
a=b^c:REM - raise b to the c power, place the result into a
a=a^b:REM - raise a to the b power, place the result into a
```

You can add, subtract, multiply, divide, and raise to a power numbers or numeric variables. You cannot add, subtract, multiply, divide or raise to a power strings or string variables, even if the string or string variable is made up entirely of numbers. (For example, you cannot perform "2" +"2", or a$-b$, where a$="171" and b$="159")

Combining Strings

The addition operator joins two or more strings together, forming a single string. (You have seen this feature of the + sign in Chapter 15.)

```
a$=b$+c$ is a legal BASIC expression.
If b$="CHUCK"
and c$="BUTKUS"
and a$=b$+c$ were executed, then
a$ would equal "CHUCKBUTKUS".
```

Division by Zero

Going back to elementary algebra for a moment, division by zero is undefined. The same with QBasic. To see what happens, get into QBasic, then type this into your computer:

```
a=0
b=99
c=b/a
print c
```

Now run the program to try this calculation on your machine.

Press **Alt+R**.

Press **Enter**.

You get an error message. Press **Enter** to clear the error message. When it encounters division by zero, a QBasic program blows up. So you should always test the divisor variable (the one you are dividing by) BEFORE doing division. If the divisor variable is 0, display a message, and skip the divide calculation.

What is Calculated First in a Formula

This is the sequence of calculation in a formula:

- Exponentiation (^) is performed first.
- Then multiplication and division (* and /). Neither has priority over the other; the question of which gets done first depends on which one is first seen by the computer, while scanning the QBasic line containing the formula from left to right.
- Then addition and subtraction (+ and -). Again, neither has rank over the other; the order of execution depends on which one the computer sees first, scanning from left to right.

Order of Precedence Example

This example shows the order of precedence in program calculations:

The sequence of calculation in

```
a=b+c*d-e/f
```

is:

1. *c* is first multiplied by *d* (name it *prod1*).
2. *e* is divided by *f* (call this result *prod2*).
3. *b* and *prod1* are added together (name this *prod3*).
4. *prod2* is subtracted from *prod3*, and the answer put into *a*.

The hierarchy of operations is probably the most common problem that programmers have with calculations. It can cost you hours of programming pain. Calculations are sometimes performed in an order different from what you intended. So, to keep the order straight you use parentheses.

The Use of Parentheses

Use parentheses (rather scrutinize the priority of operations) for each formula, to calculate correctly. The rule of parentheses overrides the operator order above in this way:

1. The formula is calculated as the computer scans it from left to right.
2. As each left parenthesis is found, it is saved, to be matched later (in Step 3 below).
3. When a right parenthesis is found, it is matched with the previous left parenthesis.
4. The expression within the parentheses is calculated according to the rule of priority of operations (discussed previously in "What is Calculated First in a Formula.")
5. The result of Step 4 is saved temporarily, and the rest of the formula is examined and processed as in Steps 1-5.
6. All of the temporary results are combined in a final calculation, and the result is stored.

Parentheses Examples

This example uses the previous calculation example from "What is Calculated First in a Formula."

```
a=b+c*d-e/f
```

Here you can see how the results differ, depending on where parentheses are placed.

1. a=(b+c)*d-e/f
2. a=b+(c*d)-e/f
3. a=b+c*(d-e)/f
4. a=(b+c)*(d-e)/f
5. a=(b+c*d-e)/f

If you understand these examples instinctively, then skip this detailed discussion and go to "Hints on Parentheses." If you have a question on 1-5 above, then read the explanations below.

Explanation of example 1

1. b is first added to c (call it *prod1*)
2. *prod1* is multiplied by d (name this *prod2*)
3. e is divided by f (label this result *prod3*)
4. *prod3* is subtracted from *prod2*, and the answer put into a.

Explanation of example 2

1. c is first multiplied by d (*prod1*)
2. e is divided by f (*prod2*)
3. b and *prod1* are added together (*prod3*)
4. *prod2* is subtracted from *prod3*, and the answer is put into a.

Explanation of example 3

1. e is first subtracted from d (*prod1*)
2. *prod1* is multiplied by c (*prod2*)
3. *prod2* is divided by f (*prod3*)
4. b and *prod3* are added, and the answer is put into a.

Explanation of example 4

1. b is first added to c (*prod1*)
2. e is subtracted from d (*prod2*)
3. *prod1* is multiplied by *prod2* (*prod3*)
4. *prod3* is divided by f, and the answer is put into a.

Explanation of example 5:

1. c is first multiplied by d (*prod1*)

2. *b* and *prod1* are added (*prod2*)
3. *e* is subtracted from *prod2* (*prod3*)
4. *prod3* is divided by *f*, and the answer is put into *a*.

Hints for Using Parentheses

1. It is better to use too many parentheses than too few.
2. Parentheses can help your understanding, and you can use them to mentally break up a complex calculation into several small ones. Use them for this conceptual clarity. Refer to Hint 1 above.
3. Make sure that you match up parentheses. In an equation, the total number of left parentheses *must* equal the total number of right parentheses.

Using the Right Data Types to Get the Correct Answer

Use the correct variable types on the left side of the equation when you are performing a calculation, or the answer will be wrong. Follow these guidelines for using the correct data types:

1. Use an integer variable on the left side when you want a whole number for an answer.
2. Use a single-precision variable when you are positive that the answer will not exceed five digits of significance. (Meaning that you only care about the first five digits of the answer.)
3. Otherwise, use double-precision variables on the left side of the equation. This ensures the highest accuracy for the answer.

These are some examples:

integer variable	a%=(b/c)+.05
single precision variable	a=(b*c)-d/e
double precision variable	a#=(b+c)^d

Rounding and Presenting the Correct Answer

Even if you have calculated the answer correctly, you can print it wrong, if you use the wrong format. For example, suppose you are printing a number, using this format:

##########.##

- If the number is an integer, and its value is 1234, it prints as 1234.00.
- If the number is a single-precision number with a value of 12.3432, it prints as 12.34.
- If the number is a single-precision number with a value of 12.3454, it prints as 12.35.
- If the number is a double-precision number with a value of 1234.1143212345, it prints as 1234.11.
- If the number is a double-precision number with a value of 1234.1154321037, it prints as 1234.12.

Normally, you calculate as precisely as possible, then round or truncate the answer for presentation. To do this follow these steps:

1. Use double-precision variables on the left side of every equation when working with decimal values.
2. Round or truncate the answer.

In calculating interest and discounts, round each interest or discount result before adding it to a total. If you do not, the total may be a value that is not the sum of the printed items. For example:

```
a=43.234
b=22.333
c=a+b
```

If these were printed out using the format #######.##, the values would display like this:

    a would print as   43.23
    b would print as   22.33
    c would print as   65.57

(The value of *c* would actually be 65.567, which rounds up to 65.57.)

To make the sum equal the printed value of each of the items, use the long integer variable on the left side of every equation and round each calculation. Using the same example, things add up:

Example Using Long Integers

```
a=43.234
a&=(a+.005)*100: REM - convert a to a rounded long
                 REM - integer. The value of a& is 4323
a=a&/100: REM - convert back to a rounded number with
          REM - two decimal places (the value of a is
          REM - 43.23)
b=22.333
b&=(b+.005)*100: REM - convert b to a rounded long
                 REM - integer the value of b& is 2233
b=b&/100: REM - convert back to a rounded number with
          REM - two decimal places. (the value of b is
          REM - 22.33)
c=a+b
```

If these were printed out using this format, #######.##, the values would display like this:

    a would print as   43.23
    b would print as   22.33
    c would print as   65.56

which is the true value of *c*. (Not just the printed value, as in the first case.)

CINT, INT, FIX, and CLNG Functions

The CINT and INT functions convert single-precision and double-precision variables (or any numeric expression) to integers.

The FIX function converts any numeric expression into a whole number.

The CLNG function converts any numeric expression into a long integer.

INT converts numbers into integers by finding the largest integer that is less than, or equal to the expression. It *rounds down*, as shown in these examples:

- INT(12.6) is 12
- INT(12.2) is 12
- INT(–12.2) is –13
- INT(–12.6) is –13

CINT converts numbers into integers by rounding up (.5 or greater rounds to the next higher digit, whether positive or negative), rather than truncating.

- CINT(12.6) is 13
- CINT(12.2) is 12
- CINT(–12.2) is –12
- CINT(–12.6) is –13

FIX converts numbers into a whole number by taking all the digits left of the decimal point and creating a whole number. It truncates, rather than rounds, whether the expression is positive or negative.

- FIX(12.6) is 12
- FIX(12.2) is 12
- FIX(–12.2) is –12
- FIX(–12.6) is –12

CLNG converts numbers into a large integer by rounding the numeric expression, like CINT.

- CLNG(100012.6) is 100013

- CLNG(100012.2) is 100012
- CLNG(–100012.2) is –100012
- CLNG(–100012.6) is –100013

INT Syntax

The syntax for the INT function is:

```
INT ({n})
```

where {n} is any numeric expression

INT Examples

```
i%=INT(12.6):REM — i% = 12
a=12.34:REM — give value to a
b=123.45:REM — give value to b
c%=INT(a+b):REM — c% = 135
```

CINT Syntax

The syntax for the CINT function is:

```
CINT ({n})
```

where {n} is any numeric expression.

CINT Examples

```
i%=CINT(12.6):REM — i% = 13
a=12.34:REM — give value to a
b=123.45:REM — give value to b
c%=CINT(a+b):REM — c% = 136
```

FIX Syntax

The syntax for the FIX function is:

    FIX ({n})

where {n} is any numeric expression.

FIX Examples

    i = FIX(12.6):REM — i = 12
    a=12.34:REM — give value to a
    b=123.45:REM — give value to b
    c=FIX(a+b):REM — c = 135

CLNG Syntax

The syntax for the CLNG function is:

    CLNG ({n})

where {n} is any numeric expression.

CLNG Examples

    i& = CLNG (12.6):REM — i& = 13
    a=12.34:REM — give value to a
    b=123.45:REM — give value to b
    i&=CLNG(a+b):REM — i& = 136

Comparison Examples

These are some comparison examples of INT, CINT, FIX, and CLNG.

number {n}	INT({n})	CINT({n})	FIX({n})	CLNG({n})
123.4	123	123	123	123
123.7	123	124	123	124
−123.4	−124	−123	−123	−123
−123.7	−124	−124	−123	−124

Math Functions

QBasic supports these mathematical functions:

ABS, ATN, COS, EXP, SGN, SIN, SQR, TAN

The syntax for all of these functions is:

{fn}({n})

where

{fn} is any of the math functions (ABS, ATN, COS, EXP, SGN, SIN, SQR, or TAN)

{n} is a numeric expression.

Refer to your QBasic manual for further explanation if needed.

String Functions and Calculations

String functions are used in calculations to pick out numbers that are contained within a string. Some applications are:

- Editing data that is entered by someone
- Picking numbers out of strings with intermixed alphabetic characters, such as:
    - dates
    - ZIP codes
    - phone numbers

STR$ converts a number into a string, which can then be processed using:

- LEN, to get the total number of characters.
- LEFT$, to get a specific number of characters, starting with the leftmost character position.
- RIGHT$, to get a specific number of characters, starting with the rightmost character position.
- MID$, to get a specific number of characters, starting with a certain position.

- VAL, to convert a string, or part of a string into a number. (Refer to Chapter 15 for a review of these functions.)

Here are some examples:

```
a=1234.56:REM - give value to a
a$=str$(a):REM - string a$=" 1234.56"
print len(a$):, REM - will print 8, which is (the
                REM - number of digits, plus one space
                REM - for the decimal point, and one
                REM - space for the sign in front of
                REM - the number.)
print left$(a$,3):REM - prints  12
print right$(a$,3):REM - prints .56
print mid$(a$,3,5):REM - prints 234.5
print val(mid$(a$,5,3)):REM - prints  4.5
```

The syntax for the STR$ function is:

```
STR$({n})
```

where {n} is any numeric expression.

Date Calculations

The main operations involving dates are:

- Date comparisons
- Elapsed days between two dates

To compare two dates, you first change their formats. The format of a date is six characters, in which the first two are the month, the next two are the day, and the last two are the year. You show this format as MMDDYY, MM being month, DD the day, and YY the last two digits of the year. To compare dates, change the date to YYMMDD, where YY is the last two digits of the year, MM is the month, and DD is the day of the month.

Conversion Example (assume the date is in variable name *d*):

1. `d$=STR$(d):REM` — convert d to a string
2. `w$=MID$(d$,2):REM` — get rid of blank sign character
3. `d$=w$:REM` — move it back into d$
4. `IF LEN(w$)<6 then d$="0"+w$:REM` — make it 6 characters
5. `w$=RIGHT$(d$,2)+LEFT$(d$,2)+MID$(d$,3,2) REM` — convert
   `REM` — the
   `REM` — string
   `REM` — into
   `REM` — YYMMDD
   `REM` — format
6. `d1=val(w$):REM` — convert it into a number

The *d1* variable is now a numeric variable in YYMMDD format, ready to compare (for a less than, greater than, or equal to condition) with any other date in the same format. Before a date can be compared, it must be in YYMMDD format.

To calculate the number of elapsed days between two dates:

1. Convert both dates into YYMMDD format.
2. Use the following routine:

Assume that *d1* and *d2* are the dates, already in YYMMDD format.

```
******      DATE CALCULATION ROUTINE       ******
REM - datecalc  060194
REM - This is not an exact calculation.
REM - It assumes a 30 day month.
     d1 = 930101: REM - date is 010193
     d2 = 911031: REM - date is 103191
     w$ = MID$(STR$(d1), 2): REM - make 1st date a string
     w1$ = LEFT$(w$, 2): REM - get the year of 1st date
     w2$ = MID$(w$, 3, 2): REM - get the month of 1st date
     w3$ = RIGHT$(w$, 2): REM -  get the day of 1st date
```

```
    x1 = VAL(w1$)
    x2 = VAL(w2$)
     x3 = VAL(w3$):REM – change year, month, and day of
              REM – 1st date into separate numbers
    w$ = MID$(STR$(d2), 2): REM – make 2nd date a string
    w1$ = LEFT$(w$, 2): REM – get the year of 2nd date
    w2$ = MID$(w$, 3, 2): REM – get the month of 2nd date
    w3$ = RIGHT$(w$, 2): REM – get the day of 2nd date
    x4 = VAL(w1$)
    x5 = VAL(w2$)
    x6 = VAL(w3$): REM – change 2nd date into separate
              REM – numbers
    w1 = x1 - x4: REM – subtract the years
    w2 = x2 - x5: REM – subtract the months
    w3 = x3 - x6: REM – subtract the days
IF w3 < 0 THEN
    w3 = w3 + 30
    w2 = w2 - 1
END IF: REM – if the days are less than 0, add 30 to the
    REM – days, and subtract 1 from the month
IF w2 < 0 THEN
    w2 = w2 + 12
    w1 = w1 - 1
END IF: REM – if the months are less than 0, add 12 to
    REM – the months, and subtract 1 from the year
w = w1 * 365 + w2 * 30 + w3: REM – sum the days
PRINT w: REM – print the answer
END
*    *    * END OF DATE CALCULATION ROUTINE * *      *
```

This is not an exact calculation. It assumes a 30 day month for all months. But as a simple method of aging invoices, determining time-to-payment, and finding elapsed days between any two dates, it works easily, and well.

Summary

1. The operators include:
   - \+ is the addition operator.
   - – is the subtraction operator.
   - * is the multiplication operator.
   - / is the division operator.
   - ^ is the exponentiation operator.
2. You join two or more strings into one by using the addition operator.
3. Avoid dividing by zero; it stops the program. Test the divisor before every divide.
4. The order of calculation is:
   1. Expressions in parentheses are calculated first, as each right parenthesis is matched with a left parenthesis.
   2. Exponentiation.
   3. Multiplication, or division, whichever is found first.
   4. Addition or subtraction, whichever is first as the computer scans the formula from left to right.
5. Use parentheses to ensure that the formula is calculated properly, and to clarify the calculation in your own mind. Do not worry about too many parentheses.
6. Data types are important in your calculations. They can give a right, or a wrong answer.
7. QBasic can cause rounding problems. Do your own rounding to avoid them.
8. INT, CINT, FIX AND CLNG are similar, but not identical. Know when to use each.

9. QBasic has math functions.
10. STR$ converts a number into a string.
11. Put a date into YYMMDD format before comparing it to another date, or calculating the number of days between two dates.

These topics are simplified to better explain the essence of calculations. If you want to use additional complexity, look to your QBasic manual.

The Book in Review

1. Design and program thoughtfully.
2. To examine any QBasic program, break it up into blocks. Then study each block separately, and finally look at the logic that controls all the blocks.
3. QBasic gives you a complete working environment, which encourages writing programs in building-block fashion.
4. Blueprint your program before you write the first line of code.
5. Data names should be meaningful, short (but not cryptic), consistent, and clear.
6. The QBasic Editor is top shelf. Use the keys, rather than the menus, and you will be productive.
7. Program organization is crucial. Blueprint, assign the tasks to routines, then program each routine.
8. GOSUB subroutines; CALL procedures. GOTO a line name that is within the same routine as the GOTO statement.
9. Keep your IFs simple, and easy to read.
10. Loops are critical to good programming. You can destroy their structure with the wrong GOTO. Never GOTO somewhere outside the loop.
11. Group like items together, describe them, and you have the start of a file.
12. Learn random files well; they are the foundation of all file work.
13. The linked list structure is for transaction-type files.
14. Edit new data thoroughly or your program dies.
15. Set up standard edit procedures and use them.

16. Design each report with the least amount of data to achieve its purpose.
17. Does this layout make the screen easier to read? If not, do not use it.
18. **Understand and test all your calculations exhaustively.**

CHAPTER 19

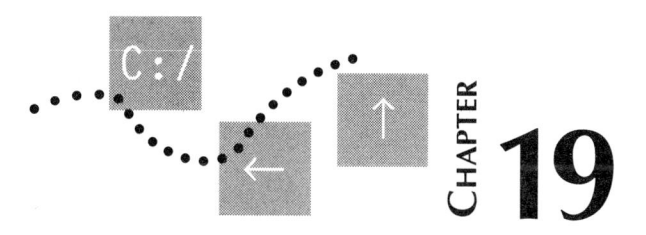

Tables

This chapter teaches you about the different dimensions of tables. You learn how to define and use tables in your QBasic programs. The topics include:

- One-dimensional tables
- Two-dimensional tables
- Three-dimensional tables
- Uses of tables in QBasic
- Defining a table
- Locating the elements in a table
- Subscripts—keeping them straight
- DIMensioning an array
- Getting values into an array
- DATA and READ statements
- Printing a table
- A table within a random file record
- A comprehensive example
- QBasic limitations for tables

Chris' Train Schedule is a Table

Chris is going to New York City for the week in order to solicit corporate business for WildWater Works. Chris is out to convince corporate executives that the New York companies should offer two- and three-day rafting trips as incentives for sales and production contests. A week-long *management experience* is being promoted in which managers are placed in difficult situations as they spend a week going down the river together.

Chris is trying to figure out which train to catch. The schedule looks like this:

train	leaves ALBANY	arrives ATHENS	arrives LONDON	arrives PARIS	arrives NYC
Road Runner	6:00 AM	6:41 AM	7:14 AM	7:57 AM	8:26 AM
Earlyworm	7:00 AM	7:41 AM	8:14 AM	8:57 AM	9:26 AM
Blue Bomber	8:30 AM	9:11 AM	9:44 AM	10:27 AM	10:56 AM
Orient Express	9:00 AM	9:41 AM	10:14 AM	10:57 AM	11:26 AM
Ramblin' Ram	10:30 AM	11:11 AM	11:44 AM	12:27 PM	12:56 PM

Chris needs to catch the train that arrives in New York by 11 AM for the first meeting. Chris looks down the "Arrive NYC," column 5, for the arrival times. The third row has a train (the Blue Bomber) that arrives in NYC at 10:56 AM. Chris then scans the row over to column 1 to find the departure time from Albany. A table has just been used.

Definition of Dimension

A *dimension* of an array is a collection of locations that identify each element of that table.

A one-dimensional table has one set of identifiers, a two-dimensional table has two sets of identifiers, a three-dimensional table has three sets of identifiers, a four-dimensional array has four sets, and so on.

There is one identifier for each location, numbered 1 to the number of locations in each dimension. For example:

1. A grocery list with 10 items is a one-dimensional table, with 10 locations in the single dimension. The locations are numbered 1-10.
2. A checkerboard is a two-dimensional table, with eight locations in each dimension. The locations in the first dimension are numbered 1-8. The locations in the second dimension are also numbered 1-8.
3. The NYC train schedule in the beginning of this chapter is a two-dimensional array with 5 locations (rows) in the first dimension, and 5 locations (columns) in the second dimension.

Locating the Elements in a Table

You can locate items on the train schedule by specifying a value in each dimension:

1. The arrival time of Earlyworm in London, 8:14 AM, is found on row 2, column 3.
2. The time that Blue Bomber leaves Albany, 8:30 AM, is found on row 3, column 1.
3. The arrival time of Road Runner in New York City, 8:26 AM, is found on row 1, column 5.
4. The arrival of Ramblin' Ram in Paris, 12:27 PM, is found on row 5, column 4.

One-dimensional Tables

These are some examples of one-dimensional tables:

- A grocery list
- Schedule for a football team
- Things to do today

- List of suspects in a murder mystery weekend
- Things to take on a trip
- List of reserved words in QBasic

Two-dimensional Tables

These are some examples of two-dimensional tables:

- Train schedules
- Calendar (for one month)
- Checkerboard
- Television schedules
- Tic-tac-toe grid

Three-dimensional Tables

These are some examples of three-dimensional tables:

- Calendar (for an entire year)
- Three-dimensional chess board
- Three-dimensional tic-tac-toe board

Uses of Tables in QBasic

These are some uses of tables in QBasic.

1. Keeping a list of error messages
2. Defining the number of days in each of 12 months
3. Defining any list of weights, dollars, conversions
4. Keeping item sales for each month of one or more years

5. Storing purchases for each month, week, or day
6. Storing dollars paid for each month, week, or day

Defining a Table

A table is defined by specifying:

- The number of dimensions
- The number of locations in each dimension

The words *table* and *array* are interchangeable throughout this chapter.

It is hard to define a dimension in plain language. So here is an example. Remember the Rubik's cube? It is a good size block, made up of a lot of little blocks that you could move all around. A dimension is one row of those little blocks in a Rubik's cube.

A Rubik's cube has three dimensions; as you look at it directly, the front side has two dimensions:

- Rows across (width)
- Rows down (columns or height)

The third-dimension is the rows deep (thickness or depth). We live in a three-dimensional world, so it is hard to visualize four- and five-dimensional things. You can also use Rubik's cubes to view four, five, and six dimensions:

- Four dimensions—a row of Rubik's cubes.
- Five dimensions—a giant checkerboard with a Rubik's cube on each square.
- Six dimensions—a box filled with those cubes.

Here is a more detailed example:

Pat is searching for new rivers where WildWater Works can host their guests. Pat goes into the State map room. Each map is filed in a book. There are 10 books on each shelf, numbered 1 through 10. There are four shelves in each rack. There are three racks to a row. The room has 10 rows of books.

Crow's Eye View of Map Room

| row 1 | row 2 | row 3 | row 4 | row 5 |
| row 6 | row 7 | row 8 | row 9 | row 10 |

Pat's view of Row 1

rack 1	rack 2	rack 3
shelf 4	shelf 4	shelf 4
shelf 3	shelf 3	shelf 3
shelf 2	shelf 2	shelf 2
shelf 1	map1 map2 map3 map4 map5 map6 map7 map8 map9 map10	shelf 1

Pat checks the computer directory for maps of the Moose River; the maps are in book 8 of shelf 1, rack 2, row 1. The Interstate runs in a straight line beginning at the southern part of the state, and goes directly north to the northern boundary of the state. The Interstate exits are numbered, beginning with 1 at the southern tip of the state and ending with 61 at the northern tip. Pat has to get off the Interstate at Exit 47.

The *Interstate* is basically a straight line, and has only *one-dimension* (length). The dimensions could either be set up as length in miles, or exit numbers. In either case, only one identifier is needed to locate a point on the Interstate.

The *map* Pat is looking at is *two-dimensional* (length and width). In the case of most maps, a grid of letters and numbers is used to locate a point on the map.

The *map book* is *three-dimensional*. To locate a point on a map, first find the page (first dimension), then the grid letter and number (the other two dimensions). The *sequence number* of the map book on the shelf adds a *fourth-dimension*. The shelf number on the rack becomes a *fifth-dimension*. The *rack* is the *sixth*. The row adds the *seventh-dimension*.

Each dimension is an identifier used to find data. To completely identify a point on a map to someone who is in the map room (so that the person can go directly to the correct point on the map without searching), you have to specify seven identifiers, one for each dimension:

- Dimension 1 (1-10) for the row
- Dimension 2 (1-3) for the rack
- Dimension 3 (1-4) for the shelf
- Dimension 4 (1-10) for the book
- Dimension 5 (1-{number of pages in the book}) to specify the page number
- Dimension 6 (A-Z) to identify the grid letter
- Dimension 7 (1-20) to identify the grid number

Subscripts: Keeping Them Straight

The coordinates that give the exact location of an item in a table are called *Subscripts*. Each dimension has its own subscript. The value of the subscript determines the location (or one coordinate of the location) of each element in the array. Subscripts tell the computer how to find any item in the array directly, without searching.

In the previous example which located the elements in the train table, the subscripts are:

1. The first subscript is 2, the second is 3.
2. The first subscript is 3, the second is 1.
3. The first subscript is 1, the second is 5.
4. The first subscript is 5, the second is 4.

Now give the train schedule table the name, *Traintab$* (for use in QBasic). Then, the locations of each item above are identified as:

1. `Traintab$ (2,3):REM` has a value of 8:14 AM
2. `Traintab$ (3,1):REM` has a value of 8:30 AM
3. `Traintab$ (1,5):REM` has a value of 8:26 AM
4. `Traintab$ (5,4):REM` has a value of 12:27 PM

Dimensioning a Table

Before an array can be used in QBasic, its size must be defined in the DIM statement. The DIM statement designates the number of dimensions, and the number of elements in each dimension. The DIM statement in a program can only be executed once for each array, so place it in the OPENFILE routine, which is enabled only once.

The syntax is:

```
DIM {array name 1}({# of elements}, {# of elements, etc}),_
{array name 2}(etc)
```

where

`{array name 1}` is the name of the table, and {# of elements} is the number of items in each of the dimensions.

An array can have from 1 to 8 dimensions in QBasic.

Example of DIM

```
DIM traintab$(5,5)
```

is the DIMension statement for the train table in this chapter.

More than one array can be dimensioned in a DIM statement:

```
DIM traintab$(5,5), monthtab(12)
```

This DIM statement defines *traintab$* as having two-dimensions, with five elements in each. It defines *monthtab* as a one-dimensional array with 12 elements.

Getting Values into Arrays

There are different ways to get values into a table. Use your *Traintab$* to:

1. Assign each value.

    ```
    traintab$(1,1)= "6:00 AM"
    traintab$(1,2)= "6:41 AM"
    traintab$(1,3)= "7:14 AM"
    ```

    and so on for each element in the table.

2. Input each value.

    ```
    LINE INPUT"enter ELEMENT (1,1)";traintab$(1,1)
    LINE INPUT"enter ELEMENT (1,2)";traintab$(1,2)
    LINE INPUT"enter ELEMENT (1,3)";traintab$(1,3)
    ```

    and so on for each element in the table.

Data and Read Statements

When these methods seem cumbersome, and the values are only set once in the program, the READ and DATA statements are a good way to give values to a table. The DATA statement contains the values. The READ statement assigns those values to the table.

Example using READ and DATA:

```
FOR i%=1 TO 5
    FOR j%=1 TO 5
    READ traintab$(i%,j%)
    NEXT j%
NEXT i%
DATA "6:00 AM","6:41 AM","7:14 AM","7:57 AM","8:26 AM"
DATA "7:00 AM","7:41 AM","8:14 AM","8:57 AM","9:26 AM"
DATA "8:30 AM","9:11 AM","9:44 AM","10:27 AM","10:56 AM"
```

```
DATA "9:00 AM","9:41 AM","10:14 AM","10:57 AM","11:26 AM"
DATA "10:30 AM","11:11 AM","11:44 AM","12:27 PM","12:56 PM"
```

This assigns 25 values to the table *Traintab$*, which is the train schedule at the beginning of the chapter.

Printing Out a Table

Traintab$ can be printed by using these QBasic program lines:

```
FOR i%=1 TO 5
    FOR j%=1 TO 5
        PRINT TAB(j%*10); traintab$(i%,j%);
    NEXT j%
    PRINT
NEXT i%
```

You could also print traintab$ by specifying each table item like this:

```
PRINT TAB(10); traintab$(1,1); TAB(20); traintab$(1,2);_
TAB(30); traintab$(1,3); TAB(40); traintab$(1,4); TAB(50);_
traintab(1,5)

PRINT TAB(10); traintab$(2,1); TAB(20); traintab$(2,2);_
TAB(30); traintab$(2,3); TAB(40); traintab$(2,4); TAB(50);_
traintab(2,5)

PRINT TAB(10); traintab$(3,1); TAB(20); traintab$(3,2);_
TAB(30); traintab$(3,3); TAB(40); traintab$(3,4); TAB(50);_
traintab(3,5)

PRINT TAB(10); traintab$(4,1); TAB(20); traintab$(4,2);_
TAB(30); traintab$(4,3); TAB(40); traintab$(4,4); TAB(50);_
traintab(4,5)

PRINT TAB(10); traintab$(5,1); TAB(20); traintab$(5,2);_
TAB(30); traintab$(5,3); TAB(40); traintab$(5,4); TAB(50);_
traintab(5,5)
```

Boring, huh?. The best way to print the entire table is to use a double loop similar to the one at the start of this section. Specify individual table elements in a PRINT statement when only a few of the table items are to be printed.

A Table within a Random File Record

A table can also get its values by reading them into the program from a random file. The table can be part of the record layout contained in the FIELD statement.

For instance, 12 months of sales for each WWW T-shirt could be saved on an inventory record on disk, and read in as each T-shirt is processed.

The table first needs to be dimensioned in the FILEOPEN routine. Then the table is defined in the FIELD statement. Once the GET is executed, (and the data unpacked, if necessary) the table has its values.

In the case of the train table, the FIELD statement is:

```
FIELD 1, 8 AS traintab$(1,1), 8 AS traintab$(1,2), 8 AS_
traintab$(1,3), 8 AS traintab$(1,4), 8 AS traintab$(1,5)

FIELD 1, 40 AS fill1$, 8 AS traintab(2,1), 8 AS_
traintab$(2,2), 8 AS traintab$(2,3), 8 AS traintab$(2,4), 8_
AS traintab$(2,5)

FIELD 1, 80 AS fill1$, 8 AS traintab(3,1), 8 AS_
traintab$(3,2), 8 AS traintab$(3,3), 8 AS traintab$(3,4), 8_
as traintab$(3,5)

FIELD 1, 120 AS fill1$, 8 AS traintab(4,1), 8 AS_
traintab$(4,2), 8 AS traintab$(4,3), 8 AS traintab$(4,4), 8_
as traintab$(4,5)

FIELD 1, 160 AS fill1$, 8 AS traintab(5,1), 8 AS_
traintab$(5,2), 8 AS traintab$(5,3), 8 AS traintab$(5,4), 8_
as traintab$(5,5)
```

A Comprehensive Example

The program below illustrates almost everything in this chapter. The program, *printran*, reads the train file to get the schedule (traintab$), then prints the table on the printer.

```
REM — printran   06/01/94
stub:
    GOSUB getdate
    GOSUB fileopen
```

```
        GOSUB main
        CLOSE
        END
getdate:
        w1$ = LEFT$(DATE$,2)
        w2$ = MID$(DATE$,4,2)
        w3$ = RIGHT$(DATE$,2)
        dat$ = w1$ + "/" + w2$ + "/" + w3$
        dat = VAL(w1$) * 10000 + val(w2$) * 100 + VAL(w3$)
        tad = VAL(w3$) * 10000 + val(w2$) * 100 + VAL(w1$)
RETURN
fileopen:
    OPEN "R", #1, "trainfil.dat", 256
    DIM traintab$(5,5)
    FIELD 1, 8 AS traintab$(1,1), 8 AS traintab$(1,2), 8 AS_
traintab$(1,3), 8 AS traintab$(1,4), 8 AS traintab$(1,5)
    FIELD 1, 40 AS fill1$, 8 AS traintab(2,1),8 AS traintab$_
(2,2), 8 AS traintab$(2,3), 8 AS traintab$(2,4), 8 AS_
traintab$(2,5)
    FIELD 1, 80 AS fill1$, 8 AS traintab(3,1), 8 AS traintab$_
(3,2), 8 AS traintab$(3,3), 8 AS traintab$(3,4), 8 as_
traintab$(3,5)
    FIELD 1, 120 AS fill1$, 8 AS traintab(4,1), 8 AS traintab$_
(4,2), 8 AS traintab$(4,3), 8 AS traintab$(4,4), 8 as_
traintab$(4,5)
    FIELD 1, 160 AS fill1$, 8 AS traintab(5,1), 8 AS traintab$_
(5,2), 8 AS traintab$(5,3), 8 AS traintab$(5,4), 8 as_
traintab$(5,5)
RETURN
read1:
        GET 1, f1
RETURN
main:
```

```
        f1 = f1 + 1
        IF f1 > 100 THEN GOTO end-main :REM — up to 100 schedules
        GOSUB read1
        GOSUB prinsched
        GOTO main
end-main:
RETURN
prinsched:
        FOR i%=1 TO 5
                FOR j%=1 TO 5
                        LPRINT TAB(j%*10); traintab$(i%,j%);
                NEXT j%
                PRINT
        NEXT i%
RETURN
```

QBASIC Limitations

1. There can be a *maximum* of eight dimensions in any one array.
2. There can be a *maximum* of 65,535 bytes total space for any one array. Each integer takes up two bytes; each single-precision number uses four bytes, each long integer is four bytes long, and each double-precision number takes up eight bytes. Each character in a string is one byte. QBasic has these limitations for each type of array (table):

   - 32767 integers
   - or 16383 long integers
   - or 16383 single precision numbers
   - or 8191 double precision numbers
   - or a total of 65,535 string characters

You can never mix data types within an array.

- An integer array contains only integers.
- A long integer array has all long integers.
- A single-precision array holds only six-digit numbers.
- A double-precision array has double precision numbers.
- A string array contains alphanumeric characters, and none of the numeric types mentioned above.

Summary

1. Tables are something you see and work with regularly.
2. A table can have from one to eight dimensions. Each dimension has a number of locations, which are specified by its *subscript*.
3. Define an array with a DIM statement.
4. You can put values into an array by:
   - Assigning the values directly.
   - Keying them using the LINE INPUT statement.
   - Using the READ and DATA statement combination.
   - Reading them from a data file on disk.
5. You can print a table:
   - Within a loop.
   - By identifying each individual element to PRINT statements.
   - Within a loop and identify each individual element to PRINT statements.
6. Use tables whenever you are working with more than three like items to reduce coding mistakes.
7. QBasic limits you to:
   - Eight dimensions in any one array.
   - 65,535 bytes total space for any one array.
     - 32767 integers
     - or 16383 long integers
     - or 16383 single precision numbers

- or 8191 double precision numbers
- or a total of 65,535 string characters

The Book in Review

1. Design and program thoughtfully.
2. To examine any QBasic program, break it up into blocks. Then study each block separately, and finally look at the logic that controls all the blocks.
3. QBasic gives you a complete working environment, which encourages writing programs in building-block fashion.
4. Blueprint your program before you write the first line of code.
5. Data names should be meaningful, short (but not cryptic), consistent and clear.
6. The QBasic Editor is top shelf. Use the keys, rather than the menus, and you will be productive.
7. Program organization is crucial. Blueprint, assign the tasks to routines, then program each routine.
8. GOSUB subroutines; CALL procedures. GOTO a line name that is within the same routine as the GOTO statement.
9. Keep your IFs simple, and easy to read.
10. Loops are critical to good programming. You can destroy their structure with the wrong use GOTO. Never GOTO somewhere outside the loop.
11. Group like items together, describe them, and you have the start of a file.
12. Learn random files well; they are the foundation of all file work.
13. The linked list structure is for transaction-type files.
14. Edit new data thoroughly or your program dies.
15. Set up standard edit procedures and use them.
16. Design each report with the least amount of data to achieve its purpose.
17. Does this layout make the screen easier to read? If not, do not use it.
18. Understand and test all your calculations exhaustively.
19. **Use tables to simplify your logic and avoid unnecessary coding.**

Chapter 20

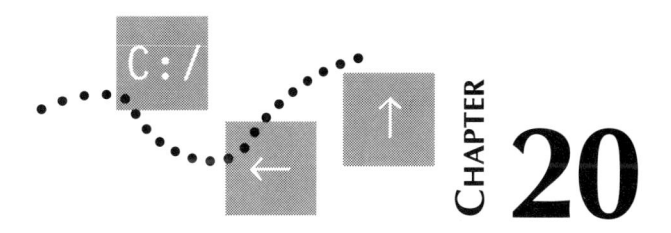

Debugging

This chapter teaches you how to test your QBasic programs for errors. You type in a program and try each of the features of the Debug program. The topics include:

- One step at a time
- Stop the action
- Action
- Quick look, quick change, then action
- A comprehensive example
- Debugger hints

Avoiding Mistakes

Remember Chris' wasted time in Chapter 6? The newsletter was typed on a regular typewriter. Eight hours was wasted because of mistakes in grammar, spelling, and newsletter organization.

Writing a program is more precise than writing in English. It would be equivalent to writing a chapter in the book on *How to Rescue People from "Death-Machine" Rapids*, written for the white water rescue teams. Every detail must be specified perfectly, or the book would be worthless, its users dead. This perfect precision is not found often in the first writing of any but the smallest programs. At first, programs have mistakes, normally in logic, but other times in typing, which prevent the program from running correctly. We call these mistakes *bugs*.

No matter how hard you try for perfection, you are likely to have some bugs in your program. Fortunately, the QBasic Debugger makes it easy to find and correct them.

First, read the explanations of each of the Debug features, then you can type in a program, and try each of the features on the program.

Press **Alt+D** to display the Debug menu.

The Debugger has both a menu and special function keys. Whenever a function key performs the same function as a Debug menu item, use the function key. Fewer screens flash before your eyes, making the debug process less confusing.

Single Stepping

Single stepping means that each time you press **F8**, one program statement is executed. As each statement is invoked, it is highlighted, to show you at what statement the program is to run.

When you first run a program, *do the single step* to see how your logic actually flows.

The Trace Feature

The Trace feature highlights each statement as the program is running. Its appearance is identical to single stepping, but it lets the program run from beginning to end, and you can see which statements are executed in what order. To stop it any time:

Press **Ctrl+Break**.

Continue your program after checking out some logic or values by pressing **F5**.

Stop the Action

You can stop the action:

- Manually
- By using the breakpoint feature

Stopping the Program Manually

You stop a running program because you want to look at data name values, verify some output, or change something in the program. To stop the execution of a program:

Press **Ctrl+Break**.

The Breakpoint Feature

The key used to mark a breakpoint statement in your program is **F9**. When the program reaches a breakpoint statement, it stops. Use breakpoints to stop a program so that you can look at variables, study screen output, or change the values of some variables.

Instant Screen

After the program is stopped, the key that switches between program statements and the screen output of the program is **F4**. Use this key to look at the screen output that was produced up to the stopping point.

While the program is stopped, use **F6**, then some PRINT statements, to print out the values of any of the program's variables. There is more information about that later in this chapter.

Action

The key that starts the program, and continues it after stopping, is **F5**. The key to start or restart your program in single-step mode is **F8**.

The Set Next Statement command allows rerunning a program at a statement that is different from the one where the program stopped. There is more information on this later in this chapter.

Quick Look, Quick Change, Then Action

The Immediate window is used to look at or change the values of variables, so that logic segments can be checked out quickly. After the program has been stopped:

Press **F6**.

The program displays the Immediate window. Then use QBasic PRINT statements to look at variables and assign a new value to the variable if you want.

Press **F6**.

The program closes the Immediate window. To continue the program.

Press **F5**.

A Comprehensive Example

Now you can use the debugger. First, type in the simple program below, then use the debugger to "test" it. This helps you develop confidence with the debugger.

Type each line, pressing **Enter** after each:

```
a = 1
b = 2.
FOR i = 1 TO 10000
c = i * b + a
PRINT i, a, b, c.
NEXT i
PRINT "finished".
END
```

First, single-step through the program.

Press **F8**.

Keep pressing **F8**, and watch the program run, one step (statement) at a time. If an error message pops up, check your program against the one in the book, make the corrections, and

Press **F8** again.

Watch each statement being highlighted as it is executed.

Next set the Trace feature, and continue the program in slow motion, rather than single-step.

Press **Alt+D**.

Move the cursor down to the Trace.

Press **Enter**.

The Trace mode is now enabled.

Press **F5** to continue the program.

QBasic highlights each statement as it is executed, and flashes to the screen display with each iteration of the loop. Concentrate on the highlighted statements, and work to ignore the flashing display like you ignore rain or snow on the windshield of your car. You see the execution of the program, statement by statement.

When you have figured out the logic,

Press **Ctrl+Break**.

The program stops running.

To look at the screen output that the program displayed,

Press **F4**.

The program displays the screen output of the program.

Press **F4** again.

The program displays program statements.

Press **F4** again.

The program displays the screen again.

Press **F4** once more to redisplay the program statements.

The Breakpoint key sets the program line or lines at which the program stops, and gives control back to you. Set a breakpoint at the print line;

PRINT i, a, b, c

Using the Arrow keys, move the cursor down to that print line, and

Press **F9**.

The statement line is highlighted. Now

Press **F5**.

The program runs. It stops at the calculation line.

Press **F4**.

The program displays the screen output.

You can see that one more iteration of the loop has printed.

Press **F4** again.

The program displays the program statements.

Press **F5** to continue.

Repeat this process six times to get the feel of it. This run-to-breakpoint, then look-at-the-output, then run-to-breakpoint, then look-at-the-output is probably how you will test your programs.

Remove the breakpoint. Move the cursor, if necessary, using the Arrow keys to the highlighted breakpoint line and

Press **F9**.

The highlight and the breakpoint are removed. Now, move on to the next feature.

The debugger allows you to print or change the values of variables of a stopped program, then continue running the program. For instance, in a program with a loop (like this one), if you want to skip most of the iterations (and get on with the rest of the program), you just change the value of the loop counter. Right now the value of i is probably less than 200. Print the value of i, then change it to be 9950, and continue running the program until it finishes.

Press **F6** to get into the Immediate window, then

Type **PRINT i**

The value of i is printed onto the screen.

Now,

Press **F4**.

Type **i=9950**.

Press **Enter**.

Press **F6** to get back to the main window containing the program statements, then

Press **F5** to continue the program.

The program skips to $i = 9950$ and continues processing until $i = 10000$, prints *finished*, then stops.

Press **Enter** to get back to the program statements, and press **F4** to look at the screen.

Finally, here is a debug feature that you rarely need. The Set Next Statement command lets you continue running a program at a different point from where the program stopped.

To try this feature, set the cursor at the statement where you want execution to begin.

Press **Alt+D**.

Move the cursor down to the Set Next Statement.

Press **Enter**.

Then,

Press **F6**.

The program continues running, beginning with that statement.

Debugger Hints

These debug features allow thorough testing of programs without ever leaving QBasic. Here are a few hints to help you test programs with the Debugger.

1. Test the program one routine at a time. Begin with the main routine, and set up blank *dummy* routines to test the main logic.
2. Single step through each routine the first time.

3. Perform the simplest test for each routine first, then go on to more complex tests.
4. One test is not enough for any routine, a minimum of three is needed for every possible logic path.
5. Use Breakpoints.
6. Keep testing simply but thoroughly. If the input is numeric, use simple numbers like 10, 50, 100, or 1000 at first so that you can easily check the answer.
7. Quantity testing is never a substitute for quality testing. Running a thousand numbers through the same logic is not as good as running a few numbers through all the logic paths.
8. When you are positive that it is perfect, test twice more.

Summary

1. You have a powerful Debugger. Use it.
2. Heed the hints in this chapter.

The Book in Review

1. Design and program thoughtfully.
2. To examine any QBasic program, break it up into blocks. Then study each block separately, and finally look at the logic that controls all the blocks.
3. QBasic gives you a complete working environment which encourages writing programs in building-block fashion.
4. Blueprint your program before you write the first line of code.
5. Data names should be meaningful, short (but not cryptic), consistent and clear.
6. The QBasic Editor is top shelf. Use the keys, rather than the menus, and you'll be productive.
7. Program organization is crucial. Blueprint, assign the tasks to routines, then program each routine.

8. GOSUB subroutines; CALL procedures. GOTO a line name that is within the same routine as the GOTO statement.
9. Keep your IFs simple, and easy to read.
10. Loops are critical to good programming. You can destroy their structure with the use of a wrong GOTO. Never GOTO somewhere outside of the loop.
11. Group like items together, describe them, and you have the start of a file.
12. Learn random files well; they are the foundation of all file work.
13. The linked list structure is for transaction-type files.
14. Edit new data thoroughly or your program dies.
15. Set up standard edit procedures and use them.
16. Design each report with the least amount of data to achieve its purpose.
17. Does this layout make the screen easier to read? If not, do not use it.
18. Understand and test all your calculations exhaustively.
19. Use tables to simplify your logic and avoid unnecessary coding.
20. **Use all the hints with the QBasic Debugger, for the quickest results.**

CHAPTER 21

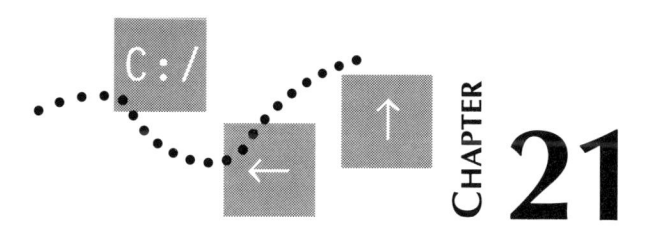

Menu Programs

This chapter concludes this book with the cement that ties all the programs together. The menu program is used to select which programs in your system are run. You learn:

- The CHAIN statement
- What a menu program does
- The WWW menu program

Terry is trying to find the meaning of a weird error message that was displayed on a program that was being debugged. The problem is, the QBasic book being used has no index, and no real table of contents. So Terry keeps skimming the book, trying to find that message.

Just as a book without an index and table of contents is hard to use for reference, so is the selection process (without a menu) for the programs you want to run. It is hard to give programs names that instantly tell you what the program does. When you have several systems, each with 10 to 20 programs, you probably won't be able to figure out each program simply by looking at the name.

A menu program that uses the CHAIN statement is the answer to organizing your system of programs.

Chain Statement

The CHAIN statement links one program to another. When this statement is executed, it exits the program currently running, and invokes the program name contained in the CHAIN statment.

This statement is used to "chain" from a menu program to the selected program, and then "chain" from the selected program back to the menu program. In this way, the only program name that you have to know is the menu program. Once you are in it, you can chain to any of its selections, which each chains back to the menu program. The statement is also used to run a series of programs that chain from one to the next in order to accomplish several different functions, one right after another.

Syntax:

```
CHAIN {program name}
```

where `{program name}` is the name of the program to be invoked.

Example:

```
CHAIN "wwwreg"
```

where *wwwreg* is the program that is invoked when the statement is executed.

NOTE: If any files are open, they should be CLOSEd before the CHAIN statement is executed.

What a Menu Program Does

A Menu program is used to describe each program in the system, so that a user can intelligently decide which program he or she wants to run. This means that:

- There must be several choices from which to pick (several programs which can be run).
- The description of the program must be clear enough that the program user can make the right decision. It is the same thing as a menu in a restaurant, describing each kind of food selection. It should be brief and clear.
- The choice should be simple to type (either a letter or number) so that the actual selection is quick and easy.
- The menu program should immediately run the selected program, which, when completed, should chain back to the menu program for further user selection.
- And one of the selections should be to exit the menu program and quit this system of programs.

Program Selection Process

Based upon the menu item the user selects, the menu program builds the name of the program to be run. This is accomplished by using a system prefix and some number to uniquely identify the program. For instance:

- WWW01 might be the first program selection.
- WWW02 might be the second program selection.
- WWW03 might be the third program selection.
- WWW04 might be the fourth program selection.

The WWW Menu Program

Now type in a sample WWW menu program:
  TYPE:

```
REM — program "WWWmenu.bas" — created 060194
REM —  (Step #1- displays the menu)
CLS : REM — clear the screen
PRINT "* * * * * WILDWATER WORKS * * * * *"
PRINT "* * * * *   PROGRAMS    * * * * *"
PRINT: PRINT: REM — space 2 lines
PRINT "1   Lookup Customer"
PRINT "2   Enter a Customer"
PRINT "3   Print Mailing List"
PRINT "4   Lookup Shirts"
PRINT "5   Enter New Shirts"
PRINT "6   Print Daily Shirt Status"
PRINT "7   Print Weekly Shirt Sales/Status"
PRINT "8   Enter Shirt sales"
PRINT "9   Receive Shirts"
PRINT "10 Exit this System"
PRINT: PRINT : REM — space 2 lines
REM —Step #2, asks for the selection
pickchoice:
 INPUT "Please Enter Number (1-10) from menu"; menuselect$
   IF VAL(menuselect$) < 1 THEN GOTO pickchoice
   IF VAL(menuselect$) > 10 THEN GOTO pickchoice
   IF menuselect$ = 10 THEN END
 program$ = "WWW" + menuselect$ :REM —form the program name
```

```
    PRINT "Selecting program "; program$
    CHAIN program$ : REM — Step #3-runs that program
    END
```

The WWW menu program prints out the titles and ten items from which to select. It then asks you which number (1-10) you care to select. If the number is less than 1 or greater than 10, the choice is invalid, and the question is reasked. When a number from 1 to 10 is entered, that number is tacked on to the end of WWW to form the program name, the menu is exited, and the selected program is chained to.

Use menu programs for any series of programs of two or more to make operations easy for the person running the system.

The Book in Review

1. Design and program thoughtfully.
2. To examine any QBasic program, break it up into blocks. Then study each block separately, and finally look at the logic that controls all the blocks.
3. QBasic gives you a complete working environment which encourages writing programs in building-block fashion.
4. Blueprint your program **before** you write the first line of code.
5. Data names should be meaningful, short (but not cryptic), consistent and clear.
6. The QBasic Editor is top shelf. Use the keys, rather than the menus, and you'll be productive.
7. Program organization is crucial. Blueprint, assign the tasks to routines, then program each routine.
8. GOSUB subroutines; CALL procedures. GOTO a line name that is within the same routine as the GOTO statement.
9. Keep your IFs simple, and easy to read.
10. Loops are critical to good programming. You can destroy their structure with the use of a wrong GOTO. Never GOTO somewhere outside of the loop.

11. Group like items together, describe them, and you have the start of a file.
12. Learn random files well; they are the foundation of all file work.
13. The linked list structure is for transaction-type files.
14. Edit new data thoroughly or your program dies.
15. Set up standard edit procedures and use them.
16. Design each report with the least amount of data to achieve its purpose.
17. Does this layout make the screen easier to read? If not, do not use it.
18. Understand and test all your calculations exhaustively.
19. Use tables to simplify your logic and avoid unnecessary coding.
20. Use all the hints with the QBasic Debugger, for the quickest results.
21. **Use a menu program whenever there are two or more programs involved.**

Remember to use thought in all your programming, and you won't go wrong. Review this book again after six months of programming. You'll pick up a lot more that wasn't clear the first time. Having gone through this book, you have made a good start.

If you have mastered this book, you can easily write good programs in any language by using the principles in these chapters.

Remember, good programming never changes. Only the languages are different. Best of luck!

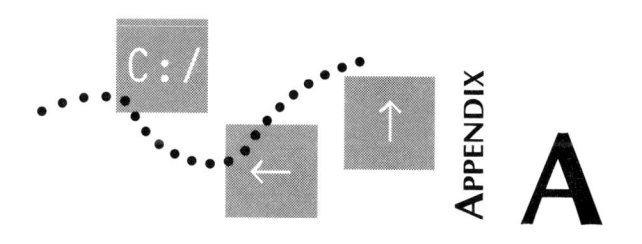

QBasic Selected Statement Summary

Statement	Description
ASC	Gets the ASCII value of the first character in a string.
BLOCK IF	An IF statement with its logic spread out onto several program lines.
CHAIN	Loads and runs a program from another program. The control is passed to the CHAINed program.
CHR$	Used with LPRINT to print one or more lines, start a new page, give special commands to your printer.
CINT	Converts an expression into an integer by rounding.
CLNG	Converts an expression into a long integer by rounding.
CLS	Clears the computer screen, and locates the cursor at line 1, column 1.
COLOR	Determines the color of the computer screen foreground (characters) and backgound.
COMMON SHARED	Makes a variable available to every routine in your program.

Statement	Description
CSRLIN	Gets the current line position of the cursor.
CVD	Unpacks a double-precision number from a random file.
CVI	Unpacks an integer from a random file.
CVL	Unpacks a long integer from a random file.
CVS	Unpacks a single-precision number from a random file.
DATA	Used in conjunction with READ to get data into variable names.
DIM	Specifies the size of an array.
DO UNTIL	Begins a loop, which iterates until the specified condition is true. This loop ends with LOOP.
END	Ends a program.
END IF	Ends the logic of a block IF statement.
FIX	Converts an expression into a whole number by truncating, rather than rounding.
FOR…TO	Begins a loop that processes a fixed number of times. This loop ends with a NEXT statement.
FORMAT	A string assignment statement that lays out the print line for use by a PRINT, or a PRINT USING statement.
GET	Reads a record from a random file.
IF	A statement that causes some processing only when the specified condition is true.
IF (EOF {n})	A specialized IF which tests true when the end-of-file is found in file n.
INT	Converts a number into an integer by finding the largest integer that is equal to, or less than, the expression.
LEN	Finds the length of a string.
LEFT$	Gets a specific number of characters from the left side of a string.
LINE INPUT	Gets an input string from the keyboard.
LOCATE	Positions the cursor at a specific spot on the screen.
LOOP	Ends the logic of a conditional loop that began with DO UNTIL…

Appendix A: QBasic Selected Statement Summary

Statement	Description
LPRINT	Prints onto paper.
LPRINT USING	Prints onto paper according to the layout established by the referenced FORMAT statement.
MID$	Gets a specific number of characters from anywhere in the string.
MKD$	Packs a double precision number into random file format.
MKI$	Packs an integer into random file format.
MKL$	Packs a long integer into random file format.
MKS$	Packs a single-precision number into random file format.
NEXT	Ends the logic of a fixed loop that began with a FOR...TO.
OPEN	The statement that opens a random file for use.
POS	Gets the current column position of the cursor.
PRINT	Displays onto the computer screen.
PRINT USING	Displays onto the computer screen according to the layout established by the referenced FORMAT statement.
PUT	Writes a record onto a random file.
REM	A comment or explanation statement by the program to the person who is reading the program code. REM is ignored by the computer. It is never processed.
RIGHT$	Gets a specific number of characters from the right side of a string.
STR$	Converts a numeric expression into a string.
TAB	Used with PRINT or LPRINT to move to a specific column.
TYPE.. END TYPE	Defines the record layout of a random file—another method to use in place of the FIELD statement.
VAL	Converts a string into a number.
WIDTH	Sets the maximum number of characters for a print line.

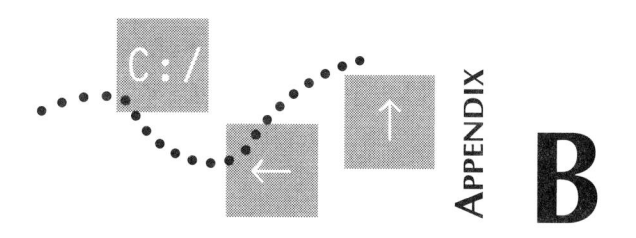

Sample Data Dictionary with Rules for Naming Data

Naming Rules

Rule examples

1. Names should be meaningful to you, the programmer.
   - Not good: `ln personslastname y`
   - Good: `lnam yr%`
   - Better: `lastname salesyr%`
2. Names should be short; not more than twelve characters.
   - Not good: `st streetaddress1`
   - Good: `stradd`
   - Better: `street`

3. Names should be consistent.

   a) All data items from the same file should use the file name as the first part (prefix). Use short file names (up to four characters).
   - Not good: `customeraddr1 name part1stprc`
   - Good: `custstr custnam`
   - Better: `custstreet custlastname`

   b) The same data item seen in several files should have the same suffix (last part) in each name.
   - Not good: `cno pnum`
   - Good: `cusno prtno`
   - Better: `custnum partnum`

   c) All items that are dates should have the same abbreviated suffix, e.g., dt, dat, or date.
   - Not good: `pdt hired bald`
   - Good: `paydt hiredt baldt`
   - Better: `paydat hiredat balancedat`

   d) All numbers that identify things, such as *customer number*, *part number*, *Social Security Number*, etc.) should have the same abbreviated suffix, e.g., no or num.
   - Not good: `cusnmb prt# socialsn`
   - Good: `cusno prtno ssno`
   - Better: `custnum partnum ssnum`

4. Names should not be cryptic. Use vowels when necessary for clarity.
   - Not good: `cutot dtst`
   - Good: `currunpdtot dtsent`
   - Better: `totunpaid datesent`

5. For each program, make a Data Dictionary containing the data names used. Place it at the very beginning of the program.

6. Make data names unique. Include enough characters to make them clear, but no more.

APPENDIX B: SAMPLE DATA DICTIONARY WITH RULES FOR NAMING DATA • **381**

Data Dictionary Example:

```
REM -- Data Dictionary
REM -- blaktrip          $ spent on Black River trips
REM -- city$
REM -- custbirthdat$     customer's birthdate
REM -- custfirstnam$     customer's first name
REM -- custlastname$     customer's last name
REM -- custstreet1$      customer's street address, line 1
REM -- custstreet2$      customer's street address, line 2
REM -- hudstrip          $ spent on Hudson River trips
REM -- moostrip          $ spent on Moose River trips
REM -- purchyr%          year of purchase
REM -- salestax
REM -- shirtsals         $ spent on shirts
REM -- st$               state
REM -- zip%              zip code
REM -- Work Variables:
REM -- c%                loop counter
REM -- tripsubtot#       trip subtotal
```

The Data Dictionary includes all the data names (variables) used in the program. Put them in two major groupings:

- Data names that are contained in files.
- Followed by "work variables" (those used by the program but not saved). Within each grouping, list the data names in alphabetical order. Look at the example Data Dictionary above.

  1. Each Dictionary entry gives the data name, then an expanded definition of its meaning. Limit the definition to 50 characters; do not write full sentences to expand on a data name.
  2. Data names should include the character suffix that defines the data type (as explained in "DATA TYPES"). The Dictionary entry *zip%*

specifies this zip code as a short, five-digit integer (instead of a long, nine-digit integer, or an alphanumeric one).

3. When there can be *no* confusion about what a data name represents, grudgingly omit the expanded definition in the Dictionary. See *city$* and *salestax* in the sample Dictionary.

4. The work variables are simple data names for the "utility" variables used in standard routines, as well as the results of calculations and loops performed within PROCESS, SUBCALC, and MASSAGE routines. Since they serve a broader, workhorse function, being used over and over, their naming is less critical. For example, you might decide that *c%* will always be a loop counter, in all your programs, from now on.

NOTE Name your data consistently throughout all your programs.

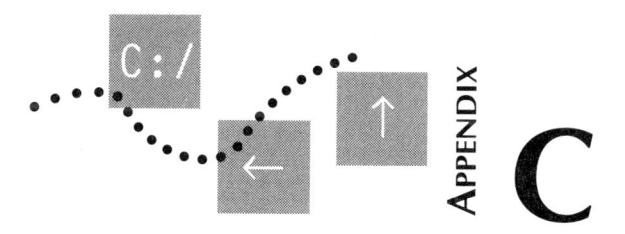

Blueprints

Step 1. Purpose

State in one simple sentence (no ands, ors, ifs, commas) the single major purpose of your program. Then, list the major tasks that this program is to accomplish, defining each task in one simple sentence. If the program has only one simple task, this section is one sentence.

Step 2. End Result (OUTPUT)

On paper, lay out each page to be displayed on the screen or printed by the printer. If a data file will be saved onto disk, specify on paper what the disk file contents will be. (Look at the disk file as if it were a report on paper.) List each data item that is output.

Step 3. Necessary Data (INPUT)

Look at the OUTPUT data (Step 2) in the end result, and determine its source (where it comes from—another file, a calculation, or keyboard input). As you are doing this, give meaningful data names to the OUTPUT data this program creates.

Step 4. Hidden Data (HIDPUT)

If a calculation (formula) is involved, then determine the source (as in Step 3) of all the data contained in the formula. The source could be another file, another calculation, or keyboard input. Keep going until every piece of data in the formulas has a source within the program. Otherwise, you will have formulas that will not work.

Step 5. LOGIC

Put your logic into simple block diagrams. Each block diagram should fit onto a single 8–1/2 inch by 11–inch sheet of paper. If it does not fit, then your logic is probably too complex. (Remember the essence of good programming: make it simple.) If you cannot fit all the functions or procedures on one sheet, then put the major logic onto one sheet and the other (more detailed) routines on other sheets. In any case, force yourself to be constrained—that is the purpose of using 8–1/2 inch by 11–inch sheets rather than large paper for the logic. Fitting the logic on small sheets forces simplicity. The rules of block diagramming are:

1. Put each step within a block.
2. Connect the blocks with arrows to show the direction of program flow. Two sample program blueprints follow. You can block diagram your programs from here on.

NOTE Take your time. The time you spend blueprinting to define the problem and its corresponding solution will pay you back tenfold at the programming stage. Conversely, every minute you think you save by not defining the problem costs you 10 or more at the programming stage. Five minutes can save an hour.

Sample Blueprint #1

Program Name: mailkey1.

Purpose: To key the magazine mailing list into our computer.

OUTPUT Result: File on disk, containing 3,000 names and addresses. The name of the file is *mail*. The description is...

Data Name	Description	Location In File (positions)	Maximum Length
mailname	prospect's name	1-30	30
mailaddr1	1st line of address	31-60	30
mailaddr2	2nd line of address	61-90	30
mailcity	city	91-110	20
mailstate	state	111-112	2
mailzip	zip	113-121	9

INPUT: Source for all data is keyboard input. The operator of the program keys in all the data on each prospect.

Data	Source
mailname	key entry
mailaddr1	key entry
mailaddr2	key entry
mailcity	key entry
mailstate	key entry
mailzip	key entry

HIDPUT (data hidden in formulas): None.

LOGIC (block diagram):

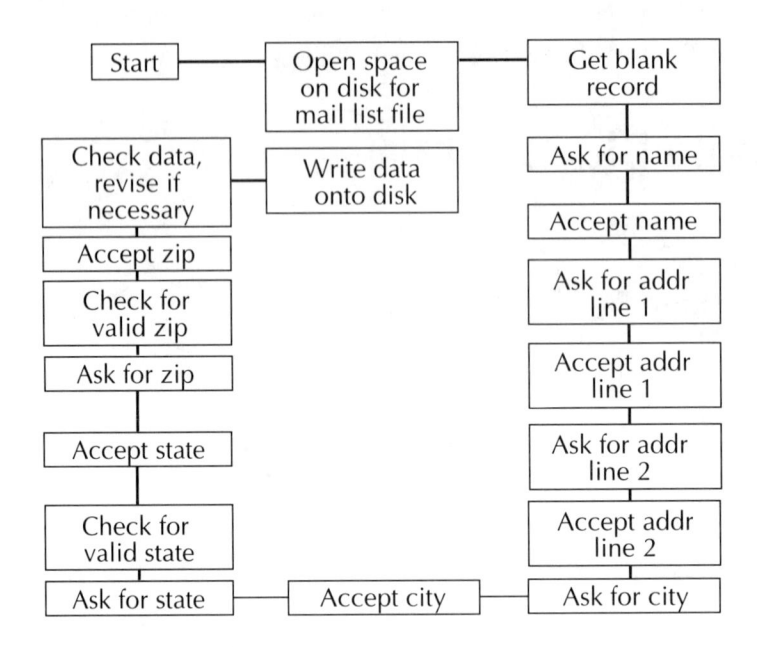

```
Start ──→ Open space      ──→ Get blank
          on disk for          record
          mail list file        │
                                ▼
 ┌──────────────────────── Ask for name
 ▼                               │
Check data,    Write data        ▼
revise if  ──  onto disk    Accept name
necessary                        │
 │                               ▼
 ▼                          Ask for addr
Accept zip                   line 1
 │                               │
 ▼                               ▼
Check for                   Accept addr
valid zip                    line 1
 │                               │
 ▼                               ▼
Ask for zip                 Ask for addr
 │                           line 2
 ▼                               │
Accept state                     ▼
 │                          Accept addr
 ▼                           line 2
Check for                        │
valid state                      ▼
 │                          Ask for city
 ▼                               │
Ask for state ── Accept city ────┘
```

Sample Blueprint #2

Program Name: `maillabl`.

Purpose: To print mailing labels for all the people in your MAIL file.

    OUTPUT Result: One mailing label for each person.

INPUT (data sources): All the data for the label is found in the file called MAIL,

```
Chuck Butkus
999 Route 9
Indian Lake   NY   12345
```

which is on your computer disk.

Data	Description	Source
lablname	prospect name	mail file
labladdr1	1st addr line	mail file
labladdr2	2nd addr line	mail file
lablcity	city	mail file
lablstate	state	mail file
lablzip	zip	mail file

HIDPUT (data in formulas): none.

LOGIC (block diagram):

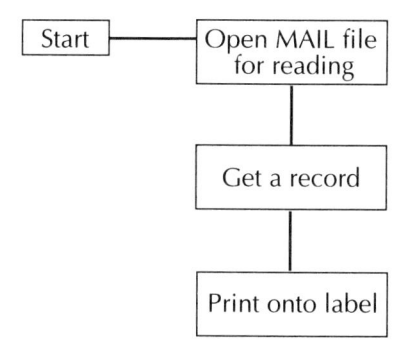

```
Start ─── Open MAIL file
          for reading
              │
              │
          Get a record
              │
              │
          Print onto label
```

APPENDIX D

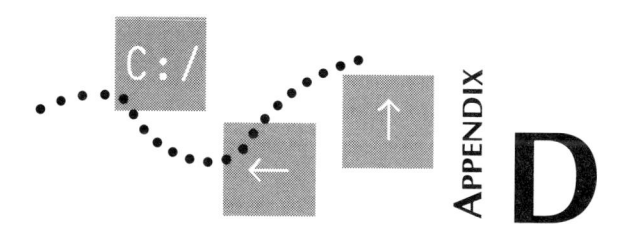

Model Program Structure

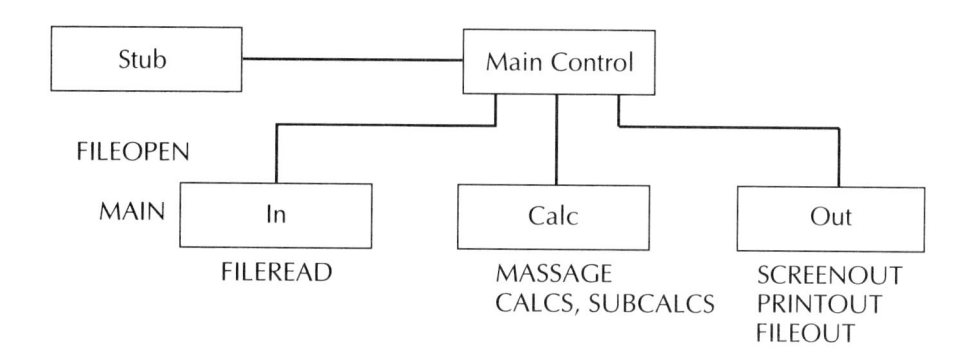

```
                    ┌──────────────┐
        Stub ───────│ Main Control │
                    └──────┬───────┘
   FILEOPEN          ┌─────┼─────┐
   MAIN         ┌────┴─┐ ┌─┴──┐ ┌┴───┐
                │  In  │ │Calc│ │Out │
                └──────┘ └────┘ └────┘
               FILEREAD  MASSAGE   SCREENOUT
                         CALCS, SUBCALCS  PRINTOUT
                                          FILEOUT
```

Model Program Routines

Routine Name	Number of Occurrences	Routines that it Enables (controls)
1. STUB	One	All others
2. FILEOPEN	One	None
3. MAIN CONTROL	One	FILEREAD, PROCESS, SUBCALC, 3 OUTPUTS
4. FILEREAD	One for each file	None
5. CALC	None to several	SUBCALC, MASSAGE
6. SUBCALC	None to dozens	None
7. MASSAGE	6 or more	Other MASSAGE
8. SCREENOUT	One per screen	None
9. PRINTOUT	None to dozens	None
10. FILEOUT	One per file out	None

Model Program Routines

Routine	Number of Occurrences	Routines which will be Enabled	Subroutine or Procedure?
1. STUB	1	All others	— neither —
2. FILEOPEN	1	None	Subroutine
3. FILEREAD	1 per file	None	Subroutine
4. MAIN CNTRL	1	FILEREAD, PROCESS, SUBCALC, 3 OUTPUTS	Subroutine
5. CALC	0 to dozens	SUBCALC, MASSAGE	Subroutine
6. SUBCALC	0 to dozens	None	Either
7. MASSAGE	6 or more	Other MASSAGE	Procedure
8. SCREENOUT	0 to dozens	None	Either
9. PRINTOUT	0 to dozens	None	Either
10. FILEOUT	1 per file	None	Subroutine

Model Program summary:

1. STUB
    - Directs program flow to:
    - FILEOPEN routine
    - MAIN routine
    - Includes CLOSE statement
    - Includes END statement
    - (But usually, CHAINs to another program)

2. FILEOPEN routine
    - Opens all files
    - Establishes the layout of each file

3. MAIN CONTROL routine
    - Enables FILEREAD, MASSAGE, CALC/SUBCALC, and OUT routines.

4. FILEREAD routine
    - Reads files
    - Unpacks information

5. MASSAGE routines
    - Any commonplace tasks that handle data
    - For example, errors, input, date, etc.

6. CALC routine
    - Changes data
    - Produces value to be saved or displayed
    - (Optionally) controls SUBCALC routines

7. SUBCALC routines
    - Detailed calculations

8. SCREENOUT routine
    - Outputs information to screen

9. PRINTOUT routine
   - Outputs information to printer
10. FILEOUT routine
    - Outputs changed data back to files

(Keep in mind that the names of these routines do not appear in QBasic. The names are used only to illustrate program organization.)

Model Program (detail):

1. The STUB.

   This is a collection of statements like this:

   ```
   REM -- program "xxxxxxxx.bas" -- created (date)
   REM -- data dictionary contains data
   REM -- item names and brief explanation of each
   REM -- data dictionary could be more than 400 REM
   REM -- statements.
   GOSUB getdate: REM -- enables (invokes) date setting_
                  REM -- routine
   GOSUB openfiles: REM -- enables routine which opens_
                    REM -- the files
   GOSUB main: REM -- enables (summons) main control_
               REM -- routine
   CLOSE: REM -- closes all files
   END: REM -- stops the program
   ```

   Every program you write should begin with a STUB of this form because it:

   - Puts descriptions (program name and date, names and explanations of all data items) at the beginning, where you can skim them at a glance.
   - Begins your program with a building-block structure, as shown by the GOSUB statements in the STUB.

> **NOTE:** The STUB is not main control. It enables MAIN CONTROL. It actually does little work, and it makes no decisions. Think of the STUB as an outline of the chapters in a book. It just points to the chapters.

A model STUB is shown on the previous page. Use it at the beginning of each new program, putting a REM in front of any statements that are not needed. (You should not need to add any.)

2. The FILEOPEN routine.

   Three types of statements normally appear in a FILEOPEN routine:
   - OPEN for all files used by the program.
   - DIM defines the size of a table of data items stored in the file.
   - FIELD defines the location of data items within a file.

   The FILEOPEN routine places the definitions of all file data in one place.

3. The MAIN CONTROL routine.

   This is the *air traffic controller* for the IN, PROCESS, and OUT routines. Actually, the MAIN routine controls everything except the STUB and its routines.

   Most of the MAIN CONTROL routine is a loop (Chapter 10) that enables FILEREAD, SUBCALC, MASSAGE, and the three OUT routines. It enables these routines repeatedly, until all the data has been processed and sent to the OUT routines.

   Since MAIN CONTROL is the focal point of your program, it is crucial to check and double-check the design of this routine. MAIN CONTROL is the routine where the more devastating errors are found. So take your time with it.

   MAIN CONTROL has the following statements:
   - GOSUB enables a subroutine.
   - CALL enables a procedure.
   - GOTO redirects the program to a QBasic line within the MAIN CONTROL routine.

- IF...THEN tests if a condition is true, then does something.
- Statements that assign (give or calculate) values, such as:
  - maxlines% = 60
  - partnum% = 1234

These are also called formulas.

4. The FILEREAD routine.

   Once a file is open, it can be read. However, some files have numeric data *packed* in (compacted), to reduce storage space on disk. So the FILEREAD routine reads the files, then UNPACKs the numeric data so that it can be used.

   Two statement types are in most FILEREAD routines:
   - GET (to read a record from a random-access file)
   - the unpack statements (which you see later on)

5-6. The CALC and SUBCALC routines.

   These are the routines that perform math calculations or data manipulation (move data from one file or data item to another). MAIN CONTROL calls the CALC routines, which then call SUBCALC routines if there are a lot of different calculations.

   Your best bet is to group routines of this type in one part of the program for readability and ease of change.

   Here are the statement types that are in CALC or SUBCALC routines:
   - CALL enables a procedure (a minor, repeated routine).
   - GOTO redirects program flow to another program line within the same CALC or SUBCALC routine.
   - IF...THEN {calculate}/CALL/GOTO performs the indicated operation only when a condition is true.
   - "Assign" statements manipulate, calculate, or move data.
   - LSET (needed to pack data into disk files before they are written)—works with the "pack" statements.
   - The "pack" family of statements (MKI$, MKS$, MKD$, and MDL$) pack numeric data to go into files.

7. The MASSAGE routines.

    There can be any number of these small, data-manipulating, utility routines. When you find yourself needing a short routine that is repeatedly called during a program, write a MASSAGE routine. Assemble these small routines in one easy-to-read group rather than scattering them throughout the program.

    That way you know where to look for any MASSAGE routine you need to change. Also, you know where to put a new one, so that you can easily find it later.

    Here is a list of some MASSAGE routines:

    - NUMERIC EDIT ensures that a number is valid.
    - DATE EDIT ensures a date is valid.
    - DATE COMPARISON finds the earlier of two dates.
    - DAYS ELAPSED calculates the number of days between two dates.
    - DATE SWAP changes a date into date comparison format: (Swap your standard format MMDDYY into YYMMDD.)
    - ROUNDING rounds off dollars and cents to two decimals.

    Appendix E contains a number of sample MASSAGE routines, ready for you to use in your programs.

    MASSAGE routines can use most statement types with the following exceptions:

    - No file GETs and PUTs
    - No GOSUBs (CALL is okay)
    - No CLOSE
    - No END

8. The SCREENOUT routine.

    Sends data to the screen. The statement types found in the SCREENOUT routine are:

    - PRINT and PRINT USING.
    - The "string" family of statements (such as CHR$, STR$, MID$).
    - LOCATE (locates the blinking cursor on the screen).

- CLS (clears the screen).
- COLOR (lets you use different colors on the screen).
- CSRLIN (tells the program what line the cursor is on).
- POS (tells the program what column the cursor is on).
- TAB (positions the cursor at a specific column on the screen).
- "format" statements that are necessary for PRINT USING statements to work.

9. The PRINTOUT routine sends data to the printer. Statements used in the PRINTOUT routine are:

- LPRINT and LPRINT USING
- The "string" family of statements (see above)
- TAB
- "format" statements

10. The FILEOUT routine.

Sends data to a disk file. The FILEOUT statements are:

- PUT
- LSET (needed for packing ALL data, not just numeric)
- The "pack" family of statements (MKI$, MKS$, MKD$, and MDL$), which pack numeric data for files

From Blueprint to Routines

The rules are:

1. The STUB is the same for every program. No new control statements go into it. Only the data dictionary definitions of the variable names should ever be added. Other than that, do not change the STUB.

2. Every program contains one FILEOPEN routine, whether there are 16 files in the program or none. All OPENS go in this routine. If there are no files to be opened, then leave the subroutine itself with only a RETURN statement.

3. Each file that is read needs its own FILEREAD routine. This routine reads and unpacks one record each time it is invoked. If you have four files in one program, then you have four FILEREAD routines.

4. The MAIN CONTROL itself does no work. It serves only as the major loop, which regulates getting data, processing it and outputting it. It controls all the reads, calcs, and writes (or prints). Therefore, assign no tasks from your blueprint to MAIN CONTROL.

5. Put ALL PRINT tasks in PRINTOUT routines, All SCREEN tasks in SCREENOUT routines. Use one master routine for each different screen layout or printed page layout. Each of the master routines may or may not control several other routines, depending on the complexity of the output.

6. Each file that is written to has its own FILEOUT routine, with minor routines, if needed.

7. The CALC routine controls calculations and the movement of data. It is invoked from MAIN CONTROL. The SUBCALCS do the actual calculations. SUBCALCS are enabled by either the CALC routine, or the OUT routines (SCREENOUT, PRINTOUT, or FILEOUT), whichever works best in your program. Put calculation and data movement tasks in the SUBCALCS, and do not worry about which routines manage the SUBCALCS until the very end. Then, do what fits more naturally in your program.

8. MASSAGE routines are usually procedures that do some specific operation (massaging) on a certain type of data. They are called many times in the same program, and frequently saved for use in other programs. Most programmers build up a library of MASSAGE routines that they use over and over in their programs.

The steps for converting a blueprint into a routine.

1. Write each step of your Blueprint down the left side of a piece of paper.
2. Using rules 1-8, assign each task to a routine.
3. You will always have one STUB, one FILEOPEN, one FILEREAD for each file read, one FILEOUT for each file written, and one MAIN CONTROL, so...
4. Get another sheet of paper, and group the tasks by each type of SUBCALC, and—OUT routines.

5. When you are all done, decide how many routines you want of each type, or whether you want to group several tasks into one routine.
6. Decide if you want the SUBCALCS controlled by one major CALC, or by the OUT routines.
7. You now have a program structure.

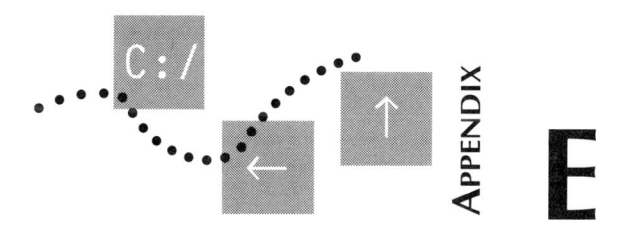

Sample Routines

1. The Error Routine (it's a Procedure):

```
SUB printerr (e$,r%,c%): REM -- e$ is the error
                        REM -- message r% is the l_
line
                        REM -- number, and c% is the
                        REM -- column number at
                        REM -- which to locate.
    PRINT CHR$(7);e$;TAB(79);"": REM -- ring the bell &
                                 REM -- print error
                                 REM --message
    LOCATE r%,c%:REM -- set the cursor at the original
                REM --location
END SUB
```

2. The Numeric Testing Routine (it's also a Procedure):

```
SUB numtest (n$,lgth%,e%): REM -- n$ is the data, lgth%
                           REM -- is the length of the
                           REM -- data item, and e% is
                           REM --an error flag (0=no
                           REM -- error, 1=error)
  e%=0:REM -- set the error flag to 0 (no error)
  FOR i%=1 TO lgth%: REM -- set up a loop to check
                     REM -- for numeric
  IF ASC(MID$(n$,i%,1))<48 THEN e%=1:REM -- testfor <0
  IF ASC(MID$(n$,i%,1))>57 THEN e%=1:REM -- testfor >9
  NEXT i%
END SUB
```

3. The Date Testing Routine (also a Procedure):

```
SUB datest (dat$,lgth%,e%): REM -- dat$ is the date,
                            REM -- lgth% is the length
                            REM -- of the date, and e%
                            REM --is an error flag
                            REM -- (0=no error,
                            REM -- 1=error)
  e%=1: REM -- set error flag to 1 (assuming that
        REM --until the date passes all the tests,
        REM -- an error has been found).
  IF lgth%<5 THEN GOTO quitdate:REM -- if the length
                                REM --<5 then leave
                                REM -- the procedure
                                REM -- with the
                                REM -- error flag e%
                                REM -- set to an
                                REM -- error
  IF lgth%=5 THEN dat$="0"+dat$: REM -- make it a
                                 REM --six
                                 REM -- character
                                 REM -- field
  w1%=VAL(LEFT$(dat$,2)):REM -- get the month
  IF w1%<1 THEN  GOTO quitdate
  IF w1%>12 THEN  GOTO quitdate
  w2%=VAL(MID$(dat$,3,2)):REM -- get the day
  IF w2%<1 THEN  GOTO quitdate
  IF w2%>31 THEN  GOTO quitdate
```

```
    w3%=VAL(RIGHT$(dat$,2)):REM -- get the year
   IF w3%>93 THEN  GOTO quitdate
   e%=0: REM -- reset error flag to 0 (no errors
         REM -- found)
quitdate:REM -- just a label to go to
END SUB
```

4. Procedure to convert lowercase to uppercase:

```
SUB upper(i$): REM -- i$ is the string to be
               REM --converted
     l% = LEN(i$)
     FOR i% = 1 TO l%
          w1% = ASC(MID$(i$,i%,1))
          IF w1% > 96 THEN
               IF w1% <123 THEN
                    MID$(i$,i%,1) = CHR$(w1%-32)
          END IF
     NEXT i%
END SUB
```

5. Procedure to test for number of days in a month:

```
SUB MOTEST(d,e): REM -- d is the date, in MMDDYY
                 REM -- format, and e is the error
                 REM -- indicator (0 = ok, 1 = days
                 REM --are greater than allowed for
                 REM -- that month)
     moda = INT(d/100)
     mo = INT (moda/100)
     da = moda MOD 100
     IF da >31 THEN
          e%=1
          goto endmotest
     END IF
     IF mo = 2 THEN
          IF da >29 THEN
```

```
                e%=1
                goto endmotest
        END IF
                IF mo = 4 THEN GOTO thirty
                IF mo = 6 THEN GOTO thirty
                IF mo = 9 THEN GOTO thirty
                IF mo = 11 THEN GOTO thirty
thirtyone:
    IF da > 31 THEN e% = 1
    GOTO endmotest
thirty:
    IF da > 30 THEN e%=1
endmotest:
END SUB
```

6. Procedure to check for a minus sign and a decimal point in a number:

```
SUB numtest (n$,lgth%,e%):  REM -- n$ is the data, lgth%
                            REM -- is the length of the
                            REM -- data item, and e% is
                            REM --an error flag (0=no
                            REM -- error, 1=error)
    e%=0:REM -- set the error flag to 0 (no error)
    w2%=0:REM -- set decimal point counter to 0
    FOR i%=1 TO lgth%:  REM -- set up a loop to check
                        REM -- for numeric
            w1%=ASC(MID$(n$,i%,1))
            IF i%=1 THEN
                    IF w1%=45 THEN
                        GOTO nexti
            END IF
            IF w1% = 46 THEN w2% = w2% + 1: GOTO nexti
            IF w1% < 48 THEN e%=1:REM -- test for <0
            IF w1% > 57 THEN e%=1:REM -- test for >9
nexti:
    NEXT i%
    IF w2% > 1 THEN e% = 1
END SUB
```

7. Date conversion (from MMDDYY into YYMMDD) procedure:

```
        SUB chgdat(d,d1)
        REM -- the date is in variable name d, the
```

```
    REM --converted date in d1
        d$=STR$(d):REM -- convert d to a string
        w$=MID$(d$,2): REM -- get rid of blank sign
                       REM --character
        d$=w$:REM -- move it back into d$
        IF LEN(w$)<6 then d$="0"+w$: REM -- make it 6
                                    REM --characters
        w$=RIGHT$(d$,2)+LEFT$(d$,2)+MID$(d$,3,2)
        REM -- convert the string into YYMMDD format
        d1=val(w$):REM -- convert it into a number
    END SUB
```

8. Elapsed days procedure:

```
SUB elapsdays (dat1,dat2,elap)
  REM -- dat1 and dat2 are the dates, elap is the elapsed
  REM -- days
  CALL chgdat (dat1,d1)
  CALL chgdat (dat2,d2)
  w$ = MID$(STR$(d1), 2): REM -- make 1st date a string
  w1$ = LEFT$(w$, 2): REM -- get the year of 1st date
  w2$ = MID$(w$, 3, 2): REM -- get the month of 1st date
  w3$ = RIGHT$(w$, 2): REM --  get the day of 1st date
  x1 = VAL(w1$)
  x2 = VAL(w2$)
  x3 = VAL(w3$): REM -- change year, month, and day of 1st
                 REM -- date into separate numbers
  w$ = MID$(STR$(d2), 2): REM -- make 2nd date a string
  w1$ = LEFT$(w$, 2): REM -- get the year of 2nd date
  w2$ = MID$(w$, 3, 2): REM -- get the month of 2nd date
  w3$ = RIGHT$(w$, 2): REM -- get the day of 2nd date
  x4 = VAL(w1$)
  x5 = VAL(w2$)
  x6 = VAL(w3$): REM change 2nd date into separate numbers
  w1 = x1 - x4: REM -- subtract the years
  w2 = x2 - x5: REM -- subtract the months
  w3 = x3 - x6: REM -- subtract the days
  IF w3 < 0 THEN
     w3 = w3 + 30
     w2 = w2 - 1
  END IF: REM -- if days < 0, add 30 to the days, and
          REM --subtract 1 from the month
  IF w2 < 0 THEN
     w2 = w2 + 12
```

```
                    w1 = w1 - 1
     END IF: REM -- if months < 0, add 12 to the months,
             REM --and subtract 1 from the year
        elaps = w1 * 365 + w2 * 30 + w3: REM -- sum the days
     END SUB
```

9. Create a date table:

```
setmonths:
         DIM motab(12)
         DATA 31,29,31,30,31,30,31,31,30,31,30,31
         FOR i% = 1 TO 12
         READ motab(i%)
         NEXT i%
RETURN
```

10. Use the date table (in 9) to test for a valid day of the month:

```
    IF da%<1 THEN {print error}
    IF da%>motab%(mo%) THEN {print error}
         where da%= the day of the month, and
               mo%= the month involved.
```

Appendix F

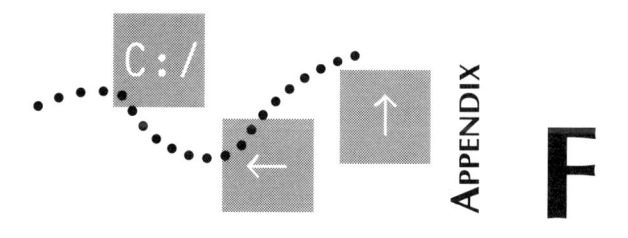

Linked File Routines

Here are the QBasic routines for reading and updating linked files.

Read the LastUsed

The LastUsed is needed for:

- reading the file sequentially (to avoid reading blank records)
- adding records to a linked file

Ironically, the very first read of a linked file gets the last record of the file to save the LastUsed value. You invoke this routine immediately after opening the linked file and executing the FIELD statement that defines the record. This makes the LastUsed available at the start of the program.

Here is the routine in use. The linked file in this program code is ORDER.DAT.

```
    OPEN "ORDER.DAT" FOR RANDOM ACCESS READ WRITE AS #2 LEN =_
192
   FIELD 2, 4 AS ORDRECNO$, 10 AS ORDNO$, 4 AS ORDDATE$, 4 AS_
ORDTYPE$,
      4 AS ORDQTY$, 8 AS ORDCOST$, 8 AS ORDPRICE$, 8 AS_
ORDEXTPRICE$, 8
        AS ORDEXTCOST$, 70 AS ORDDESC$, 2 AS ORDCUST$, 4 AS_
ORDSTART$, 4
        AS ORDEND$, 4 AS ORDPTR$
getlast:
   GET 2, 1000: REM ** Read the last record of the linked_
file
   lastused2& = CVL(ORDPTR$): REM ** Unpack and save the_
LastUsed
   RETURN
```

These are the very first program statements concerning the order file. The file is opened and the FIELD statement is declared. Then the last record, number 1000, is read and the LastUsed is saved. Now we are ready to use the linked file for any purposes whatsoever.

First, let's look it up.

The Query Routine

The Query routine reads a single record from the linked file. If there are no records to be read, it sets a flag (variable name) indicating that further reading can't be done.

The Query routine is invoked for every attempt to read a linked file. It might be the very first read, any subsequent reads, the last read, or the effort to read beyond the last record (when the link is zero). This one routine is used repeatedly to read all the links in the chain, from the Master link through all the connecting links down to the terminating link (a value of zero).

In this example the Master file is assumed to be file number one, and the linked file is file two. (To keep it clear, we will leave out all the Master file program statements.)

First, open the file and get the LastUsed:

```
  OPEN "ORDER.DAT" FOR RANDOM ACCESS READ WRITE AS #2 LEN =_
192
    FIELD 2, 4 AS ORDRECNO$, 10 AS ORDNO$, 4 AS ORDDATE$, 4 AS_
ORDTYPE$,
      4 AS ORDQTY$, 8 AS ORDCOST$, 8 AS ORDPRICE$, 8 AS_
ORDEXTPRICE$, 8
      AS ORDEXTCOST$, 70 AS ORDDESC$, 2 AS ORDCUST$, 4 AS_
ORDSTART$, 4
      AS ORDEND$, 4 AS ORDPTR$
getlast:
    GET 2, 1000: REM ** Read the last record of the linked_
file
    lastused2& = CVL(ORDPTR$): REM ** Unpack and save the_
LastUsed
RETURN
```

Now for the Query. Assume that the data element in the master file that contains the first link is named *masterlink1&*. The link within the order file is *ordptr&*.

The portion of the program that summons the *getlink* routine looks like this:

```
mainquery:
    f2&=999999999
readmore:
    GOSUB getlink
    IF link2%=1 THEN RETURN
    IF end2%=1 THEN RETURN
    GOSUB {some print or process routine}
    GOTO readmore
RETURN
```

And the *read* routine is:

```
getlink:
    link2%=0
```

```
        IF f2&>0 THEN
            IF f2&<999999999 THEN
                f2&=ordptr&: REM ** If this is not the_
first read,
            END IF              REM ** get the link pointer.
        END IF
        IF f2&=999999999 THEN
            f2&=masterlink1&: REM ** If this is the first_
read,
        END IF                  REM ** then use the link in_
the master file.
        IF f2&=0 THEN
            link2%=1: REM ** If the link is 0,
            RETURN:   REM ** then we are done. Set the flag_
and get out.
        END IF
    GOSUB readord:   REM Read the linked file
RETURN
readord:
    IF f2& > 999 THEN GOTO endord
    IF f2& > lastused2& THEN GOTO endord
    GET 2, f2&
                REM ** Unpack the record
    ORDRECNO& = CVL(ORDRECNO$): ORDDATE& = CVL(ORDDATE$)
    ORDTYPE& = CVL(ORDTYPE$): ORDQTY = CVS(ORDQTY$)
    ORDCOST# = CVD(ORDCOST$): ORDPRICE# = CVD(ORDPRICE$)
    ORDEXTPRICE# = CVD(ORDEXTPRICE$): ORDEXTCOST# =_
CVD(ORDEXTCOST$)
    ORDCUST% = CVI(ORDCUST$): ORDSTART& = CVL(ORDSTART$)
    ORDEND& = CVL(ORDEND$):   ordptr& = CVL(ORDPTR$):
RETURN
```

```
endord:
  end2% = 1
RETURN
```

Before Calling the Routine

Before the *getlink* routine is summoned for the first time, *f2&* is set to 999999999. The 999999999 value tells the routine that this is the first read of the linked file. The record number is found in the link of the master file (in this case, *masterlink1&*).

The Routine Itself

getlink tests to see if *f2&* is greater than zero but less than 999999999. (If the value were 99999999, it would be the first read, the start of the chain. If the value were 0, we would be at the end of the chain.) If *f2&* is between 0 and 99999999, this is not the first read (we are somewhere along the chain) The new record value of *f2&* (the record to be read) of the Order file is found in *ordptr&* of the linked file ORDER.DAT.

Next *getlink* tests if *f2&* is equal to 999999999. If so, this chain has not been started; the master link has not yet been read. Then *f2&* gets its new value from the master link, in this case *masterlink1&*.

Now *f2&* is tested for a zero value. If so, the end of the chain has been reached, and we can read no further. A flag is set and *getlink* exits.

If *f2&* has a non-zero value, the linked file is read and unpacked, and *getlink* exits. The record is available for use in the program.

Update the LastUsed

As records are added to a linked file, the LastUsed is updated to reflect each new addition. This is effected by incrementing the LastUsed by one, then saving it in the last record (in this case, record number 1000) before reading a new record from the file.

The *LastUsed* routine has only four statements:

```
LastUsed:
    lastused2& = lastused2& + 1: REM ** Add 1 to LastUsed
    LSET ORDPTR$=MKL$(lastused2&): REM ** Pack it
    PUT 2, 1000: REM Write the last record
    GET 2, lastused2&
RETURN
```

The *LastUsed* is always written before a record is added to a linked file.

Write a New Linked Record

This routine updates the pointer of the new record in the linked file.

It gets the master link, saves it in the new record, then writes the new record.

Assume that the master link is named *masterlink1&* and *lastused2&* is the next record in the linked file to be written.

```
writnew2:
    LSET ORDPTR$=MKL$(masterlink1&):REM ** Save the master_
link in the
                                    REM ** pointer new record.
    PUT 2, lastused2&:REM ** Write the new record.
RETURN
```

In this routine, *masterlink1&* has the value of the previous link, while *lastused2&* is the current link to be written. The value of the previous link (*masterlink1&*) is saved in the new record (*lastused2&*) to keep the chain intact.

writnew2 assumes that the pointers or links go backward, rather than forward. That is, the chain goes from most current to least current transaction. The first link (the one in the master file) is the most current, and the oldest is in the last linked record that is read.

Now we have to update the link in the master file.

Update the Master Record

Having written the new record with the former master link as the new record's pointer, we have to place the value of the new record number into the master link.

Here is how. Assume that the name of the master link is *masterlink1&*, and the new linked record being written has a record number named *lastused2&*.

```
mastlink:
     LSET masterlink1$=MKL$(lastused2&): REM ** save the_
record number
     PUT 1, f1&: REM ** and write the master record.
RETURN
```

The Assembled Routines

Now we will put everything together into three simple routines:

- Get LastUsed - immediately after OPEN and FIELD statements
- Reading through a link
- Writing a new record and updating the master

Get LastUsed

```
   OPEN "ORDER.DAT" FOR RANDOM ACCESS READ WRITE AS #2 LEN =_
192
   FIELD 2, 4 AS ORDRECNO$, 10 AS ORDNO$, 4 AS ORDDATE$, 4 AS_
ORDTYPE$,
     4 AS ORDQTY$, 8 AS ORDCOST$, 8 AS ORDPRICE$, 8 AS_
ORDEXTPRICE$, 8
     AS ORDEXTCOST$, 70 AS ORDDESC$, 2 AS ORDCUST$, 4 AS_
ORDSTART$, 4
     AS ORDEND$, 4 AS ORDPTR$
```

```
getlast:
   GET 2, 1000: REM ** Read the last record of the linked_
file
   lastused2& = CVL(ORDPTR$): REM ** Unpack and save the_
LastUsed
RETURN
```

Reading Through a Link

Remember to set the record number of the linked file before the first read (f2&=999999999).

```
getlink:
     link2%=0
     IF f2&>0 THEN
            IF f2&<999999999 THEN
                   f2&=ordptr&: REM ** If this is not the the_
first read,
            END IF              REM ** get the link pointer.
     END IF
     IF f2&=999999999 THEN
            f2&=masterlink1&:   REM ** If this is the first_
read,
     END IF                     REM ** then use the link in_
the master file.
     IF f2&=0 THEN
            link2%=1: REM ** If the link is 0,
            RETURN:   REM ** we are done. Set the flag and_
get out.
     END IF
     GOSUB readord: REM Read the linked file
RETURN
```

Writing a New Record and Updating the Master

Assume that the master link is named *masterlink1&* and the LastUsed is named *lastused2&*.

```
addlink2:
    lastused2& = lastused2& + 1: REM ** Add 1 to LastUsed
    LSET ORDPTR$=MKL$(lastused2&): REM ** Pack it
    PUT 2, 1000: REM Write the last record
    GET 2, lastused2&
RETURN
writnew2:
    LSET ORDPTR$=MKL$(masterlink1&):REM ** Save the master_link in the
                                    REM ** pointer new_record.
    PUT 2, lastused2&:REM ** Write the new record
mastlink:
    LSET masterlink1$=MKL$(lastused2&): REM ** save the_record number
    PUT 1, f1&: REM ** and write the master record.
RETURN
```

Index

A

alphanumeric data 77, 78, 79, 80, 196, 197, 209, 210, 213
arrays (QBasic tables) 343-357
ASC function (usually used in editing) 252, 253, 254, 272, 273, 286, 287

B

backward links 193-194, 221-245
blinking (on the screen display) 312
block diagrams of program logic 61, 63, 64
block **IF** statement (decision making) 160-168
block-line method of looking at a program 21
blueprint a program 60-64
blueprint to program routines 124-126
book in review 373, 374
Breakpoint (QBasic editor) 361, 364
building-blocks of a model program 111-127

C

calc (routine in a program) 114, 115, 116, 118, 121, 124, 125, 126
calculations in QBasic 323-342
CALL statement (for a procedure) 136-137, 140-143, 145, 146
CHAIN statement (to another QBasic program) 116, 370-371
Change command (QBasic editor) 98-99, 103-106
CHR$ function (usually used in printing) 256-262, 302
CINT funtion (convert to an integer) 333-335
CLNG function (convert to a long integer) 333-335
CLOSE statement (for random files) 117, 119
CLS statement (clears the screen) 317
COLOR statement (sets screen color) 318-320
colors, using them on the screen 312
commands (QBasic environment) 87-91, 95-108
commas and printing 303, 316
complex IF statements 161-168
concatenating strings 289, 326
concept of files 185-199
continuing a program (QBasic environment) 362, 363, 364, 365
control of routines 129-148
conventions (in this book) 14-16
copy (selected text - QBasic editor) 100-102, 106, 107
creating a random file 214-215
CSRLIN function (finding the screen cursor location) 317-318
cut and paste (QBasic editor) 99-102, 106-107
CVD function (unpacking data) 211-212
CVI function (unpacking data) 211-212
CVL function (unpacking data) 211-212
CVS function (unpacking data) 211-212

D

danger of **GOTO** 182-183
data
    editing 247-262
    in files 185-189, 194-198, 209-213
    in routines (global and local) 139-143
    using right types in calculations 330-332
DATA and **READ** statements (get data into a program) 351-352
data dictionary 84-86
data file 185-189, 194-198, 209-213
data names 74-77, 80-83
data "slot" (passing data from one routine to another) 140-143
DATA statement (gets data into a program) 351-352

415

data types 77-80
DATE$ function (gets the date) 81
date calculations 337-340
date comparisons 337-338
date swap for comparisons 337-338
date editing (testing) 253-255, 259-261, 270-271, 274-276
Debug menu (QBasic environment) 44, 363, 365
Debugger (QBasic environment) 359-367
defining a file 194-198, 209-210
defining a table 347-350
Delete selected text (QBasic editor) 95, 100-101
design
    blueprint 60-64
    file 189-198
    printed reports 294-299
    program 112-126
    screen layouts 308-313
diagrams and programming 49-70
DIM statement (defines a table) 350
DIMensioning a table (defines the size) 350
disk
    data files 189-198, 201-220, 221-246
    directory (listing of files and programs) 27
display (on the screen) 307-322
Display values of data names (QBasic debugger) 362
division by zero (bad mistake) 326-327

DO UNTIL statement (loop) 178-180

E

Edit menu (QBasic editor) 40-41, 97
editing
    data 247-266, 267-292
    keys (QBasic editor) 95-102
    levels of 249-250
Editor (QBasic) 93-110
elapsed days (between 2 dates) 337-340
elements in a table 345, 349
ELSE
    statement (goes with IF) 156-160
end of the file 215-217
END statement (ends the program) 116, 117, 119
END SUB statement (ends the subroutine) 140, 142
error
    messages 256-262
    routine 268-269
Exit command (QBasic environment) 88

F

F1 key (QBasic environment) 64-68
F2 key (QBasic environment) 95-96
F3 key (QBasic environment) 97
F4 key (QBasic environment) 361, 363-365
F5 key (QBasic environment) 362, 363, 364, 365

F6 key (QBasic environment) 361, 362, 364, 365
F8 key (QBasic environment) 360, 362, 363
F9 key (QBasic environment) 361, 364
field (data) 75-77, 187-188, 194-198
FIELD statement 209-213
file
    concepts 185-200
    design 189-198
    layout 196-198, 209-213
    opening a 202-204
    reading a 204-207
    structure 189-194
    subject categories 194-196
    writing a 207-209
File commands (QBasic environment) 87-91
File menu (QBasic environment) 87-91
fileout routine (program structure) 115, 116, 118, 123, 124, 125
fileread routine (program structure) 114, 115, 116, 118, 120, 124, 125
Find and replace command (Change in QBasic environment) 98-99, 103-106
Find command (QBasic environment) 97-98
FIX function (convert to a whole number) 333-335
FOR (...TO...NEXT) loop 176-177
format statement for printing 299-301, 313-316
functions in QBasic 333-336

G

GET statement (reading a file) 206-207
global and local data in routines 139-143
GOSUB statement (invoke a subroutine) 133-135
GOTO
  statement 143-145
  with IF statement 151, 180-183
  danger of 182-183

H

Help (QBasic environment)
  calling 64-65
  contents 65-66
  help on using it 65
  index 66-67
  menu 46
  specific 67-68
hidput (hidden data) 61
hints on using the Debugger (QBasic environment) 365-366

I

IF EOF THEN GOTO statement (end of file condition) 180-181, 216-217
IF statements (decision making) 149-170
indenting rule of **IF**s 167-168
input (from the keyboard) 247-266, 267-292
INPUT (LINE INPUT) statement (gets data from the keyboard) 250, 284-285
inserting text (QBasic editor) 95, 99-102
instant screen (**F4** in QBasic debugger) 361, 363, 364
INT function (converts to an integer) 333-335
integers (numeric type) 77-79

J

joining strings 289

K

keep it simple (reports) 298, 313

L

label (of a program statement) 18-19
laying out a page (printed output) 297-299
laying out a screen display 311-313
LEFT$ function (gets left side of a string) 287-289
LEN function (finds length of a string) 285
length test (editing data) 249, 251-252
line labels 18-19
LINE INPUT statement (gets data from keyboard) 284-285
linked files 193-194, 221-246
links 193-194, 221-246
local and global data in routines 139-143
LOCATE function (finds a spot on the screen display) 262, 317-318
locating
  elements in a table 345, 346-350
  a point on the screen 263, 317-318
  a record in a random file 204-207
logic (in programs) 50-59
long integers (numeric type) 77-79
loop is the base logic of a program 173-175
loops 171-184
LPRINT statement (prints to the printer) 300-301
LPRINT USING statement (prints to the printer) 300-301
LSET statement (used to pack data) 210-211

M

main control (of a program) 114-116, 118, 120, 124, 125
main routine (main control) is the critical loop 120, 173-175
major routines 111-127
massage routines 115, 116, 118, 121-122, 124, 125
math functions in QBasic 336
memorizing (this book) 9
menu program (WildWater Works) 369-374
menus (of QBasic) 38-47
MID$ function (getting part of a string) 287-290
minimal testing (**IF** statements) 163-165
minor routines (tasks) 135-138
MKD$ function (packing data) 210-211
MKI$ function (packing data) 210-211
MKL$ function (packing data) 210-211

MKS$ function (packing data) 210-211
MMDDYY (date format) 122, 253-255, 337-338
model program structure 111-124
moving text (QBasic editor) 95, 99-102

N

names for data (variable names) 74-86
nature of programming 56-57
New command (QBasic environment) 87
NEXT (FOR...TO——NEXT) loops 176-177
numbers (types of) 77-79
numeric
    edit 249, 252-253, 258-259, 264-265, 269-270
        testing routines 269-270
        types 77-80

O

one-dimensional tables 345-346
only criterion (for report design) 320
Open command (QBasic environment) 87, 89
OPEN statement (for random files) 202-204
opening
    an existing program 35-36, 89
    a random file 202-204
operators in QBasic (+, -, *, /, etc.) 325-326

Options menu (QBasic environment) 45
organization, program 111-128
output
    files 207-215
    print 293-306
    screen 307-322

P

packing data onto files 210-212
page layouts for reports 297-298
parentheses, use of 328-330
planning 4-5
POS function (finding the screen cursor location) 263-317
presenting the correct answer 330-332
PRINT statement (prints to the screen) 314-316
Print command (QBasic environment) 88, 90-91
print formats for lines 299-300, 313, 314
PRINT USING statement (prints to the screen) 314-316
printed output 293-306
printing out a table 352
printout routine (program structure) 115, 116, 118, 123, 124, 125
procedures (minor tasks) 135-138
program flow 50-56
program, model structure 113-124
program organization 111-128
purpose of a program 60

PUT statement (writes a random file record) 207-209

Q

QBasic
    debugger 359-368
    editor 93-110
    environment 25-48
    help 64-68
    limitations of numbers 78-79
    limitations of tables 355-356
    options 38-40

R

random file 201-220
range test (editing data) 250, 255, 261-262
reading and writing a random file 206-209
record layout 209-210
REMark (**REM**) statement for programmer's comments 83-84
repeated tasks 135-136, 138
report
    file 185-200, 201-220, 221-246
    printed 293-306
    screen 307-322
reserved words in QBasic 80-81
RETURN statement (exits a subroutine) 134-135
reusing edit procedures 267-292
right data types, using 330-332
RIGHT$ function (gets right side of a string) 288, 290

rounding numbers for the correct answer 331-335
routine selection test (subroutine or procedure?) 137-138
Run menu (QBasic environment) 43-44

S

Save command (QBasic environment) 87, 89-90
Save As command (QBasic environment) 88, 90
saving a program to the disk 33-34, 87-88, 89-90
screen
    easy to read 309-313
    layout 311
    mistakes 312
    neatness 263-265, 310-313
    output 307-320
screenout routine (program structure) 115, 116, 118, 122, 124, 125
Search menu (QBasic environment) 42-43
secrets of good programming 58-59
semicolons (in printing) 303, 316
short integers (numeric type) 77-79
specific help (QBasic environment) 64, 67-68
specific value test (data editing) 250-255-256, 262
starting a program in QBasic 35-36
starting QBasic 27-30
statement label (program line) 18-19

stopping a program 361, 363
STR$ function (converts a number to a string) 336-339
string functions in calculations 336-339
strings (data type) 77, 78, 79-80
structure, program 111-128
stub (program structure) 115-116
subcalcs routine (program structure) 114, 115, 116, 118, 121, 124, 125, 126
subroutines in QBasic (major tasks) 132-135, 137-138, 139-140
subscripts (of a table or array)
syntax checking (QBasic environment) 38-39

T

TAB function (used with print statements to go to a specific column 301-302, 316
table within a random file recored 353-355
tables (arrays in QBasic) 343-358
tasks, programming
    major (subroutines) 132-135, 137-140
    minor (procedures) 133, 135-138, 139, 140-143
testing (debugging) a QBasic program 359-368
three-dimensional tables 346, 347
TIME$ function (gets the time of day) 81
Trace command (QBasic debugger) 360-361, 363

Two-dimensional tables 346, 347
type test (numeric, date, etc.) 249, 252-255, 258-261, 264-265, 269-271
typing in a program 30-34

U

underlining on the screen 312
unpacking data from a random file 210, 211, 212

V

VAL function (converts a string to a number) 287, 289-290, 338-340
variable (data) names 74-86
View menu (QBasic environment) 41-42

W

WIDTH statement (sets printer line length) 303
WildWater Works 10
Working thoughtfully 5-6
Writing and reading a random file 204-209

Y

YYMMDD (date format) 121-122, 337-339

How to Use This Disk

Instructions for using the disk accompanying
teach yourself... QBasic, 2nd edition

The disk packaged with *teach yourself...QBasic, 2nd edition* contains 11 programs that help you learn and use QBasic. Work along with the employees of WildWater Works, Inc. to become familiar with the QBasic environment. You have all the tools you need to complete every possible programming task.

To use the disk, get into the DOS directory by typing:
cd\dos
and insert the floppy disk into your drive.

If the drive is drive a, then type:
copy a:*.*
If the drive is drive b, then type:
copy b:*.*

Now all the programs are copied, and you can use them to follow along with the book. The disk includes 11 programs:

Program Name	**Description**
PROG 3-1.BAS	Typing in a program.
PROG 6-1.BAS	Using the QBasic Editor.
PROG 8-1.BAS	A program showing a procedure.
PROG 8-2.BAS	A program with both a procedure and subroutine.
PROG 12-1.BAS	Creating a blank random file.
PROG 15-1.BAS	A program with a reusable edit procedure.
PROG 17-1.BAS	A screen color testing program.
PROG 18-1.BAS	Date calculation program (calculates the number of days between two dates).
PROG 19-1.BAS	Use of a table in a random file record.
PROG 20-1.BAS	A debugging example.
PROG 21-1.BAS	WildWater Works, Inc. menu program.